# Richard Hooker
# and the Politics
# of a Christian England

Engraving of Richard Hooker, c. 1672, reproduced from F. J. Shirley,
*Richard Hooker and Contemporary Political Ideas*
(London: SPCK, 1949), p. ii.

# Richard Hooker and the Politics of a Christian England

*Robert K. Faulkner*

**University of California Press**

*Berkeley / Los Angeles / London*

University of California Press
Berkeley and Los Angeles, California

University of California Press, Ltd.
London, England

© 1981 by
The Regents of the University of California

Printed in the United States of America

1 2 3 4 5 6 7 8 9

**Library of Congress Cataloging in Publication Data**

Faulkner, Robert Kenneth.
    Richard Hooker and the politics of a Christian England.

    Includes index.
    1. Hooker, Richard, 1553 or 4-1600.    2. England
—Church History—16th century.    I. Title.
BX5199.H813F38          230'.3'0924   [B]        79-65776
ISBN   0-520-03993-9

Publication of this book has been aided by grants from the
Trustees of Boston College and the Andrew W. Mellon Foundation.

# Contents

# Acknowledgments

I am happy to thank Thomas Perry, Rev. Ernest Fortin, A.A., and Christopher Bruell, who commented on an earlier version of this book, and Clare Cross, who gave generously of her knowledge of Elizabethan church history while trying to save an interloper from error. I have benefited especially from exacting readings made by A. S. McGrade and W. Speed Hill. Mr. Hill's several readings and many courtesies exemplify his generous services to contemporary scholars of Hooker. With respect to these benefactors, however, special force must be given to the customary exculpation: the plan and execution of the present study, its conclusions and deficiencies, are mine.

Some findings of chapters 5 and 7 have been published before, as "Reason and Revelation in Hooker's Ethics" (*American Political Science Review* 59 [September 1965]: 680–690), and as "Spontaneity, Justice, and Coercion: On *Nicomachean Ethics*, Books III and V" (*Coercion*, ed. John Chapman and J. Roland Pennock, [New York: Atherton Press, 1972], pp. 81–106). I am grateful for grants from the American Philosophical Society, the National Endowment for the Humanities, Princeton University, and Boston College, and for a faculty fellowship given by the Ford Foundation that helped me to complete the writing.

# Abbreviations
# Used in the Notes

In referring to Hooker's *Laws of Ecclesiastical Polity*, I follow John Keble's subdivision of its preface and books. Examples: Book I, chapter v, section 3, is abbreviated *Laws* I.v.3; chapter v, section 3, of the Preface is abbreviated *Laws* Preface.v.3; section 3 of the Dedication to Book V is abbreviated *Laws* V.Dedication.3. I use short titles for the smaller writings and again follow Keble's subdivisions. For example, "Mr. Hooker's Answer to the Supplication that Mr. Travers made to the Council" is cited as "Answer to Travers," 2, in *Works* III, 571. *Works* refers to *The Works of that Learned and Judicious Divine Mr. Richard Hooker*, 3 volumes, arranged by John Keble, 7th ed., revised by R. W. Church and F. Paget (Oxford, 1888).

The first four books of the *Laws* were published in 1593, and Book V was published in 1597, three years before Hooker's death. The last three books struggled into print much later, the sixth and eighth (both probably abused) in 1648, the seventh in 1662, when the *Laws* first appeared as a whole. Keble's was the first critical edition. By modernizing spelling, punctuation and paragraphing, Keble, Church and Paget provided a text easier to read without affecting its meaning. All references to the *Laws* have been checked for substantive accuracy, however, against the authoritative text in W. Speed Hill's new works: *The Folger Library Edition of the Works of Richard Hooker*, ed. W. Speed Hill (Cambridge, Mass., and London, 1977–).

In citing Aristotle's writings, I follow the standard notation of the pages, columns and lines of Bekker's edition: *Nich. Ethics* 1179$^a$ 27–32, for example, or *Pol.* 1253$^a$ 3–4. The translations are often mine. I have attended, however, to H. Rackham's edition and translation of the *Politics* (Cambridge, Mass., and London, 1932), and of the *Nicomachean Ethics* (Cambridge, Mass., and London, 1934).

Among the footnotes the reader will often be confronted with multiple citations in a single footnote. The first citation is relevant to the material noted; subsequent citations refer to information preceding the notation, in the order in which the information appears in the text.

# Introduction

Richard Hooker's reputation as "the judicious Hooker" endures into modern and secular times. I think that the common name bespeaks the uncommon quality and, moreover, that more may be learned from his judiciousness than modern scholars and intellectuals tend to believe. This study considers Hooker's important opinions and judgments. It weighs his judiciousness, so to speak. Since his *Laws of Ecclesiastical Polity* defends Elizabeth I's regime, Elizabethan particulars of church and state are discussed. Since he reinterprets Elizabethan arrangements in light of his own generalities, moral, political, and religious principles are considered. What follows is in good part theoretical, an inquiry in politics broadly construed. It is nevertheless historical at beginning and end: this study discusses first the Elizabethan problems that occasioned Hooker's work and shaped much of his rhetoric, and last the practical prescriptions for England to which his generalities pointed.

One need address little prefatory argument to thoughtful Anglicans long accustomed to respect Hooker's *Laws*. They at least will sympathize with a work taking seriously Hooker's sort of politico-religious wisdom. He shaped church ceremony and church governance so as to be politic without being merely politic, shaped belief and practice alike with a view to both piety and citizen education, and discouraged mindless zealotry as well as mindless atheism. This sort of wisdom (if such it is) has also commended Hooker's reflections to thoughtful English statesmen, aware, as the historian Macaulay put it, of the constant conjunction of "the secular history of England" with "the history of her ecclesiastical polity." By his *Laws* Hooker appeared to rise above the bitter and often querulous disputes among Puritans, Catholics, and the Elizabethan hierarchy—"like a knight of romance among caitiff brawlers," in Henry Hallam's simile that was for a time unchallenged among students of Hooker.[1] While one need not mention the praise often quoted from popes and kings, nor claim for Hooker rank with the first of philosophers, one should note the praise given by

---

1. Henry Hallam, *The Constitutional History of England from the Accession of Henry VII to the Death of George II* (Paris, 1841) I, 156; Thomas Babington Macaulay, *The History of England from the Accession of James II* (New York, n.d.) I, 57.

Leibniz and the tribute of sixteen quotations from Hooker in the most influential of philosophic works, John Locke's *Second Treatise of Civil Government*.

In this last quarter of the twentieth century, however, one perceives little or no praise and tribute from the politic and the philosophic. Outside the increasingly buffeted circles of Anglican faith and controversy, Hooker has become the property of a few scholars alone. Among even these the purport of his work now appears obscure and its value doubtful. The editor of the definitive new text, W. Speed Hill, contrasts the piously respectful attitude of 1836, when Rev. John Keble published Hooker's works, with "contemporary interest," which "has been so parceled out among various scholarly disciplines that we are in danger of losing sight of the wholeness of Hooker's vision." In the lead chapter of the volume prefatory to this new edition, W. D. J. Cargill Thompson suggests "that the nature of Hooker's achievement as a political philosopher is more open to question at the present day than at any time in the past."[2] Here is a paradox. We are to receive a new edition from exacting scholars—and yet the benefit of reading Hooker has never been less obvious to scholars themselves or more widely doubted.

Obviously we *should* wonder now about the adequacy of Hooker's vision and achievements, if only in light of the very different opinions and arrangements that now prevail. Yet the peculiarly stunted character of many scholarly estimates of Hooker serves to prevent precisely an open confrontation, a genuine weighing. Before taking up more serious objections, we need to work free of these artificial obstacles. A prefatory review leads to this conclusion: the historical scholarship on Hooker begun in the nineteenth century is beset with inherent and perhaps terminal difficulties.

The better historical scholars themselves exhibit doubts about recent scholarship. In the chapter mentioned, Cargill Thompson, for example, desires a "reappraisal of Hooker's significance in the history of thought" and is uneasily self-conscious about "developments that have taken place in the study of his political ideas" (p.3). Virtually all contemporary scholars are skeptical of at least the first phase of historical scholarship, which interpreted Hooker as a proto-liberal, an anticipatory Whig in the evolution of political liberalism. Hooker's commendation of government by law and consent was supposed to show that he was fighting the battle of toleration and popular government "in advance of his age" (as the *Cambridge Modern History* put it in 1905). He is portrayed as a sort of scout for the liberal general John Locke. The theme of Henry Hallam's *Constitutional History* (1841) is the progress in England of the liberty which has been the slow fruit of ages; Hooker's constant predilection for the "liberal principles of civil government" shows that "upon these subjects, his theory absolutely coincides with that of Locke."[3] Despite Locke's many quotations of Hooker's words, this view proved indefensible. In studies of Hooker by

2. W. D. J. Cargill Thompson, "The Philosopher of the Politic Society: Richard Hooker as a Political Thinker," in *Studies in Richard Hooker, Essays Preliminary to an Edition of His Works*, ed. W. Speed Hill (Cleveland and London, 1972), p. 3; Hill's remark is on p. ix.

3. *Constitutional History* I, 2, 159–60; Sidney Lee, "The Last Years of Elizabeth," in *The Cambridge Modern History* (New York, 1905) III, 348.

George Bull and the more influential Alexander d'Entrèves, and of Locke by Leo Strauss and Peter Laslett, Hooker's theory was shown to be the traditional medieval doctrine of consent, law, and community. It was far from Locke's doctrine of individual rights and governmental powers. Agreeing with the historicist thesis that Hooker's doctrines were "rooted in the living development of the thought of his time," d'Entrèves insisted nevertheless that his achievement was the transmission of an outlook thoroughly medieval. In the face of the Reformation's emphasis on faith alone, Hooker restored "the theory of law and government to its proper basis, which is a philosophical basis," and thus linked "modern and medieval political philosophy in England."[4] A similar thesis dwells on the classical rather than the Christian component: Hooker is called a transmitter of Renaissance humanism.[5]

These variations on a historical account proved insufficient, however, both in characterizing what was transmitted as medieval or philosophic and in supposing that the transmission was significant. H. F. Kearney and Peter Munz contend that Thomism, which d'Entrèves attributes to Hooker, is inconsistent with state control of religion; the *Laws*'s defense of royal supremacy over the church resembles instead Marsilius's anticlericalism.[6] Others argue that Hooker mixes reason with grace in a manner inconsistent with grace construed in a Christian way or with reason construed in an Aristotelian way. Still others suggest that, however consistent, Hooker's mixture is not philosophic in a modern sense; it fails to follow the epistemology of modern science.[7] Moreover, Cargill Thompson raises a different objection: Hooker is not an abstract thinker, not above the partisan brawls. He is a partisan who subordinated inquiry to an advocate's brief, a mere defender of his monarch's *status quo*.[8] Whatever the character of Hooker's pre-modern thought, in any event, its transmission into succeeding ages is less obvious than its crumbling, as Herschel Baker contended, before "the advent of science and a secularized natural knowledge." Hooker had doubtful success as a transmitter of medieval thought. Bacon, Locke, modern science, and the Enlightenment are a revolution from Christian and classical ways, not a modification of them. Some scholars do praise or blame Hooker as a conservative, skeptical of modern progress. Hugh Trevor-Roper paints him as an opponent of an international Calvinism similar to Jacobinism and Leninism.

4. Alexander d'Entrèves, *The Medieval Contribution to Political Thought: Thomas Aquinas, Marsilius of Padua, Richard Hooker* (Oxford, 1939), pp. 115–16, cf. chs. 5 and 6; Leo Strauss, *Natural Right and History* (Chicago, 1953), pp. 221–23; John Locke, *Two Treatises of Government*, ed. Peter Laslett (Cambridge, Eng., 1964), pp. 56–57; George Bull, "What Did Locke Borrow from Hooker?" *Thought* 7 (1932): 122–35.

5. Herschel Baker, *The Wars of Truth: Studies in the Decay of Christian Humanism in the Earlier Seventeenth Century* (Cambridge, Eng., 1952), ch. 5.

6. H. F. Kearney, "Richard Hooker: A Reconstruction," *Cambridge Historical Journal* 5 (1952): 300–311; Peter Munz, *The Place of Hooker in the History of Thought* (London, 1952); cf. Ernst Troeltsch, *The Social Teaching of the Christian Churches* (New York, 1960) II, 637.

7. F. S. C. Northrop, "Richard Hooker and Aristotle," in *The Meeting of East and West* (New York, 1946), p. 192; Robert K. Faulkner, "Reason and Revelation in Hooker's Ethics," *American Political Science Review* 59 (1965): 680–90.

8. Thompson, "Philosopher of the Politic Society," pp. 13–16.

## 4    Introduction

Unlike the unhistorical and ideological Calvinists, Hooker is said to be liberal and tolerant, recognizing "the legitimacy of historical change." The point has been argued by Sheldon Wolin. Wolin contends that Hooker originated British conservatism of the type that Edmund Burke eventually advocated: a cautious respect for old verities and a cautious skepticism of modern political generalities.[9] That Hooker originated conservatism is doubtful, however. Burke is far from sharing the priority Hooker gave to faith, theory, Christ, and Aristotle; nor did Hooker have Burke's regard for evolutionary progress, politics, and freedom of enterprise, to say nothing of toleration. Still, some transmission is undisputed: Hooker's teaching still influences Anglicans. Yet the significance of this influence is disputed. Cargill Thompson, a professor of ecclesiastical history, regrets that "the historical understanding of scholarship" on Hooker has been hampered by "Anglican hagiography."[10] Meanwhile, commentators such as John F. Booty, Egil Grislis, Gunnar Hillerdal, and John Marshall, in the wake of Lancelot Andrewes, John Keble, and Dean R. W. Church, continue to explicate Hooker's contributions to Anglicanism.

These successive problems in describing Hooker's contribution to intellectual history—whether as liberal, medieval, philosophic, conservative, or religious—have brought contemporary historical scholarship to an impasse. A few scholars occupy themselves not with the *Laws*'s contribution to historical development but merely with the history of the *Laws* itself: Hooker's own production of the text, the influence of his patrons and friends, the mechanics of its publication. One scholar has characterized Hooker's contribution as less what he had to say than how he said it, which misses what C. S. Lewis perceived: "Always an artist, [Hooker] is never merely an artist." Perhaps, as Georges Edelen has suggested, Hooker's orderly yet probing arrangement of clauses depends on the confidence in rational inquiry informing the substance of his thought.[11]

The most provocative of recent historical studies is Cargill Thompson's chapter. Agreeing with d'Entrèves that Hooker is no social contract theorist, pleased also to be rid of traditional hero worship, Cargill Thompson self-consciously furthers an iconoclastic twentieth-century scholarship that breaks "away from the stereotypes," refutes the myths, topples idols. While holding Hooker consistent in defending royal supremacy, he treats Hooker's consistency as but intellectual weaponry in service of the *status quo*. He reduces Hooker's thought to historical circumstance, without the older supposition of historical progress working within circumstance. In this debunking stage of historical scholarship, Hooker is presented principally as a time-server in some very obvious senses. His thought is but a sophisticated version of sixteenth-century

9. Sheldon Wolin, "Richard Hooker and English Conservatism," *Western Political Quarterly* 6 (1953): 28–47; Baker, *Wars of Truth*, p. 93; Hugh Trevor-Roper, "The Great & Good Works of Richard Hooker," *New York Review of Books*, Nov. 24, 1977, pp. 1, 8.

10. Thompson, "Philosopher of the Politic Society," p. 5.

11. Georges Edelen in *Studies in Richard Hooker*, pp. 250, 255–58; Hill, in *Studies*, p. xiv; C. S. Lewis, *English Literature in the Sixteenth Century Excluding Drama* (Oxford, 1954), pp. 451–63.

commonplaces; his purpose but a defense of the existing constitution of Elizabeth's church; his diagnosis of the Puritan threat essentially a smear; his refutation largely an elaboration of principles enunciated by Archbishop John Whitgift; his positive principles derivative from Aristotle or Aquinas or the English reformers or someone. At best, Hooker's theory is an eclectic sponge for the varying currents of his time, and on practical matters he is merely "as conservative in his political outlook as most Elizabethan Englishmen."[12]

Such an achievement deserves to be forgotten, and indeed Cargill Thompson comes to bury Hooker. We may postpone the interment, however. This novel-sounding argument is but conventional in its use of contemporary labels, has been long disputed, and is at its core untrue. Notions such as *conservative* and *status quo* are problematic contemporary residues of an uncritical faith in historical progress. Besides, in defending royal supremacy over the church Hooker sought also to reform and limit it, an effort Cargill Thompson eventually admits, as do the best commentators. Cargill Thompson does not confront the argument of A. S. McGrade, that Hooker "spiritualizes the state" more than he temporalizes the church, or of Peter Munz, that Hooker interprets actual "conditions in terms in which they would become acceptable to his general philosophical outlook."[13] He misses the connection between Hooker's thoughtfulness and his particular purpose, and thus only assumes conventional answers to the important question: to what extent does Hooker's defense embody a thoughtful case for something that may then, and may still, be worth defending?

These shifts and sparrings among historical scholars cannot resolve the underlying impasse. The problem with finding a place for Hooker in the history of thought lies less with the character of Hooker's thought than with the very aim of a scholarship oriented to the history of ideas. For particular notions of place, thought, and even history reflect different and inherently controversial opinions (liberal, conservative, religious, pragmatic, or whatever) about the true course of history. The fundamental controversy over what is true and truly good still lives, however muffled by various suppositions of historical development. Whether Hooker's fostering of Anglicanism is an achievement; whether a truly medieval teaching is Thomistic or Marsilian; whether a philosophy must be consistent and based solely on human perception and reasoning; whether the Aristotelian account of knowing is surpassed by the epistemology of modern science—these questions depend for their answers on judgments about what is holy, true, or good, and indeed on a judgment as to which of these judgments is most serious.

As doubts about the goodness of liberal and Marxist progress have multiplied, the supposition of development has become controversial. To judge Hooker's place, to determine whether thought progressed beyond him or whether his thought was limited, requires that one judge the merits of his

12. Thompson, "Philosopher of the Politic Society," pp. 5–6, 13–16, 20.

13. Munz, *The Place of Hooker in the History of Thought*, p. 102; A. S. McGrade, "The Coherence of Hooker's Polity: The Books on Power," *Journal of the History of Ideas* 24 (1963): 175.

thought. To be a historian of thought, Leo Strauss has intimated, one must try to be a philosopher.[14] Whatever the difficulties, this attempt at least cultivates an appreciative inquiry into the worth of various moral, political, and religious alternatives, instead of promoting a systematic plan for intellectual burial plots.

True, an appreciation of Hooker's practical proposals requires some grasp of Elizabethan history. I have benefited from the works of Sir John Neale, Christopher Hill, Patrick Collinson, Clare Cross, Patrick McGrath, G. R. Elton, and other recent writers, as well as from older historians such as W. H. Frere, James Froude, Henry Hallam, and David Hume. Some history, however, is not necessarily History. Precisely the residue of a belief in Mind or Law, decisively determining minds and laws, has often kept scholars from pondering Hooker's characterization of his Elizabethan circumstances. Hooker draws attention to the political defects inherent in the establishment's Reformation theology, to a novel and aggressive atheism linked to Machiavelli, and to the need, if England were to remain decisively Christian, for repeal of many of Elizabeth's (and of Henry VIII's) reforms. Recent historians tend to miss, I shall suggest, the extent to which Hooker sought to reshape as well as defend Elizabeth's church, to reduce as well as expound her ecclesiastical power, to redefine as well as assimilate the ancient learning newly reborn—all this as he waged a deep battle not only against English reformers but also against elements of the Reformation itself.

I am indebted to many students of Hooker, especially those whose work antedates or is somewhat independent of the historical approach. The commentaries of Dean Church and R. W. Bayne, the editions of Keble and Bayne, were indispensable. J. W. Allen's acerbic yet sympathetic portrayal stands out: he treats the sixteenth century without submerging Hooker in the commonplaces and mediocrities of that age. Yet he does not penetrate to the foundations of Hooker's thought. Nor does C. S. Lewis, against whose brief appreciation I have nevertheless checked and refined my own impressions. From Peter Munz, Duncan Forrester, and A. S. McGrade I learned much. McGrade's essays in particular are little models of witty interpretation enlivened by an effort to be currently useful. He is seriously concerned in our time with matters, such as formation of character and what McGrade calls "public religion," that occupied Hooker in his. In his undoctrinaire formulation, we can and should "ask what Hooker would advise us to do today—so long as we see that quotations from the *Polity* will not be much of the answer."[15] Indeed, the philosophical difficulties now discernible in modern political theories "suggest that the principles underlying earlier political theory may deserve reexamining."[16] In this spirit of serious reconsideration for causes both practical and theoretical, McGrade pro-

14. Leo Strauss, "Political Philosophy and History," in *What Is Political Philosophy* (Glencoe, 1959), pp. 56–77, esp. 66, 73–77.

15. A. S. McGrade, "The Public and the Religious in Hooker's Polity," *Church History* 37 (1968): 417, n. 33.

16. A. S. McGrade, "Hooker's *Polity* and the Establishment of the English Church," in Richard Hooker, *Of the Laws of Ecclesiastical Polity*, ed. A. S. McGrade and Brian Vickers (London, 1975), p. 20.

vides the best brief introduction to Hooker's problem and to his comprehensive intention.

This sort of reconsideration assumes that Hooker has a political-religious understanding worth weighing and to some extent perhaps worth following. Viewed coldly and clearly, this assumption will appear controversial and anachronistic beyond the tiny circle of Hooker scholars. Even scholars of "the period" give not Hooker but the chief object of his attack, the Puritans, their primary attention, if not their admiration. Yet they rarely focus on the Puritans' actual virtues or views—piety or theocratic republicanism, for example. Most commentators attend to the historical developments the Puritans are alleged to foreshadow, be it liberal toleration and middle-class republicanism, or (in recent years) the zeal of radical levelers and popular revolutionaries. After all, the progenitor of philosophy of history and modern history of philosophy, Hegel, never mentions Hooker in his *Lectures on the History of Philosophy*. Yet his account of the great revolution wrought by Luther is well known—thus modern individuality became manifest, a decisive stage of history's development. Hooker seems of the ash heap of history, "an archaic, backward-looking conservative," as Hugh Trevor-Roper phrased the prevailing attitude, "in a contest in which, by definition, the Puritans are the Moderns."[17]

That modern political activists and active intellectuals would characterize Hooker's views as reaction without reason is more understandable. The health of religion, or even the politic governance of religion, no longer seems relevant to the political establishments in liberal and social democracies, or to their various libertarian or democratic oppositions. Still, the old Adam of religious warfare remains before our eyes, not only in the ancient Middle East but in the United Kingdom. Even in the paradigm of enlightened development, the United States, fundamentalist churches and movements flourish among the populace as more respectable and enlightened churches languish. Serious students of politics will still find relevant Hooker's diagnosis of religious strife and of the civic possibilities and problems endemic to religious zeal.

Still, many attribute such troubles and enthusiasms to ghosts from an unenlightened past. Let modernization and popular education continue their sweep, it will be said, and these few remaining anachronisms can be exorcised. Here too we see a faith, albeit a faith in man-made progress. Are there not now reasons for skepticism, however, reasons not so visible to older liberals and socialists? We can see new kinds of civic sickness in the most enlightened countries, a social malaise that makes one wonder whether a rational and happy society is bred by free expression and popular education, coupled with visible progress in luxury and comfort. One sees in all developed countries, especially liberal and democratic ones, a proliferation of crime and pornography, most ominously among the young; an increase in suicides among the young; increasing unruliness and violence in schools; a radical increase in one-parent families; inattention by parents to children; a high and often rising divorce rate. It be-

17. Trevor-Roper referred to such attitudes in "Clarendon," *Times Literary Supplement*, January 10, 1975, p. 32.

comes questionable whether self-interest rightly understood, as Alexis de Tocqueville once called the Americans' chief principle of conduct, will move most citizens to more than consumption or luxury or (what Tocqueville himself most feared) soft servility. It even seems questionable whether citizens of mass democracies will be content with these gentler vices. Affluence and social democracy seem to magnify these difficulties; middling classes feel less the spur of necessity and become confident of their power to ease themselves from restraints by redistribution of wealth and authority. On this point Tocqueville had always retained doubts, despite being judged *the* authoritative friend of modern democracy by no less an authority than the more optimistic John Stuart Mill. Such doubts led to the Frenchman's famous admiration for the Americans' religious tradition, a judgment almost as out of fashion during the enlightened second quarter of the nineteenth century as in the liberated last quarter of the twentieth. Some well-meaning intellectuals of his native France, Tocqueville observed,

> sincerely wish to prepare mankind for liberty. When such as these attack religious beliefs, they obey the dictates of their passions, not their interests. Despotism may be able to do without faith, but freedom cannot. Religion is much more needed in the republic they advocate than in the monarchy they attack, and in democratic republics most of all. How could society escape destruction if, when political ties are relaxed, moral ties are not tightened?[18]

The lesson is more apt now. While liberal democracies' moral capital is depleted, the hopes of many intellectuals are more extreme. One commonly sees intellectuals attacking the invisible hand of the economic marketplace only to make sacrosanct an invisible mind, at least as corrosive of custom and belief, immanent in a marketplace of ideas. Meanwhile they question the old liberal faith in progress by production, the true opiate of the modern masses, in the name of distributive justice and of quality of life or authentic self-expression. Whether or not the democratic West is spiritually exhausted and increasingly vulnerable to a patient and cunning enemy, as Alexander Solzhenitsyn argues, the old Enlightenment faith in technology, science, and economic progress has lost much of its hold on intellectuals and peoples. Solzhenitsyn thinks ours a time like the Renaissance, a great turning point in civilization. It is at least time to reconsider serious reflections typically doubted on grounds now in doubt. Even if Hooker's premises, reasonings, and proposals have little direct application to our present political crisis, they might illuminate a truer or better way, a way for some to think and live if not for many to be governed.

The study that follows is an investigation of these possibilities, rather than an insistence upon their truth. A mixture of Christianity and Aristotelianism was the obvious target of, the great alternative to, the classic Enlightenment of Bacon, Hobbes, and Locke. Hooker exhibits such a mixture in perhaps its most

18. Alexis de Tocqueville, *Democracy in America*, trans. George Lawrence (Garden City, N.Y., 1969) I, 294.

attractive and moderate form. His teaching is reasonable and ecumenical in matters of religion, and moderate and republican (in the old sense of a mixed regime) in matters of politics. He returns judiciousness to religion, in the face of the Reformation's insistence on justification by faith alone, and keeps judiciousness above the mere calculations of self-interested statecraft. In the formulation of Hallam: the *Laws of Ecclesiastical Polity* forms

> a rampart, on the one hand against the puritan school who shunned the light of nature as a deceitful meteor; and on the other against that immoral philosophy which, displayed in the dark precepts of Machiavel, or lurking in the desultory sallies of Montaigne, and not always rejected by writers of more apparent seriousness, threatened to destroy the sense of intrinsic distinctions in the quality of actions, and to convert the maxims of statecraft and dissembling polity into the rule of manners.[19]

That Hooker sought a mean between zealotry and amoral cunning does not show that he found one, however. His was a mixture of Christianity and Aristotelianism—and it is an old question whether these two mix well, whether one might mix "faith and reason without doing violence to either," in Basil Willey's wishful formulation.[20] The most serious task of a student of Hooker is to clarify the consistency of this mixture and, fundamentally, the merits of each part. I have thought it illuminating to contrast Hooker in various points with the prince of Christian Aristotelians, Thomas Aquinas; with that Aristotelian of unorthodox Christianity, Marsilius of Padua; with that very politic Elizabethan Aristotelian, Sir Thomas Smith; and, at greater length in matters of both ethics and politics, with Aristotle himself.

19. Hallam, *Constitutional History* I, 159.
20. Basil Willey, *The English Moralists* (London and New York, 1964), p. 98.

# Part I

## Hooker's Problem:

### The English Church
### and Its Enemies

# 1

## The Church and Hooker's Purpose

Some suppose that Richard Hooker merely defends an Elizabethan *status quo* from purifying Christians bent on further reformation. They miss his more subtle battle against opponents less obvious, notably atheists and Catholics outside his church, and those clergy and laity not pulling their weight within. Actually, Hooker seems to have thought the church he defended its own worst enemy. "There are undoubtedly more estates overthrown through diseases bred within themselves than through violence from abroad," he remarks in the dedication to Book V of his *Laws of Ecclesiastical Polity*; diseases within made the English church peculiarly ill-fitted during the 1580s and 1590s to confront its enemies without.

Here Hooker agrees with many subsequent historians, although not with all. Ordinary clergy were too often sunk in ignorance and poverty and meanness. Many parishes had so fallen in income and stature, he writes, that a miserable crop of "the scum and refuse" of the whole land, "eyesores" and "blemishes" (no less), were employed about God's service, "the death of the nurse that feeds them."[1] Besides, many clerics enjoyed the revenue from a number of cures and from dispensations from living in their cure. Many parishes, therefore, had hardly any ministry. And the church's governors, the bishops, were frequently notorious, if only because they were more conspicuous. The great Lord Burghley evidently exaggerated when he wrote in 1585 that they "had no

1. Richard Hooker, *Of the Laws of Ecclesiastical Polity*, in *The Works of that Learned and Judicious Divine Mr. Richard Hooker*, 3 vols., arr. John Keble, 7th ed., rev. R. W. Church and F. Paget (Oxford, 1888), Book V, chapter lxxxi, sections 8, 9; henceforth abbreviated *Laws* V. lxxxi.8, 9.

credit either for learning, good living, or hospitality. The Bishops, who by their teaching and devotion, and relieving of the poor, ought to have won credit among the people, were generally covetous and were rather despised than reverenced or beloved."[2] Some scholars think this to overstate the case considerably. Nevertheless, Hooker's more delicately phrased comments picture an episcopacy often of "mean worth," little judgment, "utter contempt even of learning itself," and "coldness in works of piety and charity," of disdain for the ordinary clergy, "want of severity" toward "any great one," and above all a "wretched thirst for gain." A number of bishops were of the reforming persuasion, moreover, and sedulously assisted or permitted the reduction of church and of episcopacy itself at which the reformers aimed.[3]

These defects in clerical conduct were connected with the political side of the Elizabethan religious-political arrangements. Five-sixths of the ordinary clergy were appointed by lay patrons (including the crown), and the bishops by the queen herself. In varying proportions these influencers and governors were moved by devotion to the religion established, reforming theology, a purely political prudence wary of clerical power, an envy and jealousy of clerical power, and, not least, avarice. Hooker laments the "conscienceless and wicked patrons, of which the swarms are too great in the Church of England." For this and other reasons, hardly one benefice in fifteen, hardly six hundred of nine thousand livings, provided the minimal income necessary for a minister to exist without other, often manual, employment. As aristocracy and gentry scraped the ordinary clergy, moreover, Elizabeth exercised her considerable fiscal talents on the episcopacy. She permitted prolonged vacancies, extending to fourteen or nineteen or even forty-one years, during which she enjoyed the revenues. She compelled favorable leases or gifts of bishops' lands to her courtiers. More important, the queen was inclined to exchange crown lands of poor or unprofitable quality, or with revenues hard to collect, for fat episcopal holdings. At worst, Elizabeth was carrying on what A. F. Pollard describes as the "policy of Tudor government since 1529 which had been to make the church a national institution subject to the crown; its financial aspect was the confiscation or control of all religious endowments." Elizabeth was evidently no plunderer on the scale of her father, Henry VIII, or of even her brother, Edward VI. The queen's strongest defenders admit, however, that the bishops' revenues did no more than hold steady during her reign, while inflation and prosperity increased proportionately the shares of other estates.[4] At best the queen and her counsellors displayed an unenthusiastic and too often exploitative governance, which did little to relieve the lethargy of clergy and the indifference of laity that were visible features of the Elizabethan religious scene.

2. "Memorial of the State of the Realm," quoted in James Anthony Froude, *History of England from the Fall of Wolsey to the Defeat of the Spanish Armada* (New York, 1870) XII, 21. See Froude's further comments, and below, ch. 10, the third section.

3. *Laws* VII.xxiv *passim*.

4. William P. Haugaard, *Elizabeth and the English Reformation* (Cambridge, Eng., 1968), pp. 151–61; A. F. Pollard, *The History of England from the Accession of Edward VI to the Death of Elizabeth (1547–1603)* (London, 1910), p. 17. See below, ch. 10, the second and third sections, and ch. 11, the fourth and sixth sections.

The sluggish state of the Elizabethan church had complicated causes. Ignorance in laity and lower clergy under the old Catholicism contributed, as did the great swings from Papacy to reform once and again, the new power of the laity, weakness of ecclesiastical discipline, and the new ecclesiastical poverty. Right up to the civil wars "the functions of the parish became more and more secularized," according to Christopher Hill. Even the church's buildings marked a certain indifference. Hill suggests that in 1637 all but nine of the one hundred sixteen churches in Buckinghamshire were in serious disrepair.[5] Worse, the indifference of the neuters, supposed at the time to make up the bulk of the population, was aggravated by some new atheists who encouraged positive scorn for Christianity. England was Christian in profession and law, and its church, remarks Hooker, was at least free of open and blasphemous "contumelies." Nevertheless, "unless we be strangers to the age wherein we live, or else in some partial respect dissemblers of that we hourly both hear and see, there is not the simplest of us but knoweth with what disdain and scorn Christ is honoured far and wide." This grave diagnosis of an anti-Christian tendency within an ostensibly Christian England recurs, and must be counted one cause of the gloomy pessimism that Hooker's spirited efforts do not conceal. "God himself is for his own sake generally no where honoured," he writes almost despairingly, "religion almost no where, no where religiously adored, the ministry of the word and sacraments of Christ a very cause of disgrace in the eyes of both high and low."[6]

In confronting neuters, reformers, and scoffers Hooker's church bore a disadvantage more telling in the long run than its defects of ministry and discipline. While hugging the thirty-nine articles formulated early in Elizabeth's reign, the church lacked nevertheless an adequate teaching and spirit. It lacked the distinctive articulation of belief and arrangements that might move its followers, overcome indifference, and present a compelling alternative to atheists and reformers alike. A Christian should be moved by faith in Christ, by belief above all. "Nor doth any man ever believe," Hooker remarks, "into whom the doctrine of belief is not instilled by instruction some way received at the first from others,"[7] from the church in particular. The English church's doctrine of belief was burdened by a famously chequered past, however, which reminds one as much of the political-religious compromises set forth by Macaulay and Froude as of religious truth.[8]

England had been wrenched from Rome by Henry VIII because of what may be charitably called political expediency. Its ecclesiastical arrangements had then oscillated, from Henry's removal of papal governance and diminution of clerical wealth without major changes in creed, to the sudden impact of Reformation theology and anti-Romanism under Edward VI, to the restoration of

5. Christopher Hill, *Society and Puritanism in Prerevolutionary England* (New York, 1964), pp. 420, 441.

6. *Laws* VII.xv.7; V.lxv.9. On "neuters," see Patrick Collinson, *The Elizabethan Puritan Movement* (Berkeley and Los Angeles, 1967), p. 26.

7. Laws V.xxi.3; V.xxii.9; V.xlii.7; V.lxiii.1, 29; V.xxvi.7.

8. Thomas Babington Macaulay, *The History of England from the Accession of James II* (New York, n.d.) I, 57–64. Froude, *History of England* VII, 81–83.

Catholicism (pope, legate, payments, persecution, and everything possible) during Mary's years, to the reform, finally, of Elizabeth and her bishops and Commons. Above these particular variations in creed and formulae had hovered the general struggle between the theology of Rome, and first that of Germany, later that of Geneva. The politic compromises of Elizabeth's thirty-nine articles, and the failure of her churchmen ever to achieve codification of the church's common law, symbolized what many thought an uninspired muddle between the forceful causes of Rome and Reformation. In the circumstances the results were predictable: reformers newly ensconced in power under Elizabeth pressed for a more thorough Reformation; Catholics kept sulkily to the old ways and watched for a chance to free themselves, perhaps under Mary Stuart and with the aid of Spain, from their heretical supreme head and her waspish reformers.

The most notable pre-Elizabethan defense of distinctively English arrangements in religion was Thomas Starkey's *Exhortation to Unitie and Obedience* (1534). Writing some sixty years before Hooker's *Laws*, Starkey was justifying Henry VIII's attacks upon papal authority and the religious orders. He presents himself as fresh back from Italy, from studies of philosophy and the Bible. He is devoted above all to serving his "country," and is appalled above all at his countrymen's new blindness.[9] That blindness consists chiefly in a "division of sects," a growing division into sundry parties guided by superstition and arrogance of opinion. The superstitious insist that certain customs and rites of human invention (the custom of papal supremacy, in particular) are absolutely necessary to the church and salvation. The arrogant insist that any addition to God's Word of human inventions is forbidden to the church, inimical to salvation, and violative of the liberty of a Christian man.[10] While Starkey attends most to Rome's attacks upon Henry's overthrow of papal authority, he in effect holds the theologies of both Rome and Germany to be superstitious or in error. Indeed, the opinion that salvation is gained by faith without works is "a more corrupt judgment"; to it is annexed the ruin of Christian policy. It erodes customary devotion, and eventually all devotion, the most stable and sure foundation of "all civil order, and all good worldly policy."[11] Starkey encourages a mean that will avoid the civil harm, even civil war, that he fears from evil preachers. The "true preacher" in "all his preachings and teachings, sets before his eyes as chief end, concord and unity." To this end, one must sharply distinguish things spiritual from things worldly, and guide a Christian polity by worldly policy, albeit worldly policy qualified by charity.[12] Correspondingly, things necessary for spiritual salvation are to be understood as few, as defined

9. Thomas Starkey, *Exhortation to Unitie and Obedience* (London, 1534[?], 1540[?]; repr. Amsterdam and New York, 1973), pp. 15, 16 ff. References to unnumbered reverse sides are rendered by superscript [b], as 8[b]; to pages numbered in duplicate by [1], as 8[1] or 8[b1].

10. *Exhortation*, pp. 23[b]–25, 14, 29 ff., 20–23. The first citation is to the textual material noted; subsequent citations are to prior materials, in the order of their appearance in the passage. I follow the same procedure in all footnotes with plural citations otherwise unexplained.

11. Ibid., pp. 72[b], 28, 80, 81.

12. Ibid., pp. 40[b], 84, 4[b].

by a simple creed, as oriented to brotherly love, and as not requiring much inquiry into the scriptures.[13] All ceremonies, rites, customs, and ecclesiastical decrees, on the other hand, "all rites and constitutions ecc.esiastical," are but matters indifferent, needful to induce "rude and simple minds to conceive the mysteries of Christ" and yet susceptible of establishment or change by prince or common counsel.[14] To council, or pope and council, Starkey might leave interpretation of disputed points in scripture. His chief point is nevertheless this: preachers and the unlearned multitude (if the two may be finally distinguished in his opinion) should forego these curious examinations. Whether or not they perceive evil or bad policy, they should acknowledge "the authority of princes, or in every country or nation whoever have authority," to alter, reform, or abrogate custom—"all such things as be of our forefathers by tradition taken."[15] With subtlety and a cautious awareness of his prince's arbitrariness, Starkey would encourage Christian meekness rather than Christian zeal, and would transfer its object from zealous preachers toward the customs civil authority permits. The most sure knot of Christian civility is "this general knowledge of things necessary joined with meekness."[16] Starkey would supply the knowledge; a Christian people as educated by Starkey, the meekness. His mean between the warring faiths is "true order and policy."[17] His is less a comprehensive although politic understanding of the faith, such as Hooker's, than a comprehensive subordination of the faith to the necessities of politics. The development of this outlook occupies Starkey's less exoteric and more penetrating work, the so-called *Dialogue between Pole and Lupset*. Hooker would suppose such an argument to be of little use in appealing to the Calvinists of his time, who laid the constitution of the church in gospel truth. Nor would Hooker so slight the character of the true faith and sacraments. Nor would Hooker so lightly entrust Henry VIII or any monarch with such authority over religious ceremony, or deprive clerics of their worldly wealth and power. Starkey was chaplain to the king, for a time, and his work indicates a tendency in the Tudor state church that Hooker had to fear.

Elizabeth's settlement had found a variety of defenders prior to Hooker, the best of whom were his early and late patrons, Bishop John Jewel and Archbishop John Whitgift. Sir William Cecil had solicited Jewel's *Apology of the Church of England* (1564), upon the queen's rejection of a papal nuncio bearing an invitation to the Council of Trent. While Jewel's *Apology* has been called with reason the standard defense of the Church of England for most of Elizabeth's reign—it was broadly distributed to the parish churches—it was essentially a brief and often sharp catalogue of "we believes" with which "we Protestants" or "we believers" might rebut the Catholic charge of no coherent beliefs. The Papists were indeed attacked, but the Calvinists were not dealt with, as remarked the English ambassador to France, who had urged a work appealing to France's moderate Protestants. Whatever the merits of Jewel's defense, its zeal and devotion to the primitive church of the ancient fathers and

13. Ibid., pp. 19ᵇ–20, 9.    14. Ibid., pp. 43, 69ᵇ.    15. Ibid., pp. 69ᵇ, 8, 10, 70.
16. Ibid., p. 7ᵇ.    17. Ibid., p. 18.

apostles help to sow the problem that Hooker (among others) had eventually to define and confront.[18]

The works of the more generous Archbishop Whitgift set forth positions in many respects expounded by Hooker, not least because Whitgift, like Hooker, had to address restive Puritans. Yet Whitgift's works are distressingly defensive, parries to immediate blows. He wrote an *Answer* (1572–73) to the Presbyterian admonitions to Parliament, and then a *Defence of the Answer* (1574) in response to Thomas Cartwright's *First Reply*. Both first quote the opponent, or the *Answer* and the opponent's *Reply*, then rebut temperately and fairly. Despite Whitgift's virtues, it is hard to imagine a worse way of setting forth a comprehensive and winning position of one's own. The results are bulky tomes without verve or confident order, which take their bearings from an unworthy opponent and hence lose their way and (more quickly still) their audience. They intimate a defensiveness at the Elizabethan church's core. Patrick Collinson has suggested that at the inception of Elizabeth's reign the English church is better described as two churches beneath the legal rubric of one church. Furthermore, it is a commonplace among scholars that

> for most of the Elizabethan period the Church of England failed to develop a theology of its own. . . . During the whole of what might be called the formative period of reformed theology there is not something which one might call an English school of theology, but only English theologians influenced by Wittenberg, or Zurich, or Geneva, or Strasbourg. Not until the end of the reign did the Church produce in Hooker anyone who might be called a really great constructive and original thinker.

Although this theological vagueness served Elizabeth's endeavor to comprehend all faiths, it was by no means so attractive for "zealous ecclesiastics and laymen anxious to establish in England the true church of Christ,"[19] or for Catholics with their understanding of the true church.

Hooker's calm, commanding, and even majestic control of his argument is the obvious sign of a superiority that the better commentators easily acknowledge. He begins with a "Preface to them that seek (as they term it) the Reformation of Laws and Orders Ecclesiastical in the Church of England"; this preface consists, however, in an offense and not a defense. It may be the most rhetorically devastating dissection of English dissent and Calvin's church governance ever written, at least by a Christian. Never, then or later, does Hooker discuss openly the oscillations and variations of English creed and church. "Many times that which most deserveth approbation would hardly be able to find favor," he remarks, "if they which propose it were not content to profess themselves therein scholars or followers of the ancient, for the world will not

---

18. See John Jewell, *An Apology of the Church of England*, ed. J. E. Booty (Ithaca, N.Y., 1963), pp. 4; xxii, xxi.

19. Patrick McGrath, *Papists and Puritans under Elizabeth I* (London, 1967), pp. 15–16. Collinson, *The Elizabethan Puritan Movement*, ch. 1.

endure to hear that we are wiser than any have been which went before."[20] This maxim Hooker takes to heart. The reader is met throughout with a surface conservatism (which helps explain how Hooker might be read as merely an unoriginal defender of the *status quo*). Hooker's first statement of the issue: "The Laws of the Church, whereby for so many ages together we have been guided in the exercise of Christian religion and the service of the true God, our rites, customs, orders of ecclesiastical government, are called in question." His church's law appears venerable and somehow to be taken for granted. The task is first to make manifest the foundations of that law, "the very first causes and principles from which originally it springeth," then to rebut the reformers' own principles (Books II–IV), and finally to defend the church's practices and arrangements in detail (Books V–VIII). Throughout, Hooker is master of his opponent, and his intent was as much to inform and inspire his churchmen, especially "the minds of the simpler sort," as it was to win those already in conscious opposition.

As to Hooker's achievement there is a common if vague agreement among scholars who take seriously his sort of purpose. Ronald Bayne remarks: "Hooker's treatise did for the Church of England what Calvin's *Institutes* had done for the Genevan Church; it gave it a voice and a character." Philip Hughes observes:

> To the ultimately widespread effect of Hooker upon the formation of minds loyal to the religion whose heart is the Book of Common Prayer, the whole theological work of the centuries since doubtless bears witness. . . . This is to claim for Hooker, among his own, the kind of prestige which, let us say, St. Thomas Aquinas enjoys with Catholics.

And Alfred Barry says:

> Hooker first brought out in clear, explicit words, the chief principles, implied and embodied in the Reformation, which fixed our Anglican position from the first, on a basis far different from the artificial groundwork of the foreign Protestantism. . . . Hooker, although he founded . . . no special school, has, perhaps more than any other single writer, given to our Anglican theology a tone and a direction which it has never lost.[21]

With all their weight, these statements about Hooker's contribution to Anglicanism raise more questions than they answer. Hooker's work is said to be reformed yet not of the foreign (and original) Protestants, to set a tone and direction yet not that of any special school, and to remind of both Calvin's work for the reformers and Aquinas's for the Catholics. Hooker's new foundation for the English Church can be adequately grasped only after we consider the church's enemies from without: atheists, Catholics, and reformers.

20. *Laws* V.ii.3.
21. Bayne and Barry quoted by Gunnar Hillerdal, *Reason and Revelation in Richard Hooker* (Lund, Sweden, 1962), p. 10. Hughes in *The Reformation in England*, 3 vols. (London, 1963), III, 217–18.

# 2

# Atheism,
# Modern and Ancient

In an extension of Aristotelian reasoning, Hooker presents "true religion" as a mean between extremes. The extreme near at hand is unbridled zealotry, and its danger amounted in part to a grave weakening of creed and church before atheism, a less obvious, more foreign extremity. Hooker treats the distinction between religion and irreligion as fundamental, in contrast to the procedure of Starkey's *Exhortation*, discussed in chapter 1; his mean is moderated religion in a religious sense, rather than moderated religion in Starkey's political sense. The preface addressing reformers, which ushers in Books I through IV of Hooker's *Laws*, is complemented by a second preface, to Book V, confronting and to some extent wooing those who make of religion a mere instrument of statecraft. Recent historians often miss the significance of this secular movement, awareness of which pervades Hooker's work (as McGrade recently and Hallam in 1840 perceived), especially the last books on church governance. Perhaps this failure is partly due to the lingering influence of Hegel, who supposed that History's spirit (and not men's opinions) brought about even such a change in consciousness as the secularization of the once-Christian West. The change was said to be a process, inevitable and determined, and the process was supposed to have compounded Reformation and Renaissance, learning religious and secular, into the development of individualism, and then the state, or (in another formulation) humanism and civic consciousness. This persuasion may account for the common failure to follow Hooker in distinguishing a Renaissance atheism, dignified as the "judicious learning" of the "ancient sages," from a "new method" of mockery and learning, associated with the "wise malignant" Machiavelli.[1]

Atheism means godlessness. Hooker distinguishes the ordinary indifference of a man "having utterly no knowledge of God" from the active and theoretical bent of others who "study how to persuade themselves that there is no such thing to be known." Book V ignores the first, as owing to "grossness of wit," to attack the second, in those of "riper capacity." Such thinkers bemuse themselves in questioning the providence of God, the resurrection of the dead, the authority of Scripture, and the immortality of the soul. Priding themselves on victories over the pious but unprepared, their "licentious" mouths "stick not" directly to test "what the most religious are able to say in defence of the highest points whereupon all religion dependeth." Precisely this open scoffing, this mockery and scorn, distinguishes them. Hooker hints that writers of the ancient mold would pay lip service to Christian doctrines as at least salutary, as "spurs and motives unto all virtue." Starkey's *Exhortation* and *Dialogue* do at least this. But the new men are not drawn to the learning of the ancient sages; "it does not serve their turn." They lack the ancients' concern for virtue in the sense of the moral virtues, although they might display the combination of appetite and cunning that is Machiavellian *virtù*. These "trencher-mates" who are also disputers are willfully bent on low pleasure and advantage, are of "a resolved purpose of mind to reap in this world what sensual profit or pleasure soever the world yieldeth." Thus they set themselves against Christian doctrine, wishing to show that religion "is nothing else but a kind of harmless error, bred and confirmed in them by the sleights of wiser men." Just here Hooker singles out Machiavelli and his *Discourses*, as breeder of the opinion that religion is merely a tool of politics and that Christianity is a worse tool than pagan religion.

In his little sketch Hooker grasps the anti-Christian essentials of the Machiavellian scheme, especially of certain crude and diluted parts aimed at *politiques* and men of talent. The sinful combination of sly and lowered aim, with incisive penetration as to means, is beautifully caught in "wise malignancy." Hooker sees (what post-Hegelian commentators often do not) the profoundly anti-Christian bent, the armory of devilishly anti-Christian arguments, and the propaganda of secularization, all portions of the Machiavellian project for amoral and *effettuale* political enlightenment.[2]

It is hard now to estimate the power and pervasiveness, the who and the

1. *Laws* V.ii. 2–4. For the thesis that the thoughts of Aristotle and Machiavelli were somehow melded in Florentine circumstances to produce a "civic consciousness" influential in England, see J. G. A. Pocock, *The Machiavellian Movement* (Princeton, 1975). See A. S. McGrade, "The Public and the Religious in Hooker's Polity," *Church History* 37 (1968): 410.

2. Niccolo Machiavelli, *The Prince* (Milan, 1960), Dedication and chs. 11, 15; *Discourses on the First Decade of Titus Livius* (Milan, 1960), Dedication; Preface; Book I, chs. 11–15. All other studies of Machiavelli's intention are shaded by Leo Strauss's *Thoughts on Machiavelli* (Glencoe, Ill., 1958). See also Harvey Mansfield, *A Commentary on Machiavelli's Discourses* (Ithaca, N.Y., 1979). For a briefer account, see Leo Strauss, "Niccolo Machiavelli," in Strauss and J. Cropsey, *History of Political Philosophy*, 2nd ed. (Chicago, 1972), pp. 271–92; for a

how many, of those scoffing English circles to which Hooker points. At a time when "death by torture could be the penalty for plainspeaking, a certain prudence was mere common sense," and what was true of religious views, on which Lawrence Stone comments, would be doubly true of doubts about religion. To avow "atheism was merely to sign one's own death warrant," one student remarks. "Common prudence would require that the man who doubted the dogmas of the church should not jeopardize his life by putting his doubts in writing and that he should not reveal himself except to his closest friends. If news of his opinions came to the authorities he would of course deny everything."[3] The result is a record of smoke, and a few unequivocal sparks, that intimate a glowing fire. The true extent of the blaze, however, will be shown only by a scholar thoroughly versed in Elizabethan literature and politics, in the many ways of tricking out the new with the coverings of the old, and in the remarkable subtleties of Machiavelli's teaching.

The studies available suggest that Machiavelli's most important works were available in influential circles by the 1590s at the latest. Some suspect that Thomas Cromwell, the man most responsible for Henry VIII's break with Rome and the subsequent royal supremacy, had cultivated his natural proclivities by reading the *Prince*. And another influential servant of Henry, the writer-diplomat Richard Morison, may have reflected some views of the great Florentine. It is quite certain that by 1540 or so William Thomas gave to the young Edward VI (at the latter's request so it seems) a discourse of political counsel "for the King's use" that in topics and treatment is said to follow the *Discourses*. It is certain that a little treatise of the 1550s by Stephen Gardiner, a leading statesman under Henry VIII and Lord Chancellor under Phillip and Mary, quotes some three thousand words from *Prince* and *Discourses*, and borrows therefrom a number of leading arguments. One need not accept Cardinal Pole's remark (of 1540) that Machiavelli "had already poisoned England and would poison all Christendom" in order to suspect an important circulation of his works by the beginning of Elizabeth's reign. Her counsellor Cecil obtained at least some of the writings.[4] Roger Ascham's *Scholemaster* (published posthumously in 1570) could denounce the Italian influence upon England's young scions, "Epicures in living, and *athaoi* in doctrine," who besides ancient sources have "a patriarch" in Machiavel. They make "Christ and his Gospell, onelie serue Civill Policie: Than neyther Religion cummeth amisse to them: In tyme they be Promoters of both openlie: in place again mockers of both privilie."[5] Gabriel Harvey remarks as to his situation at Cambridge University:

---

bibliographical discussion, see Clifford Orwin, "Machiavelli's Unchristian Charity," *American Political Science Review* 72 (December 1978): 1217–27.

3. George T. Buckley, *Atheism in the English Renaissance* (Chicago, 1932), pp. 59, 61; cf. p. 124. Lawrence Stone, *The Crisis of the Aristocracy, 1558–1641* (Oxford, 1965), p. 725.

4. These judgments are based on Felix Raab's *The English Face of Machiavelli* (London, 1964), pp. 32–51, and on Peter Samuel Donaldson's Introduction in Stephen Gardiner, *A Machiavellian Treatise* (Cambridge, Eng., 1975), pp. 16–21. See Phillip Hughes, *The Reformation in England*, 3 vols. (London, 1963), I, 225–26.

5. *English Works of Roger Ascham*, ed. W. A. Wright (Cambridge, Eng., 1904), pp. 232–34.

Some good fellows amongst us begin now to be pretty well acquainted with a certain parlous book called, as I remember me, *Il
principe* di Niccolo Machiavelli, and I can peradventure name you
an odd crew or two that are as cunning in his *Discorsi sopra la prima
deca di Livio*, in his *Historia Fiorentina*, and in his *Dialogues della
arte della guerra* too . . . as university men were wont to be in their
*Parva Logicallia* and *Magna Moralia* and *Physicalia* of both sorts.[6]

Shortly after the beginning of Elizabeth's reign the evidence becomes more
precise (if more trifling) as local editions begin to supplement those from
abroad, according to Felix Raab (whose work remains the most particular and
accurate account). In 1563 the *Art of War* was translated and dedicated to the
queen; it was reprinted in 1573 and 1588. The government refused to license
publication of the *Discourses* or *Prince*, however, and translations of these did
not issue from English presses until 1636 and 1640 respectively. By Elizabeth's
last decades, nonetheless, some three or more manuscript translations of each
were circulating, some in several copies. Through the 1580s, various versions
of the Italian were printed in London under a false imprint, and *Florentine
Historie* (which disguises but lightly the full anti-Christian and anti-aristocratic
teaching) was printed in translation in 1595, dedicated to the royal courtier and
councillor Sir Christopher Hatton. Raab concludes: "Everything indicates that,
at least from the middle 'eighties onwards, Machiavelli was being quite widely
read in England and was no longer the sole preserve of 'Italianate' Englishmen
and their personal contacts. . . ."[7] Indeed, Hooker's friend, student, and sometime collaborator in the publication of the *Laws*, George Cranmer, displayed in
correspondence with Hooker himself an easy familiarity with the *Discourses*.[8]

It is peculiarly hard to judge the influence of all this on the Elizabethan
regime, a task involving a close examination of policies and statesmen that
remains to be done. The prohibition against translating *Prince* or *Discourses*
gives some indication of the dominant official view, no doubt, and corresponds
to a very common opinion of the wicked Machiavel. Still, near the century's
end three powerful courtiers, Hatton, Walter Raleigh, and Francis Bacon, held
Machiavelli's works in considerable esteem. Some evidence links Raleigh to a
freethinking group of poets, scholars, and courtiers, many of whom were important officeholders or of the nobility. Indeed, Raleigh was accused by a somewhat unreliable contemporary, Robert Parsons, of founding a school of atheism
which delighted in mocking Christianity. Similar rumors persisted about the
playwright Marlowe, together with other clamorous literary figures, such as
Thomas Greene and Thomas Nashe, and some say that all these joined in a

6. Quoted by Mark H. Curtis, *Oxford and Cambridge in Transition, 1558–1642* (Oxford,
1959), p. 119.
7. Felix Raab, *The English Face of Machiavelli*, pp. 53, 274. Pocock's discussion of the
influence of a new "civic consciousness" is an illustration of how history can be ruined by History,
an account of men's minds by imaginative constructions presupposing a developing mind.
8. Richard Hooker, *The Works of that Learned and Judicious Divine Mr. Richard Hooker*,
arr. John Keble, 7th ed., rev. R. W. Church and F. Paget, 3 vols. (Oxford, 1888), III, 113,
henceforth abbreviated as *Works* III, 113.

scoffing and contentious circle influenced by Machiavelli and the Epicureans.[9] Above all, however, there is Bacon, of a prince-like political ambition that finally occasioned his great fall from office, of a *Prince*-like ambition for new modes and orders that made him master of men centuries later. His political-industrial, scientific-technological project follows Machiavelli's formula, reason in service to realistic wants, even if "knowledge for the sake of power" is a distinct variation upon Machiavelli's beginnings. "So that we are much beholden," he writes, "to Machiavelli and others that wrote what men do, and not what they ought to do."[10] The rise in that spirit of the later projects of Bacon and of his secretary, Hobbes, of Locke (the great popularizer) and of Harrington and Bolingbroke, made widely visible the philosophic rebellion in England against Christian and ancient learning alike. Still, one should not underestimate more obvious and immediately influential changes. Raab chronicles the respectability gradually achieved by Machiavellian doctrines among political polemicists as the 1600s wore on. From a movement shared secretly by a few, the management of religion became the public policy of a considerable circle of dominant or nearly dominant figures, including Halifax and Bolingbroke. "They thought in terms of 'interest' . . . , not of divine politics." Raab sums up the development which Machiavelli's influence "materially" assisted: "The demand for a religious politics had changed to a general acceptance of politic religion."[11] It is a striking conclusion, even if perhaps overstated, and even if Raab considers insufficiently other teachings tending toward politic religion, notably the distinctively Baconian and the ancient.

Hooker's treatment of the ancients is more extensive, sympathetic, and subtle than his denigration of the moderns. He transforms almost invisibly the ancient authors whom Christianity needs, and of whom (*contra* the school of Machiavelli) something Christian might be made.

One must see first the irony and the drama here. Hooker asserts forthrightly that the "judicious learning" of the classics does not serve the scoffing atheists. While this may be true of the scoffers, it is scarcely true of atheists in general. The renaissance of classical learning had provoked a dramatic tension between ancients and Christians, even as "Christian humanists" like Erasmus, Colet, More, and Hooker endeavored, as Aquinas had, to demonstrate the har-

9. As to all this see Buckley, *Atheism in the English Renaissance*, pp. 80–97, 121–36; Eleanor Grace Clark, *Raleigh and Marlowe: A Study in Elizabethan Fustian* (New York, 1941), pp. 242–338. Raab, *The English Face of Machiavelli*, pp. 54–55, 70–73. Ernest A. Strathman, *Sir Walter Raleigh* (New York, 1951), chs. 2, 5, 6, 8; M. C. Bradbrook, *The School of Night* (Cambridge, Eng., 1936), *passim.*

10. Francis Bacon, *Of the Proficience and Advancement of Learning, Divine and Human* (London, 1966), Book II, chapter xi, section 9; see also *Essays or Counsels Civil and Moral*, ed. C. S. Northup (Boston, 1936), numbers 13, 19, 24, 58, 59. As to Bacon's views, and the controverted relation with Machiavelli, see Howard White, *Peace among the Willows: The Political Philosophy of Francis Bacon* (The Hague, 1968). On the influence of Bacon's scientific project, see Margery Purver, *The Royal Society: Concept and Creation* (Cambridge, Mass., 1967), part 1.

11. Raab, *The English Face of Machiavelli*, pp. 262–63.

mony of the two. *Humanism* is the name often given to the intellectual movement that springs from a longing for the revival of classical antiquity. This movement inclined to clash with that longing for the City of God.

Some scholars deny that the clash was characteristic or necessary. Basil Willey, for example, calls Hooker "a God-centered Humanist," and says, in words quoted before, that St. Thomas had "mixed faith and reason without doing violence to either." Nevertheless, Willey also notes the "latent contradiction" in Britain "between our official lip service to the Christian standard in all its rigour, and the pagan ideal of 'the gentleman' which is what we have really admired and sought to practise."[12] From the very first appearance of Paul in Athens, a *prima facie* contradiction between pagan philosophy and the Christian religion was apparent. While Tertullian's famous question may be too pessimistic and sharp—"What has Athens to do with Jerusalem?"—it nevertheless marks the divide across which such early apologists for Christianity as Justin, Clement, and Origen, and such an apologist for philosophy as Celsus, confronted one another.[13] If Thomas and Hooker achieve the unity of which Willey speaks, it is in the face of such confrontations.

During the Renaissance, the humanists advocated a rational and largely secular education based on the study of the Greek and Roman classics[14]; the place of the Bible and of theology was questioned, explicitly or implicitly. A gradual secularizing tendency accompanied fresh and firsthand knowledge of the ancient books, especially as they entered wholesale into English universities and schools. Throughout Elizabeth's reign it remained a mark of distinction for courtiers such as the powerful Leicester, ambitious for kingship itself, to patronize translations. Besides, sons of the nobility and gentry were often educated in Italy, as Starkey was, or traveled there, and lawyers often obtained some training at the law school at Bologna. The indifference and disdain of many of the nobility and gentry, the positive hostility of many lawyers, were two principal crosses of the Elizabethan church. Moreover, both the queen and her principal counsellor, Cecil, were intensely interested in classical literature. Cecil's library, along with other evidence, suggests that the Greek and Roman classics were the chief employment of his leisure. All this may be agreed upon readily enough.[15] One must dwell on the doubts that followed fresh readings of the Greek satirist Lucian, the Latin Epicurean Lucretius, and the Latin naturalist Pliny, and of such cautious wonderers at particular providence as Cicero ("Tully"), Plutarch, Plato, and Aristotle. Evidently the reception throughout Italy of the Arab Aris-

12. Basil Willey, *The English Moralists* (New York, 1964), pp. 102, 119–20.

13. Henry Chadwick, *Early Christian Thought and the Classical Tradition* (New York, 1966), pp. 22–30, 34, 49.

14. Fritz Caspari, *Humanism and the Social Order in Tudor England* (Chicago, 1954), p. 1.

15. Conyers Read, *Mr. Secretary Cecil and Queen Elizabeth* (London, 1955), pp. 11, 30. See also Caspari, *Humanism and the Social Order in Tudor England*, ch. 1; H. A. L. Fisher, *History of England, 1485–1509* (London, 1906), pp. 142–59; Kenneth Charlton, *Education in Renaissance England* (London, 1965), ch. 3; Joan Simon, *Education and Society in Tudor England* (Cambridge, Eng., 1966), part 3.

totelians, especially Averroes, peculiarly shook the faith, this crisis occasioning the synthesis constructed with masterful art by Thomas.[16] The Latin Averroist Marsilius, born a year after Thomas's death, had shown how a synthesis might artfully give priority to nature rather than grace; Starkey's work seems in that mold. Consider also the lament of that reforming classicist Ascham. He sermonizes against "our Englishe men Italianated" who "haue in more reuerence, the triumphes of Petrarche: than the Genesis of Moses: they make more accounte of Tullies offices, than S. Paules ipistles: of a tale in Bocace, than a storie of the Bible. Than they counte as fables, the holie mysteries of Christian Religion."[17]

The marvel is that Hooker reads no such sermon. He seems to welcome the ancient writers. Aristotle in particular is the very "mirror of human wisdom," "head of all philosophers," "whose eye scarce anything did escape which was to be found in the bosom of nature."[18] Yet this master of nature lacks knowledge of grace, and in general of the Christian's trinitarian, omnipotent, and providential deity. This deficiency affects his understanding of nature. Hooker knows this. He does not hesitate to revise Aristotle's judgment on the immortality of the soul, the eternity of the world, and the character of time,[19] not to speak here of the teachings concerning ethics and politics taken up in our Parts II and III. Yet Hooker never attacks Aristotle by name. While arguing against the philosopher, Hooker minimizes his differences from the Philosopher. His corrections are inconspicuous. He assimilates his Christianized doctrines to those of ancient writers generally and of Aristotle in particular, especially by indiscriminate citation of references to a nonprovidential deity, or to religious principles that find their rationale in civic utility. Although Hooker's most charming distortion implies that Aristotle's *Metaphysics* "plainly teaches" the manner in which God moves the angels,[20] like distortions are universal. Every passage from a Greek or Roman philosopher that Hooker cites in Book I to substantiate general agreement on a providential deity, in the original urges worship only as politically useful, or speaks philosophically of only a nonprovidential divinity.

Others have noted this tendency of Hooker's, to "exhibit the agreement of opposite schools" on key points by means of an "array of quotations in support of what at first sight seems a truism." In his valuable edition of Book I, R. W. Church observes that "at one point he cites an Italian jurist, a renaissance Platonist, a pre-reformation Cardinal, a 'novellist' in Natural Science, all repeating Aristotle's axiom, 'that which all men have at all times learned, nature herself must needs have taught'"[21]—an axiom, incidentally, Hooker gives a distinctly un-Aristotelian interpretation. While Keble had noted Hooker's effort to exhibit

16. Buckley, *Atheism in the English Renaissance*, pp. 22–24.

17. *English Works*, p. 232.

18. *Laws* VIII.ii.12; V.lxxi.11; I.iv.1. Again, the first citation is relevant to the textual material noted; subsequent citations are to preceding material and correspond to the order of appearance.

19. *Laws* V.lxix.1, 2; I.xi.2, 3.

20. *Laws* I.iv.1.

21. Richard Hooker, *Of the Laws of Ecclesiastical Polity, Book I*, ed. R. W. Church (Oxford, 1896), p. 116 (commentary on I.iv.1 and I.vii.3).

agreement, and Hooker's first critics, in "a Christian Letter of certain English Protestants," had protested his "cunning framed method" which had almost put them to sleep, the most acute remarks have been made by Robert Vincent Kavanagh.[22] Kavanagh accounts for Hooker's variety of citations by pointing to the variety in the audience addressed, an audience looking up to various authorities: sceptical courtiers trained in the law schools of Padua and Bologna, courtiers, lawyers, university professors, many of them more enamored of humanism than the Gospels. Kavanagh remarks: "When Hooker quotes or paraphrases Aristotle, Plato, or Tertullian on immortality, he does not make the important distinction, but takes for granted, that all these support the doctrine of personal immortality—Hooker is using Greek names and arguments to carry us as far as they can toward a conclusion first clearly discerned by Christian thinkers." Again, "Hooker knows that the careless reader will suppose that St. Matthew and Trismegistus say the same thing; the humanist will be pleased, the most exacting Christian reader can adapt Trismegistus to a Christian sense; and all will have set before them ostensibly Christian philosophy out of Egypt."[23]

In short, Hooker treats the classics not as enemies but allies, and he confronts their enmity by disguising it, making the most of their alliance and assuming more alliance than exists. This kind of treatment pervades the whole work, but is most constant and conspicuous in the "new foundation" of Book I, chapters i–x. There Hooker shows that nature itself points men toward virtue and the Christian religion. He hardly mentions unpromising ancients like Democritus, Epicurus, and Lucretius; he passes over the unpromising parts of Aristotle, Plato, and Cicero; and he develops and rectifies the promising parts in accord with a nature ruled by God's eternal law. Out of respect for his wisdom Hooker follows and reinterprets Aristotle, especially, and out of respect for his power he disguises their differences and his reinterpretation.

That Hooker or any great thinker might be sufficiently detached from the opinions of his time to insinuate into that time, in the guise of those opinions, views he thinks more salutary, is hard for scholars of our post-Hegelian time to see. We are preoccupied still with History as the shaper of men, and we incline to presuppose a fundamentally unequivocal relationship between even an extraordinary thinker and his time. We have been taught by Leo Strauss, however, that our blindness is recent, self-inflicted by historical scholarship.[24] Just as there is reading between the lines, so also there may be writing between the lines. Strauss argues that ancient and modern philosophers right down to Hegel inclined to disguise a dangerous teaching, available to the thoughtful who read carefully, beneath a relatively harmless surface. The cause was in part fear of persecution. In part also it was regard for their nonphilosophic fellows, for customs and laws morally and politically salutary if not necessarily best or true.

Hooker shows his familiarity with the philosophers' lofty art, and not only

22. Robert Vincent Kavanagh, "Reason and Nature in Hooker's Polity" (Ph.D. diss., University of Wisconsin, 1945); *Works* I, xvii, xviii, xix.

23. Kavanagh, pp. 15, 83, 72–96.

24. Leo Strauss, *Persecution and the Art of Writing* (Glencoe, Ill., 1952), p. 32. See also Werner Heisenberg, *Physics and Philosophy* (New York, 1962), pp. 140–41.

by circumspect treatment of their works. "Posidonius was wont to say of the Epicure," Hooker paraphrases Cicero, "that he thought there were no gods, but that those things which he spake concerning the gods were only given out for fear of growing odious amongst men; and therefore that in words he left gods remaining, but in very deed overthrew them, inasmuch as he gave them no kind of motion, no kind of action."[25] Cicero practiced what Cicero's work says of Epicurus. In the public discussion of the treatise *On the Nature of the Gods*, as Ernest Fortin puts the point, Cicero "sides with the pious Lucilius Balbus, who defends the gods, against the atheist Cotta, who attacks them; but in his less popular work *On Divination*, he states with approval and expounds in his own name the very theory that he feigns to reject in the former treatise."[26]

Hooker turns the tables on the philosophers. He uses their irony, not to point beyond the gods of the city to nature, but to point above a philosophic understanding of nature to God. His art lies in treating the philosophers' salutary and exoteric remarks on the gods as serious, or their serious remarks on god as implying God, and then using their authority for a new foundation of nature that points above nature. This art is only part of the Christian rhetoric to be discussed in Part III. It is a part sharing an essential premise with the philosopher's art. So few men can be philosophers or theologians that one's arguments to men in general must provide for the salutary as well as the true and good.

Nevertheless, Hooker's art differs fundamentally from the philosophers'. Strictly speaking, his works contain no esoteric teaching. The philosophers had an exoteric surface, moral, civil, and religious, and an esoteric doctrine which would not necessarily sustain morals, the polity, and religion. But Hooker's true teaching is fundamentally his surface teaching. The touchstone for theologian and ordinary believer alike is Christian belief; both theoretical man and ordinary man are believers. "Theological reason, . . . out of principles in Scripture that are plain, soundly deduceth more doubtful inferences."[27] We do not find the radical distinction between philosopher and political man, between truth and justice, between theory and practice, so characteristic of Aristotle and of Plato's serious teaching. The theologian's superiority enters with his wisdom, but only in explaining that gospel common to himself and the simple believer and to be spread by both. His concealment is secondary. He writes to uphold the faith of the faithful, concealing difficulties suggested by the faithless or discerned by faithful theologians. In general, and positively, he writes shrewdly and winningly to propagate the faith. Hooker's Christian esotericism may better be termed Christian rhetoric, political speech designed to persuade to the true faith.[28] In so speaking Hooker is among good Christian company. His art points back especially to St. Augustine's art of concealing the truth. Some passages in sacred scripture cannot be understood properly, or only with difficulty, to what-

25. *Laws* VIII.ii.15, paraphrasing Cicero, *De Natura Deorum* I, xliv.

26. Ernest Fortin, "St. Augustine," in Strauss and Cropsey, *History of Political Philosophy*, pp. 151–81. See St. Augustine, *City of God*, trans. Marcus Dods (New York, 1948) V, 9.

27. *Works* III, 594–95; cf. *Laws* II.iv.7; II.vii; III.viii.7–17, esp. 11.

28. See Ernest L. Fortin, "Augustine and the Problem of Christian Rhetoric," *Augustinian Studies* 5 (1974): 92–97.

ever length an exposition may extend. "These should never be brought before the people at all, or only on rare occasions when there is some urgent reason."[29]

The whole *Laws of Ecclesiastical Polity* is best understood as a great work of Christian rhetoric. Beginning with the faith, and theological reasoning in accord with the faith, Hooker adjusts his message, polemics, and appeals to defend his English church. Hence he disguises by a Christianizing assimilation the threat emanating from classical philosophy. We need now consider briefly his way of confronting threats that cannot be assimilated.

Machiavellian and Aristotelian alike incline to subordinate religion to political use, and even to subordinate it to other political measures. When Hooker rebuts atheists, at Book V's beginning, he contends openly and at length that religion is the "chiefest" politic instrument and *a fortiori* Christianity, the true religion. Religion is politic in the best or Aristotelian sense: it perfects virtues like justice, piety, and fortitude. "If the course of politic affairs cannot in any good sort go forward without fit instruments, and that which fitteth them be their virtues, let Polity acknowledge itself indebted to Religion." Let those know who commend "some for their mild and merciful disposition, some for their virtuous severity, some for integrity of life, all these were the fruits of true and infallible principles delivered unto us in the word of God as the axioms of our religion, which being imprinted by the God of nature in their hearts also, and taking better root in some than in most others," flourished even among the pagans. Hooker confines himself to a defense on *political* grounds, and refrains from asserting that Christianity among religions is alone politic, or even most politic, although he implies the latter. He allows himself to acknowledge that, as the errors in false religions are mixed with some truths (the souls of men do never perish, divine power has irresistible force), "although the one did turn to their endless woe and confusion, yet the other had many notable effects as touching the affairs of this present life." He concludes that "all true virtues are to honour true religion as their parent, and all well-ordered commonweals to love her as their chiefest stay."[30]

Then Hooker wheels to rebut directly the wise malignant who took aim at Christianity especially. He neglects Machiavelli's deeper argument, which questioned the political efficacy of Aristotelian virtue and of politic religion as well—while leaving a small place for some useful religious beliefs. Hooker simply picks on that place as an opening for his reply. The Florentine had urged princes to wrest all strange and rare events "to the strengthening of their religion," using, "if need be, plain forgeries." For reply Hooker contents himself with an argument of policy: treachery, guile, and deceit will be discovered, and Machiavelli admits that such disclosures and alterations impair religion's credit.[31] *Ergo*, these counsels of the prince of politicians are bound to be impolitic. For even those *politiques* who scoff at the truth of religion, then, it is impolitic to malign the English Christianity established. Brilliant. Against such

29. St. Augustine, *On Christian Doctrine*, trans. J. F. Shaw (Buffalo, 1887) IV, ch. 9, 581; cf. III, ch. 17, 563, and the references in Fortin, "St. Augustine," nn. 8 and 9, p. 180.

30. *Laws* V.i.2–5.

31. *Laws* V.ii.3–4.

a crew refined rhetoric would not suffice, however. Hooker urges more forceful measures upon his superiors in church and nation: more stringency in suppressing the "spit-venom" of these "licentious mouths."[32] But for wavering statesmen, and Christians not yet completely torn from their old faith, a politic refutation of unchristian policy might do some good.

32. *Laws* V.ii.2.

# 3

# Rome

Although the enmity toward his church of believers was more conspicuous than that of doubters, Hooker attacks only the doubting atheists with the bitter strokes reserved for thoroughgoing enemies. Puritans and Papists are addressed sympathetically as all members of the church of Christ, whatever secondary differences may exist. This moderation to Rome (as it seemed among reformed thinkers) was startling at the time. Even to the princes of reform the pope had been "anti-Christ" and his church the "whore of Babylon," the very objects to be protested and reformed. This fundamental suspicion of things Roman pervaded the outlook of even such prominent defenders of Hooker's English establishment as Bishop Jewel and Archbishop Whitgift. To Walter Travers, the Puritan leader in England and Hooker's rival at Temple Church until silenced, Hooker's teaching was not moderation but scandal. He accused Hooker to the Privy Council of "setting forth the agreement of the church of Rome with us, and their disagreement from us, as if we had consented in the greatest and weightiest points, and differed only in certain smaller matters."[1] Although he also charged that Hooker taught a doctrine of predestination that violated the "Word of God," relied in matters of faith upon his reason, and thought assurance by sense more certain than by the Word, Travers's central accusation concerned Hooker's teaching that Rome was a "true Church."

Hooker's treatment, then, seems impressively evenhanded. It is more: his Laws portrays the sectaries of reform as the great enemy. He touches the ecclesiastical and theological differences between Canterbury and Rome sparingly and secondarily, and leaves unmentioned the practical struggle in England. He

---

1. "A Supplication made to the Council by Master Walter Travers," in Works III, 562; see pp. 559–64.

seldom refers to the Catholic campaign involving recusants and schismatics, or to secular priests and Jesuits infiltrated from abroad, or to the only fearsome rebellion of the reign, or to pope and Rome endeavoring with Spain and intermittently with France to overthrow the heretic Elizabeth and her church, or to the invasions frequently threatened, repeatedly attempted, and once landed in Ireland. Hooker's virtual silence about the practical dangers posed by Catholics and the Catholic powers has not been adequately explained, especially by those who would portray him as merely defending the "autonomy of the Church of England."[2]

One cause, no doubt, is the weakness by 1590 of the Catholic threat compared to the Puritan threat. Starting with fearsome strength, the Catholic forces played their cards as if foreordained to blunder, to be suckers for the near-omniscient Elizabeth and Cecil. In turn came a series of political and military disasters: the Bull of Excommunication, plots involving the impossible Mary Stuart, the Spanish Armada, mismanagement of the English priestly mission. England's power and pride rose with the precipitous decline of Spain's and the divisions, especially religious, in France. By the end of Elizabeth's reign the pope himself showed signs of thinking the queen and English heresy a force to be reckoned with, at best to be managed, not to be overthrown.[3] Within, a religion dependent upon clerical governance and ministrations never recovered from the conformity of nine-tenths of its priests to the 1559 settlement.[4] Ten years and more elapsed before the Papacy encouraged the entry of priests from abroad. While the several hundred who entered after 1574 had remarkable effects upon morale and conversions, they were merely fighting, according to Patrick McGrath, a "brilliant rear-guard action" after the "main battle" had been lost. True, the Marian episcopate (with one exception) disappointed Elizabeth's hopes by declining her settlement. Cardinal Pole had left unfilled a number of vacancies, however, and the bishops were in any event generals without an army; their departure allowed the wholesale entry of Elizabeth's own generals, many in the full enthusiasm of reform.

Despite gravely renewed danger in the 1580s, as priests and their martyrs inspired the laity to make a stand for the old devotion, the Catholics were hemmed in by potent forces. McGrath remarks wisely that Elizabeth's *via media* was less between Catholic and Protestant than between different forms of Protestantism.[5] True in theology, it was truer in church government (if we may separate the two here). The Catholics were branded *Papists*, and their tie to the pope ensured that they would be outsiders to queen as well as church and without the patronage and protection so profitable to the reformers. Commons and Council excluded them, whereas the reformers dominated or had powerful friends in both. Seminarians could be trained only in exile and imported with

2. Cargill Thompson, "The Philosopher of the Politic Society," in W. Speed Hill, ed., *Studies in Richard Hooker* (Cleveland and London, 1972), p. 55.

3. Patrick McGrath, *Papists and Puritans under Elizabeth I* (London, 1967), p. 293.

4. Arnold Oskar Meyer, *England and the Catholic Church under Queen Elizabeth* (London, 1916), pp. 59–72; McGrath, *Papists and Puritans*, p. 8.

5. McGrath, *Papists and Puritans*, p. 13.

immense difficulty, while reformers converted whole colleges at Oxford and Cambridge. Catholics printed and distributed literature only in secrecy and fear; all sorts of official presses were available to publicists of reform. Finally, Catholic priests were restricted to "household religion," living secretly with their gentry, while reformers could preach publicly and to great numbers throughout the localities.[6] Also, fiscal and other penalties were imposed on the laity for not conforming, and priests suffered persecution, torture, and martyrdom. By the eighties and nineties a drift toward conformity and even conciliation had appeared, some Catholics doubting the pope's deposing power, and most being loyal to nation and queen against pope, Spain, and France.[7] The assimilation was aided by continual governmental pressure for uniformity and reform, and a politic exploitation of rifts among the Catholics.

There are reasons, then, why the Catholic threat did not force itself into Hooker's work. They fail to account, however, for the complete absence of particulars about a threat grave in the eighties and by no means impotent in the nineties. Furthermore, why does Hooker not join the reformers in pressing more upon the English Catholics? And why the almost sympathetic treatment of the Roman church that sustained its English brethren?

Hooker evinces first a reticence concerning the whole issue, then a visible desire to breathe some fire into the "feeble smoke of conformity" between Canterbury and Rome (in England and without). Eventually he presents a less visible but firm criticism of Rome, most conspicuous in Book VIII concerning matters of church governance where no compromise was possible.

Just as it was "safer to discuss all the saints in heaven than M. Calvin," so it was safer to praise any church, even the "Turks," ahead of Rome. Before he wrote the *Laws*, Hooker had experienced Travers's complaints to the Privy Council. Hence his reticence, no doubt. Yet the sympathy that occasioned Travers's accusation is present in the *Laws*. It becomes more apparent, notably as Hooker criticizes, throughout Book IV, the reformers' doctrine that the way to be near Christ is to be far from Rome. One reason is the terrible danger of religious warfare: the shooting wars that originate with these heated ghostly conflicts. Hooker reminds his zealous opponents of the state of continental Christendom: "flaming in all parts of greatest importance at once." Attempts at "extreme alteration" had enraged "the adverse part," and led each side to see a solution only in "utter oppression and clean extinguishment" of the other. Hooker acknowledges this great European tragedy, one cause why later philosophers (like Locke in his pieces on toleration) revolt against otherworldly politics by separating church from state and in effect displacing religion from its age-old priority. Yet Hooker's solution is not the politics of religious toleration but the politics of moderate establishment. He invites comparison of the Continent's broils with England and Elizabeth's *via media*. "These eager affections in some" have been stayed, "a course more calm and moderate" chosen.[8] Political moderation helps account, then, for Hooker's failure to rake up old offenses of an

6. Ibid., ch. 13.
7. Ibid., p. 363, ch. 10; Meyer, *England and the Catholic Church*, ch. 4.
8. *Laws* IV.xiv.6.

English Catholicism no longer fundamentally dangerous, and for his failure to vent his spleen with the old pejorative, *Papist*.

Other results of the reformers' warfare, however, require Hooker to call for reconciliation with Rome and not simply for moderation in repression. "When we are in a fretting mood at the church of Rome, . . . we are sure to have always one eye fixed upon the countenance of our enemies, and according to the blithe or heavy aspect thereof, our other eye sheweth some other suitable token either of dislike or approbation towards our own orders." Preoccupied with Rome's affronts, as the names *Protestant* and *reformer* imply, the reformers were but squinty-eyed in taking aim at what they loved. Inadvertently they were undermining the customs and institutions that bore up Christianity in an unpromising age. "Under colour of rooting out popery, the most effectual means to bear up the state of religion (may) be removed, and so a way made either for Paganism or extreme barbarity to enter."[9] Unlike Starkey, Hooker condemns less the reformers' corrosion of customary observances and more their bitter attacks on church authority, hierarchy, and wealth (matters to be later detailed). In fomenting religious wars, or through a perverse zeal that prefers even pagans and Turks to Papists, the reformers ignored dangers shared with Catholics, especially the danger from those who hate Christianity. In general, they ignored the common problem of spreading the faith and even more generally, the common faith in Christ as savior.

Hooker takes his bearings from the main and common ground, with a deep prayer for reconciliation with Catholicism. Despite Rome's sundry "gross and grievous abominations, yet touching those main parts of Christian truth wherein they constantly still persist, we gladly acknowledge them to be of the family of Jesus Christ."[10] The reformers in their anger forget that Rome is "a part of the house of God, a limb of the visible Church of Christ." Hooker takes Calvin specially to task for a "crazed" opinion that "children of Popish parents" may not be baptized. Even, "yea, a cardinal or a pope" will be saved by a merciful God, if the churchman repents his sins and heresies.[11] English Catholics who outwardly conform are not to be treated as "'dogs, swine, beasts, foreigners and strangers' from the house of God," to be excluded for un-gospel-like behavior from the English church's communion. The reformers thus confuse crimes with errors, suffer their indignation at the faults of the church of Rome to blind and withhold their judgments from seeing it as a church, dive into men's consciences unduly, and repel those in whom should be cherished and encouraged whatever smoke of conformity may appear. It follows that some old English rites are not to be discarded merely because they give encouragement to a few Romanists "not scoured of their former rust." Instead Hooker urges churchmen to seek unity with the Catholics, "to build wheresoever there is any foundation, to add perfection unto slender beginnings."[12] That counsel could summarize his posture toward Rome in general and the English Romanists in particular. The

9. *Laws* IV.ix.3, 2.
10. *Laws* III.i.10.
11. *Laws* III.i.12; V.lxviii.9; Sermon II, 35, in *Works* III, 541.
12. *Laws* V.lxviii.9, 5; IV.ix.1.

English church should follow Christ and reason whether or not Rome does, and sometimes Rome in preference to reform. "We had rather follow the perfections of them whom we like not, than in defects resemble them whom we love."[13]

Although he presents Rome as an enemy to be wooed from enmity, Hooker knows nonetheless the depth of her enmity, and the massive differences from a church of England even well-understood. The bitter venom of a proud style was not the reformers' alone. Hooker bridles under the gibes of novelty and the charges of heresy leveled at England by Rome and English Romanists like Cardinal Allen.[14] He refrains from replying in kind, encouraging instead a quiet if crucial presumption of English sufficiency and even superiority. English churchmen need not be defensive about their ways. Some seem to imagine

> that we have erected of late a frame of some new religion, the furniture whereof we should not have borrowed from our enemies, lest they relieving us might afterwards laugh and gibe at our poverty; whereas in truth the ceremonies which we have taken from such as were before us, are not things that belong to this or that sect, but they are the ancient rites and customs of the Church of Christ.[15]

It is Rome that departed from the old and true ways, even if politic churchmen like Hooker (and unlike the reformers) will not focus principally upon her departures. "Heretics they are," he acknowledges, even as he justifies English ceremonies like Rome's.[16] Through all of Hooker's genuine efforts at conciliation runs the presumption of Roman "abominations" requiring to be "reformed."

Nevertheless, Philip Hughes may go too far in saying that "on every one of the points of belief at issue between Rome and the Reformation [Hooker] is stoutly, and as by a second nature, on the side of the Reformation." Among other proofs he observes that "Holy Order is not, for Hooker, a sacrament."[17] He misses, however, the mediating subtlety whereby Hooker, "although he does not make ordination a sacrament, . . . endows it with all the characteristics of a sacrament."[18] The example is not uncharacteristic of Hooker. Still, he accepts some massive reformed principles and presents himself in the *Laws* and everywhere as belonging to the reformed tradition.

According to Hooker, pope and priest have enjoyed untoward civil and spiritual authority over the ordinary believer. The *Laws* is sprinkled with attacks upon the inordinate sovereignty of the pope, this Bishop of Rome who usurped authority over all churches and even over temporal rulers like the king of England. These papal authorities are derived not from Scripture, as he claims, but from worldly policy.[19] The need for uniformity of the faith affords a reason for that policy. It is a reason outweighed by the potential for tyranny that goes with

---

13. *Laws* V.xxviii.1; IV.lx.1.
14. *Laws* III.i.10; IV.ix.1, 2; VI.vi.11; Sermon V, 15, in *Works* III, 674–80.
15. *Laws* IV.ix.1.
16. *Laws* III.i.10; IV.vi.2; Sermon VI, 31, in *Works* III, 697.
17. Philip Hughes, *The Reformation in England*, 3 vols. (London, 1963), III, 224–25.
18. John S. Marshall, *Hooker and the Anglican Tradition* (Sewanee, Tenn., 1963), p. 117.
19. Sermon V, 15, in *Works* III, 674–80; *Laws* VIII.iii.5, VIII.iv.9, VIII.viii.4.

an imperial sway. Better general governance by "one law, to stand in no less force than the law of nations doth," obtained through the verdict of the whole church orderly taken, and set down in the assembly of some general council. Church law by church councils would at least avoid "those woeful inconveniences whereunto the state of Christendom was subject heretofore, through the tyranny and oppression of that one universal Nimrod who alone did all." Church government at its heights is largely a matter of policy, not Scripture, and "such authority over all churches is too much to be granted unto any one mortal man."[20]

Hooker backs away also from the spiritual authority of Roman priest and church, in favor of the more direct and reformed relations between a just and merciful God and erring but faithful man. A marginal comment about the Eucharist shows Hooker's spirit: "Whereas popish doctrine doth hold that priests by wordes of consecration make the reall, my whole discourse [in Book V, chapter lxvii] is to shew that God by the Sacrament maketh the mysticall bodie of Christ. . . ." A similar thread ties together Hooker's deprecation of the Mass, of the equation of unwritten verities with the Scripture of God, and of the worship of images and the calling upon saints as intercessors. He adopts expressly the formula of justification by faith alone, criticising the Roman church for suggesting that the righteousness within us is our own. Yet these differences in formulae conceal a mediating interpretation noted by knowledgeable theological commentators. If Rome should undergo some reform, Canterbury should accept some counter-reformation. With proper caution C. J. Sisson has rightly called Hooker a pioneer in "that development of the Reformation in England which in some ways became a counter-Reformation."[21]

20. *Laws* IV.xiii.8; VIII.iii.5.
21. C. J. Sisson, *The Judicious Marriage of Mr. Hooker and the Birth of the Laws of the Ecclesiastical Polity* (Cambridge, Eng., 1940), p. 100; *Laws* V.lxvii.6, n. 2; Sermon II, 11, 3, 4, 6, in *Works* III, 497–98, 485–91.

## 4

# Reform

**The Movement**

In light of his church's weaknesses, of a swelling secularism, and of the need to heal a Christendom racked by sectarian strife, Hooker's deep fear of his principal opponents becomes intelligible. Who they are is not so obvious as one might think. Hooker never sets off his opponents from the church by a distinctive name like Presbyterians or Calvinists, or calls them Puritan, which they resented. He does identify "the Brownists," whom the broad middle on both sides regarded as extreme. He resorts to circumlocution and to speaking in his opponents' words. His preface is addressed "to them that seek (as they term it) the reformation of laws and Orders Ecclesiastical in the Church of England." His chief opponents are not Brownists or Barrowists or Catholics, all clearly separated from the English church, but those equivocally within, seeking or even "panting" (a little sardonic irony shows through) after "reformation." That famous word with all its connotations is no mean indication, despite the circumlocution. Hooker confronts in England the religious movement set off by Luther's and later Calvin's purification of Christianity from additions merely human, especially from Rome's. Hooker certainly can express "deep social truth," as Christopher Hill put it. He was nevertheless far from reducing society in Christian polities to economic arrangements, or disputes apparently religious to matters psychological, political, or social. These reformers are moved by Reformation doctrine, and Hooker will reinterpret their watchword "justification by faith alone." However, he begins his diagnosis with the reformers' status as an English religious movement, a semi-political sect of leaders and led, and only later and cautiously considers and corrects the fundamental leaders, Luther and Calvin.

Beside preachers like Travers, the reformers include a great number of "the ordinary sort of man" swayed by preachers' rhetoric. Hooker examines that rhetoric to remove its credibility. This does not necessarily imply that he "smears," else a penetrating rebuttal would not differ from a smear. Hooker's account penetrates.[1] First, the preachers win the affections of the "common sort among you" by "ripping up the faults especially of higher callings" and imputing all faults and corruptions, "wherewith the world aboundeth," to the official church. Having introduced their moral superiority, and undermined respect for the hierarchies established, they propose their discipline, move men to believe all Scripture authenticates it, and persuade the credulous that "it is the special illumination of the Holy Ghost, whereby they discern those things in the word, which others reading yet discern them not." The many thus believe themselves alone "God's children," "the godly" as distinct from the remainder of mere time servers. They are fervently devoted to the cause and equally fervent haters of its detractors, "for fear of quenching that good spirit."[2] So moved by God's Spirit, as they think, they ignore all argument to the contrary as temptation purveyed by merely worldly intellects.

The preachers, "you whose judgment is a lantern of direction for all the rest," Hooker acknowledges as men not altogether moved "out of a politic intent or purpose" to thus govern. They were "first overborne with the weight of greater men's judgments." Their views were determined by the theologian second only to Luther in the Reformation begun but seventy-five years before, John Calvin, "to whom of all men they attribute most."[3] Such preachers were the leading and inevitably dissenting edge of a tendency that cut through the whole Church of England, struggling and pressing against contrary belief and practice. This conforms with the usual perception of Puritanism, which "was not so much an organized system as a religious temper and a moral force," as Collinson puts it, "and, being such, it could enter into combinations and alliances of varied kinds." The movement should not be confused with the nonconforming party. Sir Maurice Powicke described it thus:

> The Puritan element . . . could speak with authority and was entrenched in responsible positions, in Parliament and council chamber, in bishops' houses and cathedral chapters and benefices, in the Inns of Court and the universities. It ran through all shades of opinion, from docile submission to frank rebellion and the line between permissible and illegal criticism was only gradually revealed.[4]

Calvin's exposition of God's word had entered England somewhat prior to Elizabeth's rule. Indeed, sparks from Luther's revolt had already found their way into the church from the time of Henry VIII's assumption of the headship

---

1. Cf. W. D. J. Cargill Thompson, "The Philosopher of the Politic Society," in W. Speed Hill, ed., *Studies in Richard Hooker* (Cleveland and London, 1972), pp. 14–15.
2. *Laws*, Preface iii.5–16.
3. *Laws* III.xi.13; Preface iv.8.
4. Maurice Powicke, *The Reformation in England* (Oxford, 1963) III, 147; Patrick Collinson, *Elizabethan Puritan Movement* (Berkeley and Los Angeles, 1967), pp. 21–58; J. Brown, *The English Puritans* (Cambridge, Eng., 1910), p. 1.

in 1535. Still, Henry's orthodoxy in tenets other than papal power, and that of such leading clergy as Stephen Gardiner, obstructed the more enthusiastic Lutheranism of Henry's Archbishop of Canterbury, Thomas Cranmer. Cranmer's views nonetheless wriggled into a number of official creeds and articles. With Henry's death, there came the Protectorate of a less orthodox Somerset over an impressionable and religious Edward. Gardiner found himself in the Tower. Cranmer moved the church and its doctrines decisively into the reformers' camp, in which Calvin, his Geneva a school of theological practice and theory, was becoming increasingly prominent. The commentators speak of England as flooded with divines from the continent, come to join and guide this new conquest to God's word. The flood receded abruptly with Mary's accession. A chastened Gardiner returned to Catholicism, became Lord Chancellor and for a time the queen's leading counsellor. Some few divines, like the future Archbishop Parker, managed quietly and privately to survive Mary's reign, and pockets of reforming worship remained. However, the most notable activity of English Protestants was the famous departure of some eight hundred, including Thomas Cartwright, Walter Travers, and the future Archbishop of Canterbury, Grindal, following their erstwhile guests to the continent. For five years they worshipped, published tracts hopefully for use in England, and waited, generally in Calvinist centers, because the Lutherans could not stomach their doctrine of the Eucharist. Upon Mary's death in November 1558, the exiles returned, having been exposed to Calvin's teaching although only a quarter enjoyed his personal guidance in Geneva; the influence of "international Calvinism," as Trevor-Roper puts it, systematically spread throughout Elizabeth's England.

Some statistics collected by Charles Davis Cremeans are revealing. Of the eighty-five editions of the Holy Scripture printed in Elizabeth's reign, sixty were the Geneva Bible, with its extensive notes and summaries reflecting the new doctrines—"a book undertaken at the instance of a Calvinist congregation, by Calvinist scholars, for Calvinist readers."[5] Between 1575 and 1640 thirty-eight editions of Luther's writings and thirty-eight of Bullinger's issued from the English presses, while no fewer than ninety-six editions of Calvin's and fifty of his successor at Geneva, Beza, appeared. One or more of the Genevan's works appeared almost every year from 1548 to 1634; in the middle years of Elizabeth's reign, 1578–81, six to eight appeared annually. Cremeans concludes that no other writer was nearly so often published; Calvinism became "the ruling theology of England."[6]

This popularity reflected the influence of certain devoted bishops, clergy, and magnates, and not any wish of the monarchy. Historians now incline to agree that neither Elizabeth nor Cecil was intensely religious, although their precise opinions on theological matters are obscure, and Cecil intervened quite often on behalf of the godly. Elizabeth was put off by the intemperate "Blasts" of Goodman and Knox (one of which was so zealously impolitic as to oppose

5. H. W. Hoare, quoted in Patrick McGrath, *Papists and Puritans under Elizabeth I* (London, 1967), p. 82.

6. Charles Davis Cremeans, *The Reception of Calvinistic Thought in England* (Urbana, Ill., 1949), pp. 120, 82; see all of ch. 4.

the "monstrous" rule of women) and by popular elements in the new creed. Thus there existed neither direct correspondence between Calvin and the English monarch, like that under the Protectorate, nor conspicuous and continual monarchical meddling in matters of creed, such as that which had occupied Henry. In spite of this, perhaps because of this, Calvin's influence grew apace.

For reasons as politic as religious, Elizabeth allowed a doctrinal looseness that would retain her many Catholics as well as the reformers now riding high. Thus the shaping of doctrine was left in good part to the practices of the clergy and especially the chief clergy, the bishops. For many years, furthermore, until her Archbishop Whitgift was allowed to require from all holding benefices an oath to support his "Three Articles" of 1584, the queen forbade the bishops to require any set beliefs from the lower clergy, except an oath recognizing her supremacy and, from candidates for the ministry, an agreement to read the new service book. The leading clergy, however, were by no means fully sympathetic with the state-directed church, not yet thoroughly purified, and foreign to that strict separation of political from religious office which Calvin advocated. They thought it "but halfly reformed," as Collinson titles his fine chapter on the subject. Almost all the Marian bishops had been swept away. A scarcity of available Protestants, together with the stature of those just returned, gave to the Calvinists a place prominent as well as large in the Anglican church. Thus the various formulations of the articles of belief and the most popular catechisms after 1570 tend to be rather pure Calvin, the queen insisting upon the impurities. His *Institutes* succeeded Bullinger's *Decades* as the manual of the clergy and the text used by students of divinity in both Oxford and Cambridge. While the queen soon set her face against "the least alteration in matters of religion," remarks S. J. Knox, she was powerless to prevent the "infiltration of presbyterian ideas, and so the amazing situation was that the Elizabethan church which was *via media* in worship was actually Calvinistic in theology."[7]

The spread of new and different opinions about what seemed the most important issues could not but provoke profound conflict with the old ecclesiastical order. Calvin had followed Luther in urging justification before God by faith alone, the scriptural word of God as the sole source of religious knowledge, and the priesthood of all believers. He differed from the German divine notably in finding the essentials of true church polity in the Scripture's account of the apostles' practices. Much history of the Elizabethan nonconforming movement lies in the rubbing of these tenets, as held by men of neither Calvin's theological subtlety nor his sobering practical responsibilities, against the compromises of doctrine and practice that Elizabeth desired to preserve. The "vestiarian controversy" was provoked by scrupulous reformers who refused to wear certain garb prescribed by church regulations but unprescribed by Scripture; it began a series of attacks on Anglican ceremonies, which Book V of Hooker's *Laws* was meant to meet, and on priestly prerogatives, the concern of Book VI.

The reformers received the second Elizabethan Archbishop of Canterbury, Grindal, as one of themselves. A Marian exile, he was reluctant to follow Eliza-

---

7. S. J. Knox. *Walter Travers: Paragon of Elizabethan Puritanism* (London, 1962), pp. 114–15; Cremeans, *Reception of Calvinistic Thought*, p. 60; cf. p. 120.

beth and his predecessor, Matthew Parker, in enforcing even external conformity to the church's doctrine and dress. He it was who first licensed the Genevan Bible that Parker had in effect suppressed.[8] Grindal even resisted Elizabeth's express command to halt the burgeoning "prophesyings"—instructional meetings of godly ministers for theological self-help in understanding (in a properly reforming manner) Holy Scripture. The queen was a Tudor, as the historians say, and Grindal suffered for it. Yet the nonconformists retained latitude to pray together, to organize, and above all to instruct the young and promising in God's pure teaching. Dissatisfied with their progress, reformers in general came to insist that the chief obstacles, lordly bishops, be replaced by a biblical government of presbyters, called invisibly by God, but invested visibly by the congregation. Elizabeth's staunch support for her chief clergy then led the reformers' vanguard to question, at least surreptitiously, the vesting of the church's supreme headship in a civil ruler, that old and crucial accomplishment of Henry VIII that Calvin had called "blasphemous."[9]

A new generation of young, largely university trained Calvinists grew increasingly frustrated with the church's obstinacy and launched "admonitions" to Parliament, supplemented by various "defenses." They demanded, as the first admonition said in 1572, elimination of episcopal prerogatives and of ignorant ministers incapable of preaching the Word, introduction of "that old and true election" by the congregation, "the ancient purity and simplicity" in all customs, and "finally, that nothing be done in this or any other thing but that which you have the express warrant of word of God for."[10] With this holy warning, and a follow-up composed by Thomas Cartwright, discontent with the church became hostility to the church (as W. H. Frere put it). The decisive step received positive direction from Walter Travers in his *Book of Discipline* (1574). Modeled on Calvin's Geneva, it claimed a strict New Testament warrant that Calvin did not exactly claim. From then on, the rift between conformists and nonconformists widened as the controverted question of polity, made central by Cartwright, had been given by Travers an answer unequivocally different from that of the English church. The *classis* movement then arose. It comprised an underground organization of devoted preachers who catechized and instructed their congregations in the pure Word of God, and linked themselves in synods to maintain the true discipline. This is the ecclesiastical equivalent of taking the government into their own hands, and not merely an analogue since the queen was head of the established church.

The work of Whitgift under Elizabeth and that of Bancroft under James I ended the Puritan movement and party, Collinson suggests—the visible tendency to reform creed, ceremony, and discipline, often "without tarrying for the magistrate." Yet many bishops were still sympathetic, "and under their indulgent rule the conversion of England continued."[11] William Haller actually calls the

---

8. Collinson, *Elizabethan Puritan Movement*, pp. 164–65.

9. Cremeans, *Reception of Calvinistic Thought*, pp. 18–23.

10. Quoted by W. H. Frere, *The English Church in the Reigns of Elizabeth and James I* (London, 1904), p. 179.

11. Collinson, *Elizabethan Puritan Movement*, p. 464.

years 1590–1603, more or less when Hooker was writing and publishing his work, the time of "the great growth of the Puritans." Down from the universities came earnest and zealous pastors, "balked of their ambition to rule the church," who spread the doctrine among the people and wrote to spread farther.[12]

Now the reforming movement exhibited a variety of virtues, and received much of its opportunity from the vices of the establishment. The Elizabethan hierarchy inclined to be worldly, ignorant, avaricious, and in its arrangements oligarchic. It slighted the poorer clergy, allowed "great decay in the parish churches," and harrassed parishioners with mean fees. The reforming clergy tended to be earnest and devout and of a zealous Christian character. And, toward the century's end at least, they were considerably more educated than their orthodox counterparts.[13] Prophesyings and a flow of popular religious literature testify well enough to their zeal to know and to teach the Word of God, and to their success. Moreover, reforming laymen banded together to buy up impropriate lands, ecclesiastical properties fallen out of ecclesiastical possession, thus sustaining the ministry and restoring religion to the poor. The efforts of devout patrons such as the Earl of Huntington, therefore, bore very important fruits. R. G. Usher has calculated the livings of godly preachers to be worth, as a rule, four to five times those of loyal clergy.[14] In doctrine, appeal, and arrangements, then, the reforming clergy was far more attractive to the middling man, just when Reformation doctrine demanded his active religious participation. Most important of all, the reformers were fiercely devoted to their narrow and distinctive discipline. By comparison churchmen too often appeared compromising in doctrine, lax in devotion, and deserving of a wandering flock.

In Elizabeth's national church, moreover, powers other than the clergy favored the purifiers. Positive encouragement even to nonconformists came from the highest circles of governance (excepting the queen herself). The Privy Council often harbored Puritans or obstructed bishops. Some councillors, Sir Francis Knollys, Sir Walter Mildmay, and Sir Francis Walsingham, were devout protestants. Others hungered for the plums reformers might cut from the church, or wished to reduce the authority of bishops and religion generally. A few, such as the Earl of Leicester and Sir William Cecil, enjoyed some mixture of these motives difficult to discern. The great Cecil patronized repeatedly Walter Travers, who tutored Cecil's son Robert, later himself a Principal Secretary. Cecil recommended Travers for the influential Temple Church where his preaching, to England's future lawyers and judges, would eventually move Hooker to rebuttal and then to the *Laws*. Travers had already composed the *Ecclesiastical Discipline*. He went on to write the "Directory of Church Government," a tract which is supposed to have guided the Westminster Assembly of 1644–45, which met,

12. William Haller, *The Rise of Puritanism* (New York, 1938), p. 93; see chs. 3–5.

13. W. H. Frere, *English Church*, pp. 168, 269; R. G. Usher, *The Reconstruction of the English Church*, 2 vols. (New York, 1910), I, 240, 269.

14. Usher, *Reconstruction of the English Church* I, 274–75; Claire Cross, *The Puritan Earl* (London, 1966), passim; Christopher Hill, "The Feoffes for Impropriations," ch. 11 of his exhaustive study, *Economic Problems of the Church* (Oxford, 1956).

in the triumph of Presbyterianism over episcopacy and monarchy, to plan a godly England.[15]

Many of the greater nobility were hardly sustainers of religion, and some remained faithful in their hearts at least to the old Catholicism. Others, such as the Earls of Warwick, Bedford, Pembroke, and Huntingdon, were great patrons of the new theology. Lawrence Stone finds it "very significant that of the thirty peers who between 1558 and 1641 showed signs in their wills of strong religious feelings, no fewer than seven were recusants or schismatics, and twelve were Puritans or Puritan sympathizers."[16] Those earls devoted to reform Neale calls "the flower of the nobility."[17] At a time when many nobles were indifferent or checkmated by a government remembering Mary and fearful of papally-inspired risings, the reformers' high-minded devotion to godly ways profoundly and disproportionately affected English religious practice. Claire Cross has shown how Huntingdon, brought up at court in a rigorous Protestantism by the very tutors Henry VIII chose for his son Edward, devoted his life to a more thorough reformation of the English church; he fostered over a broad area a Calvinism that almost constantly sprouted forth nonconformity. President of the Council of the North from 1572 to 1595, the earl was the queen's lieutenant in five counties, and he promulgated his religion through all the branches of his family as well. Huntingdon patronized ministers and preachers that had been dismissed from livings elsewhere. Cross calls him "the Apostle of Leicestershire." He beneficed as his preacher Anthony Gilby, who was constantly organizing in the van of the reformers at least until the advent of Field, Cartwright, and Travers. Gilby was unofficial "bishop" of an enthusiastic circle, many of them appointed with Huntingdon's encouragement or connivance. Cross says: "This little band of zealots led by Gilby assisted by other like-minded ministers changed the religious climate of the county within a generation."[18] Many of them declined to wear the surplice and subscribed only in a qualified fashion to Whitgift's "Three Articles." Besides planting such preachers throughout the North, the "Puritan Earl" gave several livings to the new and specifically Protestant college at Cambridge, Emmanuel. He founded many schools sprinkled with radical Protestant masters, cooperated genially with Grindal when the then Archbishop of York instituted exercises and prophesyings, and feuded with his arch-episcopal successor Sandys, who sought compliance to Elizabeth's settlement from Protestant as well as Catholic.[19]

If zealous Protestantism could root in the mellow earth of an earl, its capacity to flourish among the members of the House of Commons was less surprising. Reforming nobles never controlled the House of Lords, but reform was a principal aim of the Elizabethan Commons from its first session. Sir John Neale suggested that the House began by trying to purify the queen's politic

---

15. Knox, *Walter Travers*, pp. 54–58, 148–49.

16. Lawrence Stone, *The Crisis of the Aristocracy 1558–1641* (Oxford, 1965), p. 727.

17. J. E. Neale, *The Elizabethan House of Commons* (London, 1949), p. 223.

18. Cross, *The Puritan Earl*, p. 137; cf. ch. 4 and, indeed, all of part 2.

19. Cross, *The Puritan Earl*, pp. 249–53, 227–28, 41, 24, 32, 131, 157, 140.

compromise, succeeded considerably, and was beaten off afterward only by Elizabeth's monarchical power and steadfastness of will.[20] The theme of his *Elizabeth I and Her Parliaments* is the point and counterpoint of the Commons's pressure for religious reform, extending in some members' hopes to "a complete and radical revision of all orders," against the queen's unbending refusal to allow Parliament authority over her church and her bishops.

While the reformers in Parliament had little but initial success, their prominence throughout Elizabeth's reign indicates the temper of many gentry, lawyers, and officials. Indeed, the reforming proclivities of the Commons reflect complicated causes yet a problem for historians. The lower house was dominated largely by some two hundred fifty country gentlemen reflecting the preeminent power and wealth of the nobler few and the upper gentry, and by some seventy-five royal officials and a sprinkling of fifty or more lawyers.[21] Four-fifths of the members were chosen from boroughs or towns, rather than counties, and yet not more than a sixth were merchants or borough officials, Neale has shown. Through a clientage of tenantry and other dependents, nobles and upper gentry virtually controlled county elections and exercised strong sway over the boroughs, especially smaller boroughs cowering among wealthy neighbors who were landlords and employers. Aristocratic control was complemented and sometimes supplemented by the influence of the queen, her Council and officials, and her circle of courtiers. The royal power nominated from such fiefs as the Cinque Ports, the Duchy of Cornwall (fourteen members), and the Duchy of Lancaster. By word of mouth to notables, and letters to sheriffs responsible for holding local elections, it could also influence to a mild and varying degree members chosen elsewhere.[22]

Queen and Council preferred Protestants to Catholics in selecting candidates for the Commons—and Protestantism at that time tended toward Calvinistic reform. Besides, a goodly number of Councillors were devoted reformers, including the first Elizabethan Warden of the Cinque Ports, and the first Elizabethan chancellors of the Duchy of Lancaster, who enjoyed a viceroy's powers in Lancashire.[23] Moreover, the devout nobles had a great effect. Cross shows Huntingdon helping pure spirits like his Puritan brothers Sir Francis and Sir Edward Hastings to obtain seats, county as well as borough. And Neale remarks that the Earl of Bedford, an outstanding personality in the state and a very active man, "made no small contribution to the strong puritan complexion of Elizabethan parliaments" as he relentlessly promoted the candidacies of an active Puritan physician, Marian exiles, and such other leaders of the cause as Walsingham and Nicholas Throckmorton.[24] Here as always, will and spirit tend to overcome indifference and lethargy, and the godly nobles' efforts bore disproportionate fruit in a regime suspicious of the Catholic nobles. The same is true of the somewhat less stately Puritan gentry, families like the Knightleys, or the

20. J. E. Neale, *Elizabeth I and Her Parliaments: 1559–1581* (New York, 1958), I, part 1.
21. Neale, *Elizabethan House of Commons*, pp. 146–47, chs. 7–13.
22. Ibid., ch. 14.
23. Ibid., pp. 214–15, 222–23.
24. Ibid., pp. 70, 197–200; Cross, *Puritan Earl*, pp. 117–19.

Knollyses, who at one time numbered seven in Parliament. If Huntingdon's brother Sir Francis is typical, the zealous gentry was itching for membership in the Commons, thus to reform the laws and all England. Yet enthusiasm cannot do all. Quite a number of leading citizens of county and borough must have leaned toward religious reformation well beyond the boundaries that Elizabeth had marked. In a lucid if somewhat exaggerated discussion, R. G. Usher shows that the reforming proclivities of a shire depended more on its gentry's beliefs than on any spontaneous leaven among the people at large. He traces the non-conformists' influence to their "enthusiastic proselytizing of a few influential gentlemen."[25] When this work of godly laymen is added to the political prose-lytizing that Collinson exhibits in godly ministers, the power of reform among the Commons becomes intelligible.

Besides their influence upon Council and Parliament, nobility and gentry, the reformers gained a foothold and then dominance in those molders of opin-ion, the universities. Attending Oxford and Cambridge became ever more the custom for young gentlemen and even young nobles. Even at the start of Eliza-beth's reign, Cambridge "as a haven of Reformation doctrine might rival Wit-tenberg or Marburg,"[26] and the rule of reforming theology strengthened, essen-tially unchallenged until the turn of the century. Cambridge had produced about twenty-five of Mary's martyrs and about a fifth of the Marian exiles, including Cartwright and Travers. Cartwright has been called the most influential man in Cambridge during Elizabeth's first years.[27] True, Cartwright and other open as-sailers of the establishment were eventually deprived of chairs and fellowships. Yet the new spirit spread. "Of much more importance in the long run than the brief impact of a heated sermon and the passing glory of the academic martyr was the sustained influence over many years of puritan masters, tutors and col-lege lecturers," Collinson remarks. The best of many, Laurence Chaderton, was "the pope of Cambridge puritanism." In the sixties and seventies he made Christ's College a Puritan seminary in all but name; in the eighties he carried the tradition over to Emmanuel; later he accepted no pupils but worked to find pulpits for them; and, in general, he was "preoccupied with the higher strategy of harnessing the university to the supply of learned preachers." This example is more characteristic than exceptional. The three largest colleges were those with the strongest Puritan element; Trinity educated both Cartwright and Trav-ers. What was true of Cambridge seems also true of Oxford, to a lesser extent. Oxford's own Chaderton, John Reynolds, was president of Corpus Christi where Hooker had been student and fellow. A number of the most radical preachers, including John Field, were Oxford men. Collinson concludes that "clerical puritanism, as a cohesive, national movement, was created in the uni-versities."[28] Nor did the universities solely produce preachers. By 1593 appre-ciably more than half the lower house of Parliament had attended Oxford or

25. Usher, *Reconstruction of the English Church* II, 277; 269–81, 140.
26. Quoted by Knox, *Walter Travers*, p. 16.
27. Ibid.
28. Collinson, *Elizabethan Puritan Movement*, pp. 127, 122–30. For details, H. C. Porter, *Reformation and Reaction in Tudor Cambridge* (Cambridge, Eng., 1958).

Cambridge, up from less than a third in 1563. These were mostly from Cambridge, and reflected in good part the influence of Laurence Humphrey. This Puritan scholar stocked his college with a generation of nonconformists, Neale tells us, and "his influence was reflected in the strong puritan tone of the Elizabethan House of Commons."[29]

Reforming theology had nearly captured the heights that govern or at least influence the religious opinions of a Christian people. While the reformers were rarely radicals, they were always cool to the established discipline. Collinson remarks on the preachers come down from Cambridge:

> These pastorally-minded puritans cared deeply about the failings of the established Church as they knew them at the parochial level: the lack of preachers, the shortcomings of the poorer clergy and the carelessness of the wealthy and non-resident, the powerlessness of the pastor with no weapon of discipline in his hand. And although the label "nonconformist" does not begin to describe what was distinctive about these men, nonconformists they were, and they could be stung into defiance by too peremptory a demand to conform. Presbyterians in an active, militant sense most of them were not, but they had little sense of loyalty to their ordinaries or to the Church conceived in an Anglican, hierarchical way; and by contrast a strong sense of belonging to their fellow preachers, gathered in conference.[30]

### The Movement and Its Theology

Against this movement, whose spirit is well and sympathetically caught by Collinson, Hooker sets himself in the *Laws*. He had no impotent or unworthy opponent, he knew, as the famous pessimism of his work's first words shows:

> Though for no other cause, yet for this; that posterity may know we have not loosely through silence permitted things to pass away as in a dream, there shall be for men's information extant thus much concerning the present state of the Church of God established amongst us, and their careful endeavour that would have upheld the same.[31]

Encouraged by powers within the church and without, the reforming movement and its allies brought England to civil war less than fifty years after Hooker wrote and won a decisive if short-lived triumph, an opportunity to make old Britain into a godly commonwealth. Hooker exhibited deep sympathy with the reformers' devoutness, their godly devotion to the faith. Yet he thought their movement profoundly dangerous precisely for the prospects of Christianity in England.

Hooker did not disguise his fear that the peril at hand could reach even in his time to a civil war, and this a "flaming" religious war, "for the most part

---

29. Neale, *Elizabethan House of Commons*, p. 304.
30. Collinson, *Elizabethan Puritan Movement*, pp. 128–29.
31. *Laws* Preface. i.1.

hotlier prosecuted and pursued than other strifes."[32] Considering the pettiness of the disputes, some might "marvel how a thing in itself so weak could import any great danger." Indeed, the wisest had not troubled themselves. Nonetheless, Hooker saw the peril as grave, grave as his somber pessimism. More than once he chronicles like instances from Christian history, especially Protestant history. Heresies little regarded and less confronted had so increased their hold upon the faithful that bitter schism and even war had resulted. Hooker admired Whitgift's enforcement of conformity within the church, and Bancroft's suppression of the *classis* movement designed to reduce the church from without. Their deeds were insufficient, however necessary. If the partakers of religious error "be terrified and not taught, their punishment doth not commonly work their amendment."[33]

The English reformers so misinterpreted justification by faith alone, Hooker thought, as excessively to throw themselves upon God's providence and excessively to neglect human provision. Theirs was a political naiveté, albeit one that affected ecclesiastical polity: the church in the world suffered from their godly otherworldliness. In the name of scriptural simplicity reformers sought to level the church's property—and they demanded most of all the displacement and reduction of lordly bishops. So stripping away worldly power, the reformers would leave church and faith defenseless in the world, without power in a country where landed property and lordly landowners rule. This danger, always grave, was compounded by the spreading "atheism"; the reformers' naiveté played into the hands of the *politiques*, as well as of those with "the sacrilegious intention of church robbers, which lurketh under this plausible name of Reformation."[34] On the other hand, the reformers' zeal led them to disregard the counsel of the prudent in favor of the "spirit" of any godly man, and to foment all sorts of theological quarrels—"these fruitless jars and janglings"—rendering Christians improvident and divided, again to the pleasure of their enemies.[35] We may sum up this preliminary diagnosis in Hooker's own words:

> The scope of all their pleading against man's authority is to overthrow such orders, laws, and constitutions in the Church, as depending thereupon if they should therefore be taken away, would peradventure leave neither face nor memory of the Church to continue long in the world, the world especially being such as now it is.[36]

Hooker's response can be simply stated: he deflates a preeminently theological rebellion by exposing as unchristian and unreasonable its theology, and replaces the source of the difficulty, his church's Calvinism, with a blending of faith and philosophy adjusted to English circumstances. The remainder of this chapter discusses Hooker's theological alternative; Part II considers the ethics, or moral philosophy, of his alternative; Part III, the politics. We begin with a

---

32. *Laws* V.Dedication.50; IV.xiv.6.
33. *Laws* VIII.Appendix 2; *Works* III, 462; V.Dedication.3, 4, 9.
34. *Laws* VII.xxi.1.
35. *Laws* II.vii.6; II.viii.6.
36. *Laws* II.vii.1; V.lxxix.17; cf. V.lxxi.4; V.lxxv.4.

comment on some subsidiary strategies, however, which chiefly involve dividing the reformers, and separating them from their principal supporters.

The movement included preachers and flock, and Hooker, who could reach only the preachers and of these only the more open-minded, frequently reminds them of the defects of the common sort of men. The preachers would tear down old hierarchies and rebuild through election by a simple congregation of believers. They weigh insufficiently "with themselves how dull, how heavy and almost how without sense the greatest part of the multitude every where is."[37] Similarly, Hooker holds up to the moderate reformers their immoderate extremes, the Anabaptists, or the Barrowists who utterly refuse to conform to English rituals. Like other apologists for the church, he takes pleasure in suggesting that these extremes are the movement's natural fruits. But as usual his sardonic reflection is unusual.

> These men's hastiness the warier sort of you doth not commend; ye wish they had held themselves longer in, and not so dangerously flown abroad before the feathers of the cause had been grown; their error with merciful terms ye reprove, naming them, in great commiseration of mind, your "poor brethren." They on the contrary side more bitterly accuse you as their "false brethren"; and against you they plead, saying: "From your breasts it is that we have sucked those things, which when ye delivered unto us ye termed that heavenly, sincere, and wholesome milk of God's word, howsoever ye now abhor as poison that which the virtue thereof hath wrought and brought forth in us."[38]

Hooker woos the moderates by dwelling on the conflicts between their creed and their other devotions: loyalty to England and its customary arrangements, to the queen's supremacy, the precedence of the nobility, the flourishing universities, and the authority of law and lawyers. He is careful not to smear, not to presume that the revolutions to come are intended by most reformers; yet he seeks to awaken moderates to the corrosive premises they share with radical brothers who will push on. "Only therefore I wish that yourselves did well consider," for example, "how opposite certain your positions are unto the state of collegiate societies, whereon the two universities consist."[39]

Nevertheless, Hooker knew full well that a decisive barrier stood between them and his argument or any argument:

> Against all these and the like difficulties your answer is, that we ought to search what things are consonant to God's will, not which be most for our own ease; and therefore that your discipline being (for such is your error) the absolute commandment of Almighty God, it must be received although the world by receiving it should be clean turned upside down.[40]

---

37. *Laws* V.lxviii.2; cf. VI.i.2.      38. *Laws* Preface.viii.1.
39. *Laws* Preface.viii.3; cf. V.lxxx.5.      40. *Laws* Preface.viii.5.

The root of the church's problem, and of Hooker's fears, is the conviction of preacher and believer that through the Spirit of God they speak the Word of God. Another of these remarkable passages offers his deepest diagnosis:

> When the minds of men are once erroneously persuaded that it is the will of God to have those things done which they fancy, their opinions are as thorns in their sides, never suffering them to take rest till they have brought their speculations into practice. The lets and impediments of which practice their restless desire and study to remove leadeth them every day forth by the hand into other more dangerous opinions . . . for which cause it behoveth wisdom to fear the sequels thereof, even beyond all apparent cause of fear.[41]

The connection between the movement's fearsome effects and its reforming core is explored in the third chapter of Book V. There Hooker matches a dissection of atheism with a longer dissection of the other extreme, superstition. While superstition is religious, unlike atheism which ignores God or denies him, it is mistaken or perverse in relation to true religion: "Superstition is, when things are either abhorred or observed with zealous or fearful, but erroneous, relation to God." All religion involves the affections zeal and fear, dedicated ardor to serve the deity in hope of obtaining the best of goods, terror in giving offense lest this invite the worst of evils. The zealot pursues without limit the unlimited good; ill guided, he is filled with excesses of righteous indignation at what he conceives to be sin. Zeal, when it confronts things "imagined to be opposite unto religion, useth the razor many times with such eagerness, that the very life of religion is thereby hazarded." Fear also can lead to a frenzy. Since it

> doth grow from an apprehension of Deity endued with irresistible power to hurt, and is of all the affections (except anger) the unaptest to admit any conference with reason . . . therefore except men know beforehand what manner of service pleaseth God, while they are fearful they try all things which fancy offereth.

In short, both affections breed superstition, if they "have not the light of true understanding concerning God, wherewith to be moderated. . . ." Hence the importance in this world of theology as to the next, the true understanding of God by reason that Luther and Calvin, in their horror of the Aristotelian church, sought to kill off.

Perhaps no guidance oriented to the other world can take adequate account of this. One can appreciate Hooker's accomplishment only if one sees that the difficulty intrinsic to religion is heightened in the religion of Christ. The end is Christ's kingdom beyond this world. The means (principal or exclusive) is faith in otherworldly sustenance, in Christ's saving grace. True, Christ's messages to his followers suggest earthly duties. Yet *the* duty is to spread the true faith. Christ's chiefest care "was that the spiritual law of the Gospel might be pub-

41. *Laws* Preface.viii.5, 12.

lished far and wide."[42] Both the end above and the duties below put a premium in this world on zeal and true belief as to the other world. Although Francis Bacon cannot be called an adequate authority on these matters, there is truth in his remark that

> the quarrels and divisions about religion were evils unknown to the heathen. The reason was, because the religion of the heathen consisted rather in rites and ceremonies, than in any constant belief. For you may imagine what kind of faith theirs was, when the chief doctors and fathers of their church were the poets. But the true God hath this attribute that he is a jealous God, and therefore his worship and religion will endure no mixture nor partner.[43]

These difficulties inherent in the true faith were exacerbated when early churchmen resorted to Greek philosophies. Mysteries unintelligible by their mysteriousness were expounded by nonphilosophers with theoretical doctrines and distinctions. Disputes became exquisite and profound, as well as zealous and popular, and it did not take the polished enlightenment of a Gibbon to grasp the harm of this for Christianity.[44] Hooker laments the peculiar "monsters" of the Eastern heresies,

> the chiefest cause whereof doth seem to have lien in the restless wits of the Grecians, evermore proud of their own curious and subtile inventions; which when at any time they had contrived, the great facility of their language served them readily to make all things fair and plausible to men's understanding.[45]

To discern the mean between atheism and superstition seems the work of theology. To discern the mean prudent as well as true is hard, and yet necessary, for he who clarifies Christian mysteries is also watchful guide of the Christian flock. This connection between theory and practice, between Christian theology and the quest of all for salvation, is the great theme explored in our study of Hooker's politics, and precludes any separation of Hooker's politics from his theology. Hooker never forgot the connection. A great theologian was then the church's boon. Thomas is praised as the greatest of the "school-divines." Augustine is esteemed most highly of all, as "without any equal in the *Church of Christ from that day to this*." But a misguided theologian is a terrible sore. "So true we find it by experience of all ages in the church of God, that the teacher's error is the people's trial, harder and heavier by so much to bear, as he is in worth and regard greater that mispersuadeth them." What is true of misguided

---

42. *Laws* VIII.vi.13.

43. Francis Bacon, "Of Unity in Religion," essay 3, in *Essays or Counsels Civil and Moral: The Works of Francis Bacon*, ed. James Spedding, Robert Leslie Ellis, and Douglas Denon Heath, 15 vols., (Boston, 1964), XII, 86–87.

44. Edward Gibbon, *The History of the Decline and Fall of the Roman Empire*, ed. J. B. Bury, 7 vols. (London, 1909), II, xxi.

45. *Laws* V.iii.3.

theologians in general, is true of the reformers Luther and Calvin in particular: their error is the English people's trial, or so Hooker believes.

The suggestion has been made before. To rebut Cartwright and Travers and defend the Elizabethan settlement might have been Hooker's immediate object, Herschel Baker said flatly, "but ultimately he was marshalling all the artillery of history, reason, and Tradition against the heresy of Calvin."[46] Still, one should speak more warily. For Hooker never reveals a comprehensive attack upon the theology of Luther or Calvin. He confronts openly enough the seven leading theses of the English reform movement in Books II–VII, deflating its pretensions to true Christianity, exhibiting its self-contradictions and its impossibility in light of the new foundation laid in Book I. Yet his references to the movement's continental masters are both rare and generally favorable. This is surprising, considering that his opponents nailed Calvin's name and opinions to their masthead, and that Hooker was pioneer of something like a counter-Reformation and follows St. Thomas in important respects. F. D. Maurice alone has felt the strangeness of "the caution and hesitancy of Hooker in finding fault with the foreign Reformer, when he was most disposed to be severe upon his English imitators."[47]

In his preface Hooker does set forth the origin in political prudence of the Genevan arrangements for which Calvin claimed biblical warrant. The assessment is succinct. "That which Calvin did for establishment of his discipline, seemeth more commendable than that which he taught for the countenancing of it established." Hooker suggests that it was pride which led Calvin to sanctify with holy Scripture his own discipline. "But what argument are ye able to shew, whereby it was ever proved by Calvin, that any one sentence of Scripture doth necessarily enforce these things, or the rest wherein your opinion concurreth with his against the order of your own church?"[48] This paragraph is the one really conspicuous attack by Hooker on Calvin. It was unavoidable. The sanctity of the discipline was the most massive and dangerous dogma of the reformers. Nothing discredits a massive claim to sanctity like a revelation of human, all too human, motivation. For English reformers the evidence of sanctity was less a thing of reason than of authority, the authority of Calvin, and a paragraph discredits the crucial authority. Yet a passage immediately follows praising Calvin's virtue (albeit with a touch of irony), in particular his industry in "composing the *Institutes*" and expounding Scripture accordingly. Even the dissection of the discipline's origin begins with resounding praise, "incomparably the wisest man that ever the French Church did enjoy, since the hour it enjoyed him," although it too is followed with a touch of irony, "But wise men are (still) men." Be this as it may, Hooker never extends his criticism of Calvin or Luther to the fundamental points of reformed teaching.

46. Herschel Baker, *The Wars of Truth* (Cambridge, Mass., 1952), p. 93; *Laws* V.lxii.9; III.ix.2; "Fragments of an Answer to the Letter of Certain English Protestants," *Works* II, 580.

47. Frederick Denison Maurice, *Moral and Metaphysical Philosophy* (London, 1890) II, 191.

48. *Laws* Preface.ii.7.

No references to them occur in Book I, where Hooker sets forth his own fundamentals, mixing Christianity and Aristotle, nor in Book II, where he attacks his opponents' orientation by the Word of God alone. In the whole work two references to Luther or Lutheranism occur, both essentially approbatory; this despite an intimation in a sermon that Lutheranism destroys, if only indirectly or "by consequent," the foundation of the faith.[49] According to Keble's index there are eleven explicit references to Calvin in the *Laws*, apart from those in the preface. One criticizes the Genevan's insistence on re-baptism of baptised Catholics. Another remarks his labeling as blasphemous the royal supremacy, as Hooker exposes the reformers' attempts to evade treasonous implications of the phrase. A third notes Calvin's stature among the reformers. The remaining eight references are favorable, insofar as they are more than neutral, and often embrace Calvin's authority as warrant for Hooker's own doctrines. Hooker trots out Calvin's name repeatedly to attest a church's "right to choose according to its own discretion such subsidiary rules as in its circumstances seem wise."[50]

Hooker departs from reformed theology, then, reticently and on the whole not explicitly. His Christian rhetoric assimilates the authority of reformers as well as Papists, theologians as well as atheists. Precisely this manner of writing distinguishes Hooker from the masters of reform and is one sign of the basic distinction: he restores practical judgment to reformed theology.

The reformers had been firebrands, and their chief, Luther, the hottest of all with his sweeping, vivid, bitter, and sarcastic rhetoric, spiced with assaults upon the "monsters" and "fair speaking toadies" of the papal "anti-Christ." Even Calvin exhibited the "abundant invective" to which a modern editor refers, a "bitterness" in theological combat and in his nature about which Hooker expressly remarks.[51] If one may judge from his practice to the contrary, Hooker thought these excesses the chief cause of a Christian Europe "flaming at all points at once." Religion arouses powerful passions and is susceptible of infinite divisions. Christianity in particular is hard to formulate in a creed that can be followed by the multitude, whether or no it be understood by them. Cautious prudence is more appropriate than fiery zeal. "In matters of so great moment, whereupon the peace or disturbance of the Church is known to depend, if there were in us that reverend care which should be; it is not possible we should either speak at any time without fear, or ever write but with a trembling hand."[52] We need to be especially reluctant to stir up strife and disputation among the bulk of believers. Hooker solemnly warns his opponents: "Let the vulgar sort amongst you know, that there is not the least branch of the cause wherein they are so resolute, but to the trial of it a great deal more appertaineth than their conceit doth reach unto."[53]

49. Sermon II, 17, in *Works* III, 503; *Laws* VII.xiv.11; III.i.10.
50. *Laws* III.xi.11; IV.xiii.3; V.lxxviii.5. See Index heading "Calvin," *Works* III, 744.
51. Hooker, MS note, in *Works* I, 133–34, n. 2; John Calvin, *Institutes of the Christian Religion*, ed. J. T. McNeill (Philadelphia, 1960), p. lxii.
52. *Works* III, 463.
53. *Laws* Preface.iii.3.

At the beginning of the Reformation Erasmus had protested Luther's "fierce outcries." His "license of pen" was likely to lead to "tumult and general dissidence throughout the world"; in "an issue sharp by its very nature," he was "divulging everything and making public even to cobblers what is usually treated among the learned as mysterious and secret." To a young man drawn to Luther, Erasmus wrote that Christianity requires a "holy artfulness." Even "the evangelical spirit of Christ has its own prudence," including gentleness and politeness. Jesus himself "speaks one thing to the more uncultivated crowd, another to his disciples, and he gradually leads these very men, bearing with them for a long time, to an understanding of heavenly philosophy." Deceit and dissimulation in the philosopher-king were not displeasing to Plato, "provided that his wiles were employed for the public good"; while the Christian should perhaps be free of every deceit, "nevertheless, it happens sometimes that the truth may well be silent."[54]

It is hard to explain Hooker's reticence with respect to Luther and Calvin, and his manipulation of Calvin's authority, unless for aims similar to Erasmus's. His church's strifes are caused principally by a reforming creed widely preached and pushed, and believed in various degrees by almost all churchmen including bishops and the chief bishop. Hooker wishes to mend the strifes without rending the fabric; hence his enveloping tone of sweet reasonableness.

> Think not that ye read the words of one who bendeth himself as an adversary against the truth that ye have already embraced, but the words of one who desireth even to embrace together with you the self-same truth, if it be the truth, and for that cause (for no other, God he knoweth), hath undertaken the burdensome labour of this painful kind of conference."[55]

Hooker also suggests conferences of the conventional kind, councils of the various churches. His book breathes a spirit of peace; he encourages religious statesmen to dwell on common essentials while reconciling for the public good their differences. Reformers as well as Romanists should "build upon the weak grounds we have in conformity." Yet the reformers' zealous dogmatism makes the grounds weak and likely to get weaker. Harmony itself, as well as a more generous and wise Christianity, dictates a reform of the Reformation. But Hooker's reform is directed in part to a nontheological multitude. Therefore Hooker exaggerates harmony by judicious quotation from the masters of reform and is quiet even to silence about his departures from their teaching. He instructs the flock and even the bishops, revising their beliefs while damping their disputes. He presents his theology as in accord with the best theologians, Calvin and Luther included. There is no accidental cause of what S. J. Knox remarks, if it is true: "Nearly all denominations, not only Anglicans but also Puritans and Armenians, have tried to claim him as the secret propagator of their views."[56]

54. Letter to Judocus Jonas, May 10, 1521, in Desiderius Erasmus, *Christian Humanism and the Reformation*, ed. John C. Olin (New York, 1965), pp. 151–63.

55. *Laws* Preface.i.3.

56. Knox, *Walter Travers*, p. 87.

The form of Hooker's teaching reflects its substance. Reasoning (and thus prudence and governance) obtains a vital place in non-Roman theology. Luther and Calvin did not provide this, Hooker seems to think, to the perpetual self-contradiction and peril of their followers.

The reformers' insistence on justification by faith alone is inconsistent with the reasoning needed to understand the faith. They trace faith only to God's good spirit. "God breathes faith into us only by the instrument of his Gospel. . . ," Calvin writes. "It is necessary, therefore"—to give another sample—"that the same Spirit, who spake by the mouths of the prophets, should penetrate into our hearts, to convince us that they faithfully delivered the oracles which were divinely entrusted to them." The church is simply those who know they are of it, or, rather, those who believe they know: we who are "fully convinced we are members of it." By reading the Scriptures, every predestined believer participates through God's spirit in the Word of God. The true church is a secret elect, drawn by an "inner call" unsullied by merely human consideration. The intrusion of judiciousness into faith is not godly; it is even ungodly. "We seek not arguments or probabilities to support our judgment," writes Calvin, "but submit our judgments and understandings as to a thing concerning which it is impossible for us to judge."[57] The old syntheses of Christianity and ancient philosophy are positively repugnant. Luther himself had pronounced "Aristotle's *Ethics* to be worse than any other book, being the direct opposite of God's grace, and the Christian virtues. . . . I cannot avoid believing that the Evil One introduced the study of Aristotle. The whole Aristotle is to theology as darkness to light."[58]

Without naming its authors, Hooker remarks that

> an opinion hath spread itself very far in the world as if the way to be ripe in faith were to be raw in wit and judgment; as if reason were an enemy unto religion, childish simplicity the mother of ghostly and divine wisdom. A number there are who think they cannot admire as they ought the power and authority of the word of God, if in things divine they should attribute any force to man's reason.[59]

This attack upon human capacity, Hooker suggests, has the practical consequence of unsettling all human institutions. The paradoxical doctrine that "the doctrines of men are to be rejected" inevitably "shaketh kingdoms, churches and . . . whatsoever is now through the providence of God by authority and power."[60] We are reminded of the "greatest danger of all" from the English reformers—their persuasion "that it is the will of God to have those things done which they fancy." The great reformers were far from being sober guides of the

57. Calvin, *Institutes* I.vii.4–5; II.i.2; pp. 1013–15.

58. "Disputation Against Scholastic Philosophy," clauses 6, 10, 17, in *American Edition of Luther's Works*, ed. Jaroslav Pelikan and Helmut T. Lehman, 55 vols. (St. Louis, 1959), XXXI, 3–16; "An Appeal to the Ruling Class of German Nationality as to the Amelioration of the State of Christendom," in *Martin Luther: Selections from His Writings*, ed. Dillenberger (Chicago, 1961), p. 471; see "Pagan Servitude of the Church," *ibid.*, pp. 268–69.

59. *Laws* III.vii.4.

60. *Laws* V.lxxi.5, 4.

flock; according to Hooker they exacerbated its zeal and fear, while diminishing its deference, judgment, and moderation.

Some criticize Hooker for ignoring the conditions and qualifications Luther and Calvin put on their doctrine of justification. Luther insisted on the separate authority of the civil magistrate, and Calvin required church organization and even hierarchy of a kind. Both praised reasoning and the pagan authors in areas removed from the Word of God, and Luther acknowledged that the heathen "are far more skilful in such matters as secular government than the Christians."[61] Hooker evidently thought these qualifications insufficient. They either separate temporal affairs from religious, neglecting a politic provision for religion on earth, or subordinate temporal affairs to a simplistic and doctrinaire biblical fiat. The qualifications could not evade the difficulty at the core of Reformation theology: the removal of reason from theology. Hooker thought the mistaking of the proper relation of nature and grace the chief cause of those disputes which troubled his church.

Gunner Hillerdal has suggested that Hooker's own reconciliation of nature and grace has its difficulties; the argument deserves respect. Yet Hooker's objection to the reformers' teaching seems valid. "He was violently fighting all tendencies," as Hillerdal puts it, "to regard the Scripture as the self-evident illuminative word of God which does not need reason for its proper understanding and interpretation."[62] Hooker fights with an argument difficult to refute. His opponents "never use reason so willingly as to disgrace reason." The contradiction will not go away. Repeatedly Hooker shows the English reformers violating their self-denying ordinances. "They have long pretended that the whole Scripture is plain for them," he remarks, and nevertheless they bring forth the authority of learned men, or offer their own judgments concerning meaning and interpretation. "That which by right exposition buildeth up Christian faith, being misconstrued breedeth error: between true and false construction reason must shew."[63] Hooker finally disposes of the English reformers gently but firmly, in a long passage as conclusive about his handling of their masters, Calvin especially, as instructive in his mingling of reason and spirit.

> Neither can I think [he writes] that when grave and learned men do sometime hold, that . . . there is no proof but by the testimony of the Spirit, which assureth our hearts therein, it is their meaning to exclude utterly all force which any kind of reason may have in that behalf; but I rather incline to interpret such their speeches, as if they had more expressly set down, that other motives and inducements, be they never so strong and consonant unto reason, are notwithstanding uneffectual of themselves to work faith concerning this prin-

61. "Psalm 101," in *American Edition of Luther's Works* XIII, 198, 199, 179. For the references in this note and in note 58, I am indebted to Duncan Forrester, "Martin Luther and John Calvin," in Leo Strauss and Joseph Cropsey, eds., *History of Political Philosophy*, 2nd ed. (Chicago, 1972), pp. 290, 280.

62. Gunner Hillerdal, *Reason and Revelation in Richard Hooker* (Lund, Sweden, 1962), p. 23.

63. *Laws* V.lxxii.14, 15; III.viii.4.

ciple, if the special grace of the Holy Ghost concur not to the en-
lightening of our minds.

Otherwise, Hooker says laconically, men may "think that the Spirit of God doth
testify those things which the Spirit of error suggesteth." He concludes: "There
is a strong presumption that God hath not moved their hearts to think such things
as He hath not enabled them to prove."[64]

Hooker agrees with the essential creeds of Reform. We are "justified by
faith without works, by grace without merit." From Scripture alone we learn of
the mysterious way through faith, hope, and charity. "There is not in the world
a syllable muttered with certain truth concerning any of these three, more than
hath been supernaturally received from the mouth of the eternal God."[65] As the
authorities say, however, Hooker so qualifies the reforming formulae as to move
toward Thomism, although not to Thomism. A key equivocation: "We teach
faith alone necessary: wherein it is not our meaning, to separate thereby faith
from other quality or duty, which God requireth to be matched therewith."[66]
Human effort as well as divine grace is needed and in some sense worthy:
"rewardable," as John Marshall puts it. Tradition and the church and nature
guide us, then. "When supernatural duties are necessarily exacted, natural are
not rejected as needless." Hooker ends by urging what would revolt the chief
reformers: "Our good or evil estate after death dependeth most upon the quality
of our lives." Salvation requires a certain minimum level of conduct, "accessory
augmentation of our bliss" requires higher levels, and these duties are discov-
erable by "the very light of Nature alone."[67]

Such is the purport of the new foundation in Book I: to set grace and
revelation in the context of nature and reason. These first nine chapters remind
of Aristotle's outlook, as infused by Thomas with a Christian understanding of
God's providence. Various natural things, such as horses or men, are distinguished by kind, and yet Hooker's is not simply the Aristotelian account of
heterogeneous natures. Hooker's theme is not manifoldness but unity, not the
various natures but God's law and the various ways in which his creatures obey.
Hooker proceeds through God's plan (the eternal law), to the law governing
natural creatures ("which keep the law of their kind unwittingly"), to that which
governs purely intellectual creatures (angels), to the law of reason which directs
man to his good (treated in our Part II), and finally to human laws which direct
men in society (treated in Part III).

Hooker builds his discussion of grace and revelation on this new foundation. God's mercy alone could atone for sin, and could make fallen men worthy
in His eyes. Yet grace does not surpass nature but restores it, or perhaps supplements it. Even in matters theological Hooker suggests we should "gather by
reason from the quality of things believed or done, that the Spirit of God hath

---

64. *Laws* III.viii.15.
65. "Fragments of an Answer," in *Works* II, 553; *Laws* V.x.1.
66. *Works* II, 553; see also Sermon II, 31, in *Works* III, 530.
67. *Laws* V.xlvi.1; I.xi.5–6; Marshall, *Hooker and the Anglican Tradition*, p. 112; *Laws*
I.xii.1.

directed us in both."[68] Although faith produces justification, and grace produces faith, grace does not act by intuitive illumination as to the Word. Prophecy has passed with the gift of Scripture; grace illuminates now by prompting reason. Original sin causes "sloth" in the reason; only in a roundabout way does it corrupt the appetites, or destroy the will. Grace cures as a "spur of diligence" in reasoning. Industry in investigation shows God's grace; truth is grace's fruit. A remarkable statement: "There is not that good which concerneth us, but it hath evidence enough for itself, if Reason were diligent to search it out."[69] After the sin that God "hath threatened eternally to punish," however, God added a new and revealed way to salvation, "a way which could never have entered into the heart of man as much as once to conceive or imagine, if God himself had not revealed it extraordinarily."[70] Once revealed, however, the mysterious way can be understood as necessary and thus demonstrable, Hooker alleges. At first a man believes the tradition of his church. Should he reflect on the mysteries of his belief, however, "the thing itself doth answer our received opinion concerning it." Nor is it "greatly hard" to maintain "the authority of the books of God by arguments such as unbelievers themselves must needs think reasonable," arguments not to be denied "without denying some apparent principle such as all men acknowledge to be true." The Christians, Hooker concludes remarkably, possess "a demonstration sound and infallible" as to the authenticity of Scripture as Word of God.[71]

Now Hooker's new foundation had to overcome serious difficulties. Some very assiduous reasoners had been familiar with the Christian revelation and yet not persuaded by it. Hooker knew this. "Not only the carnal and more brutish sort of men, but the wittiest, the greatest in account for secular and worldly wisdom, *Scribes, Philosophers, profound disputers,* are the chiefest in opposition against God."[72] Moreover, the disjunction between Christian truth and reason's findings is more serious than Hooker at times allows. He himself observes that "the mysteries of our religion are above the reach of our understanding, above discourse of man's reason, above all that any creature can comprehend."[73] Does Hooker rely on an understanding of reason informed by sources other than reason?

A discussion of grace in a carefully wrought but unpublished reply to some reforming critics intimates such a reliance. Hooker distinguishes sharply the "special illumination" of prophecy from the "general assistance and presence" of God assisting our reasoning; yet the latter too involves special illumination. God's general aid not only prods reason better to calculate means to

68. *Laws* III.viii.15; II.vii.2, 4; "Fragments of an Answer," 13, in *Works* II, 554; John S. Marshall, *Hooker and the Anglican Tradition* (Sewanee, Tenn., 1963), pp. 137–40; Hillerdal, *Reason and Revelation*, pp. 126–47.

69. *Laws* I.vii.7.

70. *Laws* I.xi.5.

71. *Laws* III.viii.14.

72. "Fragments of an Answer," 9, in *Works* II, 545. See *Laws* III.viii.9.

73. *Laws* V.lxxiii.1; cf. V.xxii.5; I.xii.2; "Fragments of an Answer," 7, 9, in *Works* II, 543–44; V.xxii.8, 9; V.li.3; V.iii.1; V.liv.6; VI.vi.11.

ends, but also suggests better ends. Grace is not only "a spur to quicken reason," but also "shall put in us good desires": that "knowledge, approbation, and love of things divine, the fruit whereof is eternal life."[74]

Difficulties of this kind gave rise to criticisms; still famous are Hobbes, Descartes, Spinoza, and other enlightened critics of mixing religion with philosophy. Still, the evolution of modern philosophy intimates that reason is more touched with mystery than enlightenment thinkers had assumed. Their methodological canon of clear and distinct ideas lacks a clear and distinct basis; the canon of knowledge by experiment is not justified by experiment or experiences; the method of science cannot account for the judgments of quality inherent in common sense and good judgment; certainty of progress by useful science decays with doubts as to progress, as to perilous accumulations of man-made power, as to an orientation by mere utility and power, and as to the certainty and comprehensiveness of scientific hypotheses. Finally, the distinction between values and the facts with which science is concerned leaves mysterious the value of science and its facts. One cannot defer to historical development, since men alone judge, even of what is development and not perversion or mere change. It has come to seem that human existence inextricably involves choice and commitment. More, it seems that humans experience in speech and poetry and music something transcending them as individuals, although the character of this being, and thus of the ground for all choices and commitments, remains mysterious. The development of an anxious and obscure existentialism on the ruin of the enlightenment's hopes, then, should caution us from dismissing, on grounds now doubtful, Hooker's blend of reason with our mysteries.

74. E. Grislis has noted Hooker's difference from Thomas Aquinas, who held that within "its own proper sphere, reason *qua* reason does not need the assistance of Grace." "Richard Hooker's Image of Man," in S. J. Heninger, ed., *Renaissance Papers, 1963* (New York, 1964), p. 80; "Fragments of an Answer," in *Works* II, 548; cf. *Laws* VIII.vi.7; III.viii.12.

# Part II

## Christian Ethics

# 5

## The Character of Hooker's Ethics

In healing his church's disease Hooker sought to restore measure to zeal—"justification by faith alone," indeed, but prudently or wisely understood. We now turn to his combination of faith with an Aristotelian understanding of prudence and wisdom. Part II treats of the resulting moral teaching: what is good (chapter 5), and how it is grasped by a combination of desire (chapter 6) and reasoning (chapter 7). Part III discusses Hooker's general political teaching and his particular prescription for England.

### Generalities

The theologian Hooker regarded the philosopher Aristotle as "head of all philosophers." If the heathen thinker was unaware of the mysterious revealed Way, his "eye scarce anything escaped, which was to be found in the bosom of nature."[1] One cannot agree with the occasional opinion, discussed in the introduction, that Hooker was a transitional figure who held "enlightened" views about natural rights and a social contract. Nor should one treat him (wearily to author and reader) as but another mixture of faith and reason modeled on Aquinas, or as but another Aristotelian of his time. That would miss his freshness and penetration. Besides, Hooker admires Augustine among churchmen more than Aquinas, and differs markedly from Aquinas. Finally, those who suppose Hooker a conventional product of Thomism or Aristotelianism, themselves conventional, should show us another such mixture of such unconventional penetration, or should show us why Hooker was not a Calvinist of the sort prevailing in his old

1. *Laws* VIII.ii.12; V.lxxi.11.

college, Corpus Christi.[2] But enough of these unanswerable questions as to how ordinary conventions determine an extraordinary thinker.

Broadly speaking, Hooker's teaching about human things follows the path set forth by Aristotle. Our species is said to incline by nature to a twofold perfection, of intellect (philosophy) and of character (the moral virtues). "Speculation of truth" and "exercise of virtue" are the activities "beseeming man's excellency." Speculation is the finer or higher of the two, since it manifests directly and not mediately man's distinctive intelligence. It is that "wherein the excellence of his kind doth most consist," in Hooker's words, "the virtue of the best part in us," in Aristotle's.[3] Hooker proceeds with Aristotle, nevertheless, to the unplatonic affirmation that moral virtue is a genuine human excellence, if not quite measuring up to philosophy. There is virtue of character, exercised in deeds, apart from the activity of intelligence, knowing.

Hooker and Aristotle agree also about the existence of moral duties minimal as well as admirable, oriented to natural necessity as the virtues are to natural excellence. One might suppose Hooker to say, "You can lay down a flooring of actions dictated by the needs of men, and known by men generally, and a ceiling of finer dispositions that the best inclinations call for, and present in only the better men. Presuming that you perform the things that necessity demands, you should try to be as excellent a fellow as circumstance permits." The lower level of good conduct is prescribed by Hooker's well-known law of reason, his equivalent of the natural justice of *Nicomachean Ethics*, Book V.

These similarities are only that, however. We name our parts "ethics" and "politics," after Hooker's philosophic master, and yet this should not obscure differences profound enough to affect division of the sciences. The sharp division of ethics from politics that we will describe is foreign to Aristotle, whose *Nicomachean Ethics* begins as "in a sense the study of politics."[4] Equally alien is Hooker's unification of the two subjects within an account of God's comprehensive governance. Both fit within the famous divine jurisprudence of *Laws* I, the account of laws as they emanate from divine commands. The theologian reshapes a philosophic ethic and politics to comply with the doctrine of Christian salvation.

In general, Hooker interprets distinctively even the opinions that remind most of Aristotle. A supernatural end and plan, and the supernatural virtues of faith, hope, and charity, somewhat displace all of the natural excellences. The natural duties come to be deduced from God's law; they lose their principal claim to intrinsic worth.[5] Moreover, Hooker's ethics is legal and clear-cut in spirit and therefore dogmatic and certain. Correspondingly, priority of law displaces human judgment from its crowning place in practical virtue. For this

2. See Cargill Thompson, "The Philosopher of the Politic Society," in W. Speed Hill, ed., *Studies in Richard Hooker* (Cleveland and London, 1972), pp. 21–22, 26–27.

3. *Laws* I.x.12; see also I.v.3; I.xi.1, 3, 4; I.viii.5 (end); V.lxxvi.3; *Nicomachean Ethics*, 1177ᵃ 12–18, hereafter *Nich. Ethics*, 1177ᵃ 12–18.

4. *Nich. Ethics*, 1094ᵇ 11–12.

5. Harry V. Jaffa, *Thomism and Aristotelianism* (Chicago, 1952), chs. 3, 7, esp. pp. 142–48.

reason, Hooker's ethics is deductive in tone; it can dispense with Aristotle's insistently imprecise and somewhat dialectical orientation by various opinions, especially those most widely prevalent, or that seem to have some argument in their favor.[6] In addition, by his essentially individual (and spiritual) understanding of happiness, Hooker displaces friendship from its Aristotelian prominence. The *Ethics* seem to progress through the moral virtues and practical judgment to friendship, as embracing in its better forms a higher pleasure and happiness; only then it advances the claims of philosophy. Hooker's natural ethics focuses unequivocally upon morality and philosophy. Finally, Hooker accords a distinctive preeminence to the necessities of conduct.

### The Law of Reason

The definition of reason's law is succinct, whatever the complications implied.

> The nature of Goodness being . . . ample, a Law is properly that which Reason in such sort defineth to be good that it must be done. And the Law of Reason or human Nature is that which men by discourse of natural Reason have rightly found out themselves to be all for ever bound unto in their actions.

By reasoning we discern universal duties so compelling that our performance is more than advised; it is commanded as by a law. Although these things so commonly necessary are but common, of "so mean a degree of goodness" that all men can perform them,[7] they enjoy a place even literally central in Hooker's new foundation. Of the sixteen chapters in Book I, chapters 5, 6, and 7 prepare for discussion of the law of reason, 8 and 9 discuss it, 10 exhibits the political consequences, and 12 explains why God's written revelation bothered to aid us with many of these laws supposed to be discernible by our unaided reason. Moreover, this law of conduct is clear in its demands. The two main precepts are express: "worship God" and "love your neighbor"; worship of God is primary because ultimately God (and not, say, the political ruler) rules. "Presuming some knowledge," Hooker remarks as he deduces this precept from his natural theology, "not only that there is a God, but also what power, force, wisdom, and other properties that God hath, and how all (benefits) depend on him (as their principal cause)," each man can be brought to perceive that God ought to be honored. The result is a broad prescription chiefly religious in tenor: "That which is simply against [the law immutable of God and nature] . . . can at no time be allowable in any person, more than adultery, blasphemy, sacrilege, and the like."[8] The secondary place of politics is even explicit. Hooker sharply distinguishes primary from secondary precepts of reason, a procedure made needful by the fall. Primary precepts such as "love your neighbor" are called forth by unspotted nature, while secondary precepts afford guidance with respect to the evils abounding in man's fallen state. "Men always knew" that they might defend themselves from force and injury, and keep others from injuring a third

6. *Nich. Ethics*, 1095ᵃ 29–30.
7. *Laws* II.viii.2; I.viii.8.
8. *Laws* VII.xv.14; I.viii.7; V.lxxix.2.

party, and that no one might decide his own case, or rule others without their consent.[9] Among secondary precepts alone does concern for political matters appear.

By contrast, the *Nicomachean Ethics*'s discussion of natural justice is neither central nor conspicuous nor very clear, and the context of discussion is political. Book V discusses justice, and is the last of four books on moral virtue, the next to last of five books on the practical virtues, moral and intellectual. The discussion of justice is part of the first solution (noble and just deeds) to the problem of happiness, a solution succeeded by at least two additional, and contradictory, suggestions. The discussion of natural justice proper occupies only a slight and obscure passage in Book V. The book's argument moves from justice in its general and obvious sense—what the law says—to justice in its more subtle and better sense, a person's equitable disposition. After treating of legal justice Aristotle discusses in turn distribution of common goods, restoration of equal shares in private transactions, and reciprocity in exchange of goods and in punishment of evils. He then wonders whether a man may *do* acts of injustice without *being* unjust, thus preparing the transition from *actions* to *dispositions*. Yet he halts. "But we must not forget that the subject of our investigation is at once justice simply and political justice."[10] Aristotle then discusses political justice, and natural justice as part of political justice. Justice is only in polities and in the commands of rulers, and can be fully defined only by taking up the requirements of polities and rule.

One such requirement is law. To live together or live well together requires certain fair actions from everyone, not merely fair intentions. One demands repayment and not merely an intention to repay. That is why justice is most obviously what specific laws prescribe, but also why a discussion of justice must investigate the political preconditions of law. This interpretation of the general argument is supported by an otherwise inexplicable sentence, immediately preceding Aristotle's sudden turn to political justice: "The relation of reciprocity to justice has been stated already." He had explained reciprocity in exchange and punishment as only tit for tat, a product of desire for one's own and not of an opinion about what is due another. While not justice strictly speaking, a mutual exchange of goods and evils is necessary for society's existence, and thereby for law and justice in stricter senses.

Another prerequisite for a just relationship is proportionality in political power. Only those more or less equal in power will agree to accept law (*nomos* or agreement) from one another. Nothing is due to one's slave—according to the harsh political reckoning that usually obtains between master and slave. Slaves, children, and women either are excluded from participating in justice, being ruled more or less without their consent, or participate in lesser degree. Such is Aristotle's contention. Justice can exist among the oligarchs in an oligarchy, but not between the oligarchs and their slaves, and only in lesser degree between the ruling oligarchs and the subservient poor. When the argument reaches this point Aristotle distinguishes two kinds of political justice, natural

9. *Laws* I.x.4, 13.
10. *Nich. Ethics*, 1134ᵃ 25–26, 1137ᵇ 34, 1138ᵃ 2.

and conventional. Natural justice has the same validity everywhere and does not depend upon opinion. Conventional justice may be settled one way or the other, "though having once been settled it is not indifferent; for example, that the ransom for a prisoner shall be a *mina*, that a sacrifice shall consist of a goat and not of two sheep, and any regulations enacted for particular cases, for instance the sacrifice in honor of Brasidas, and ordinances in the nature of special decrees." Shortly afterward, Aristotle observes that "it is easy to see" which justice is natural and which conventional. One's exasperation with this blithe assurance is not reduced by Aristotle's brevity, or by his failure to provide a single example of natural justice; the discussion lacks the clarity and explicitness of Hooker's. Still, one might follow the commentary of Thomas Aquinas, who infers examples of natural justice from the illustrations of conventional justice that we have just quoted. It is naturally just that a citizen who suffers in the line of civic duty should be aided, and that the highest honors or sacrifices be paid to the city's heroes or the city's gods.[11] If Thomas is correct, natural justice consists in those duties necessary to every polity. This solid root explains why it "has the same validity everywhere, and does not depend upon our opining it or not." Contrariwise, "the justice ordained not by nature but by man is not the same in all places, since regimes are not the same, though in all places there is only one regime that is natural, namely, the best." While conventional justice varies with political choice, natural justice is fixed by the minimal but general requirements for political existence. Yet it is difficult to regard such requirements as simply natural. Although generally discernible, they call for a certain art in discerning, and in establishing. They too are creatures of opinion and choice, not simply products of nature—nor *so* generally given. Aristotle shortly replaces the distinction between convention and nature with that between convention and expediency.[12] Providing for the necessities of polities cannot be separated from a rudimentary wisdom in political choosing, from an elemental political prudence.

The distinctive clarity and content of Hooker's law of reason are due to divine establishment and divine insistence. To begin with, the legal form differs from the counsels of Aristotle's vaguely couched natural justice. Hooker's legalism is clearly a moderate one; we have noted his introduction of statesmanlike discretion into a reformed Christianity grown insufferably doctrinaire. The effort has its Aristotelian parallel. An overly rigorous religious morality is one target of the *Ethics*'s many allusions to chance, natural weakness, inexactitude, and the frequent need for flexible discretion.[13] Admitting the similarity, one must note the difference: the discretion on which Hooker insists is bounded by an irreducible minimum of unchanging law expressing God's unchanging gov-

11. *Nich. Ethics*, 1134$^b$ 21–24; cf. Aquinas, *Commentary on the Nicomachean Ethics*, trans. C. I. Litzinger (Chicago, 1964), Book V, Lecture XII, ch. 1024.

12. *Nich. Ethics*, 1133$^b$ 35–1134$^a$ 1, 1132$^b$–1133$^a$ 2, 1135$^a$ 3–6. See also Leo Strauss, *Natural Right and History* (Chicago, 1953), pp. 156–64; Strauss, "Marsilius of Padua," in Strauss and Joseph Cropsey, eds., *History of Political Philosophy*, 2nd ed. (Chicago, 1972), pp. 251–70; Marsilius of Padua, *Defensor Pacis*, trans. Alan Gewirth, vol. 2 of Gewirth's *Marsilius of Padua, Defender of Peace* (New York, 1951), II.xii.7; I.iii.4; I.xix.13.

13. *Nich. Ethics*, 1165$^a$ 14–35.

ernance. Laws of reason are literally indispensable. "Natural laws direct in such sort, that in all things we must for ever do according unto them." This unequivocal generality is not due to their grand dignity, for the laws of reason prescribe things of a "mean . . . degree of goodness." Ordinary in themselves, these duties are nevertheless required by God for the most heavenly of goods; the laws are superior to human discretion, because superior to earthly considerations. Also, law as distinguished from counsel implies mandatory counsel, an order from one who can enforce his command with sanctions. Only if "the law of nature and God" is obeyed does a provident God reward with a happiness more perfect than earthly, and refrain from punishing with unearthly torments. "The light of nature," we are admonished, "is never able to find out any way of obtaining the reward of bliss, but by performing exactly the duties and works of righteousness."[14]

Whatever the translators say, the *Ethics* in its thematic discussions never speaks of natural rules or immutable law. Aristotle contrasts natural justice with justice "not natural, but legal and conventional," and says expressly that all justice is changeable. "With the gods" this is perhaps not true, "while with us there is something that is just even by nature, yet all of it is changeable."[15] This passage is hard to understand. Perhaps every maxim of justice has to be broken when in an extreme case the existence of the polity is at risk. An attempt to rescue a war hero captured by the enemy, for example, might entail a potentially disastrous defeat. When his discussion in Book V reaches the perspective of equity, Aristotle says that "all law is universal but about some things it is not possible to make a correct universal statement. . . . The error is not in the law nor in the legislator but in the nature of the thing, since the matter of practical affairs is essentially irregular."[16] Not law but equitable judgment ought to rule; in the ensuing Book VI Aristotle investigates practical judgment. Contrary to Hooker, Aristotle treats law as fundamentally a political phenomenon; he discusses it mostly in the *Politics*. Moral phenomena chiefly concern activities, dispositions of soul, and fortunate circumstances; only indirectly do they concern the mere prescriptions in words of law. Besides, the quality of law varies with the lawmaker, and law inevitably errs somewhat in dealing with various and variable particulars. A discussion of equity concludes Aristotle's account of justice, and equity is both a qualification of strict legality and a manifestation of considerate judgment.

### Philosophy, Friendship, and Moral Virtue

Hooker seems far from reformed doctrine in the prominence he allows virtues other than faith, hope, and charity. "The gospel of Christ requireth" only the performance of "virtuous duties" for the attainment of immortal happiness. Those who commend the love of equity and right, "though they speak not of

14. *Laws* I.xi.5; cf. I.ix.1; II.viii.2; *Works* III, 599, 619. Cf. *Laws* I.viii.5, 8, 11; III.ix.1; VII.xv.14; V.ix.1; V.lxxi.4; IV.lx.5, 6, 7.
15. *Nich. Ethics*, 1134$^b$ 26–33.
16. *Nich. Ethics*, 1137$^b$ 18–20.

religion, do notwithstanding declare that which is in truth her only working." Such teachings help to account for the rationalism which some commentators discern, and surely account for Hooker's reliance on Aristotle. Yet his reliance is qualified, just as the wisdom of philosophers is qualified. Hooker is not altogether unlike Calvin in knowing of a light above "the great darkness of philosophers who have looked for a building in a ruin, and fit arrangement in disorder." [17]

Although Hooker praises and admires "speculation of truth," he understands theoretical inquiry as guided and illuminated by a revealed way. The queen of the sciences is theology, "which out of principles in Scripture that are plain, soundly deduceth more doubtful inferences." The queen of the sciences serves the King of Kings—and is not to exceed the bounds of service. "The foolishness of the cross of Christ is the wisdom of true believers," Hooker remarks, and again: "It is not the deepness of their knowledge, but the singleness of their belief, which God accepteth." [18] Thus a revealed happiness in the next life guides inquiry in this life. While good in itself, knowledge is chiefly good as a means; knowledge of our dependence upon God's power enables us to know and perform our natural duties. Perhaps this explains why Hooker prefers the word "knowledge," neutral as to means or end, to "wisdom," more indicative of a good in itself. Inquiry or philosophy is finally subordinate to practical activity, then, especially to acts obedient to the divine commands of faith and righteousness. It follows that "the highest advancement" for mortal man is "service," particularly ecclesiastical service; the highest natural activity, contemplation, serves to advance the ministry of Christ. [19]

Similar considerations cause Hooker's distinctive treatment of friendship. Hooker fails to include friendship among the chief goods discussed in Book I, although he mentions it later as an "external good." Friendship involves a mutual disposition in friends to take pleasure in one another's company. Such a love of another human and of things human might be thought to distract from love for a happiness higher than human. Perhaps friendship had to seem dubious to Hooker as an end and distracting as a means, whereas something more serviceable to the Christian may be made of philosophy and moral virtue.

Aristotle had distinguished friendships of low pleasure and of utility from the best friendships, those of the good who love one another's fine actions or character or thoughts. [20] These things are good, and the pleasure that accompanies love for them and the person embodying them is also good. The *Ethics*'s paean to friendship, Books VIII and IX, is surrounded by two long discussions defending pleasure and clarifying the kinds of pleasure. The better friendships

17. John Calvin, *Institutes of the Christian Religion*, trans. Beveridge (London, 1949), I.xv.8, quoted by Duncan B. Forrester, "Martin Luther and John Calvin," in Strauss and Cropsey, *History of Political Philosophy*, p. 307; see *Laws* V.i.2, 3; V.lxxi.2; II.i.2; Preface.iii.2; Preface.iv.8; I.i.5, 6. I have benefited from Forrester's remarks.

18. *Laws* V.xlvi.3; *Works* III, 594–95; *Laws* V.xxii.17. Cf. *Laws* V.viii.2; V.iv.8; esp. I.ii.5, 6; II.iv.7; II.vii; III.viii.7–10; III.ii.12–17.

19. *Laws* V.lxxx.6; cf. V.lxxvi.10; V.lxxvii.8.

20. *Nich. Ethics*, 1155$^b$ 17–1157$^a$ 35.

involve the better pleasures; discussing friendship Aristotle says that "life is sensation and thought."[21] Sharing a friend's sensations and thoughts, the better friendships involve true living as well as the better pleasures.

Hooker thinks good deeds and true thoughts chiefly but means to a spiritual good in another world, however, and pleasure in this-worldly things but a chain to this temporal world. True life is beyond men, their perceptible bodies, and their thought, and therefore beyond mutual participation in perceiving and thinking. The human desire for good is infinite; "no good is infinite but only God; therefore he our felicity and bliss."[22] Hooker does look forward to a final union with God in both "understanding and will." Then men will find their longings satisfied in the "rich treasures of all wisdom" and the "sea of goodness."[23] Yet this union is hardly friendship, if only because of the disparity even in the other world between the parties. The disparity in this world is unutterable, because self-love prevents humans from loving the good itself, and thus God Himself.

Aristotle had finally traced friendship not simply to love of others but to self-love. One loves in others what one desires for oneself, be it money or bodily pleasure or noble deeds or true thoughts. Precisely this conditioning of love by love of self has to repel Hooker. One might for God's sake love men at large or even the more godly: charity and the community of Christ displace friendship. These approximate the selfless love of the life to come. "Whereas we now love the thing that is good, but good especially in respect of benefit unto us; we shall then love the thing that is good, only or principally for the goodness of beauty in itself."[24] As the divine is above man, so the thing loved is above man, and this displaces friendship for the self no less than friendship for other men.

With respect to moral matters in the strict sense, Hooker advocates a righteousness less political and more dutiful than the aristocratic manliness outlined in Books III–V of the *Ethics*. This should not be overstated. Hooker is in another world, as it were, from Machiavelli's powerful attacks on an orientation by noble character and aristocratic politics. The Christian divine explicitly follows the "Grecians" in praising the gentlemanly excellences, for their "beauty" no less than for their fitness for use.[25] He counsels "the cherishing of those virtues . . . wherein if nobility do chance to flourish, they are both an ornament and a stay to the commonwealth wherein they live."[26] Hooker praises not only courage, moderation, and prudence, which are politically necessary, but also liberality and grandeur of soul, more splendid virtues less closely tied to utility.

---

21. *Nich. Ethics*, 1170ᵃ 19–20.

22. *Laws* I.xi.1–3; cf. *Nich. Ethics*, 1159ᵃ 3–5. See 1162² 4–5, considering friendship of men for gods as conferers of greatest benefits.

23. *Laws* I.xi.3.

24. *Laws* I.xi.3; *Nich. Ethics*, 1168ᵃ 28–1169ᵃ 18.

25. *Laws* I.viii.1.

26. *Laws* VII.xviii.10, cf. VII.xxiv.5.

Liberality, even magnificence, befit prominent men. They "always know that great things are at their hands expected. . . . For actions which must be great, mean instruments will not serve." Devout magnificence, for example, is a fitting tribute to the deity. Charity to the poor may be a necessary work, but the splendid raising of churches is even in God's eyes an honorable work. Hooker's words point toward one peak of moral virtue for Aristotle: magnanimity or greatness of soul. Knowing its own excellence, noble pride pursues what Hooker like Aristotle calls "the chiefest" of earthly blessings, reputation or honor.[27]

Other and contrary tendencies are more prominent in Hooker's discussion, however. He praises humility and penitence. Magnanimity, as Aristotle describes it, involves a proud consciousness of one's unflawed excellence. "The good man never finds fault with himself at the moment of his act, like the incontinent, nor the later with the earlier man, like the penitent, nor the earlier with the later, like the liar."[28] Such serene pride clashes with the suppositions that all men are flawed by sin, and that man's well-doing is owed to God. The Christian remains humble before his divine superior; human pride is human sin. Hooker calls vanity the mother of all vice, not (as Aristotle suggests) merely one kind of vice. He repeatedly exhorts his readers to meekness and tenderness of heart. "God doth load with his grace the lowly, when the proud he sendeth empty away."[29] Also, Hooker interprets honor distinctively: the tribute paid by opinion to beneficial virtue. "Honour is no where due, saving only unto such as have in them that whereby they are found, or at the least presumed, voluntarily beneficial unto them of whom they are honored."[30] In discussing magnanimity Aristotle had treated honor principally as the tribute paid to nobility, to virtue as such and not to the use or beneficence of virtue. Honor is the "prize of excellence." It manifests in opinion the admiration evoked by nobility of character, deed, and thought. Hooker implicitly depreciates nobility, especially the grandeur of soul and deed that most evokes awe. He interprets honor in light of the useful benefits given one another by men aspiring above a merely human nobility. Eventually Aristotle speaks of honor as compensation for the labor of political office, as the coin of gratitude to parents and others, and as the *douceur* paid to gods, and those of birth, wealth, and power, in hope of benefit. Yet his account retains its deference to qualities noble in themselves. "Honor is the reward paid to virtue and beneficence," he finally says.[31] Ultimately, Hooker's own esteem for liberality and magnificence is decisively qualified: one's intention is crucial in God's eyes, not the grandeur of one's means.

27. *Laws* V.lxxvi.2, 3; V.lxxvii.14; V.ii; V.xxiv.18; V.v; V.xv.3, 4; V.xv.5; V.lxxix.14; V.lxxv.3; V.lxx.3; V.lxxx.16.

28. Aristotle, *Eudemian Ethics*, trans. H. Rackham (Cambridge, Mass., and London, 1952), 1240$^b$ 21–24.

29. See Hooker's interpretation of Luke xviii, 10–14, in Sermon VII, 1, at *Works* III, 702. Cf. Sermon IV, at *Works* III, 647; Sermon III, at *Works* III, 614; *Laws* Preface.i.3; I.iv.1, 3; III.ix.3.

30. *Laws* VII.xvii.2, 3.

31. *Nich. Ethics*, 1163$^b$ 1, 1095$^b$ 27–31, 1134$^b$ 7.

> The meanest and the very poorest amongst men yielding unto God
> as much in proportion as the greatest, and many times in affection
> more may be assured . . . that in his sight from whom all good is
> expected, they are concerning acceptation, protection, divine privi-
> leges and pre-eminences whatsoever, equals and peers with them
> unto whom they are otherwise in earthly respects inferiors.[32]

In short, the more splendid virtues culminating in magnanimity are shaded by
Hooker's advancement of patience, humility, and dutifulness. Greatness of soul
is somewhat presumptuous for men subject to divine justice.

Distributive justice in the Aristotelian sense is similarly shaded. Actually,
Aristotle's accounts of magnanimity and of fair distribution of office and privilege are inextricably connected; the claims of the outstanding man justly extend
to predominance. While the floor of Aristotle's ethics is linked to the necessities
of politics, the ceiling (so far as moral virtue is concerned) is linked to the best
in politics, the best regime. The peak of aristocratic virtue is matched by the
peak of distributive justice, a distribution of office to the best men. Such a
coincidence of power and quality is unlikely, however. The disparity causes
Aristotle to reconsider the goodness of justice and of political rule, the worth of
moral virtue, and in general the practical and political life so often obstructed.
Not so for Hooker.

> It is both commonly said, and truly, that the best men otherwise are
> not always the best in regard of society. The reason whereof is, for
> that the law of men's actions is one, if they be respected only as
> men; and another, when they are considered as parts of a politic
> body.[33]

Man is not a political animal in the Aristotelian sense, and thus the character of
the polity, the form of the government, who dominates, is not crucial. "The
kinds [of regiment] being many, Nature tieth not to any one, but leaveth the
choice as a thing arbitrary." Hooker's only thematic elaboration of justice passes
up human justice, summed up as distributive, commutative, and corrective, to
dwell on divine justice. Justice is the bond of the very world whereby each thing
benefits from the rest. God's distributive justice "yields unto each person that
which is due according to the difference of their quality."[34] God's corrective
justice punishes sins, and man must himself provide some satisfaction to God
for sins, and to men for injuries. The satisfactions of God consist in penitence,
and Hooker discusses at length the several works of repentance.

Hooker's principal concern is "the justice of God rewarding the worthiness
of (man's) deserts with the crown of eternal glory."[35] For duties performed and

---

32. *Laws* V.lxxix.8.
33. *Laws* I.xvi.6.
34. *Works* III, 615 ff.; cf. *Laws* I.ii; I.iii.
35. "In the natural path of everlasting life the first beginning is that ability of doing good,
which God in the day of man's creation endowed him with; from hence obedience unto the will of
his creator, absolute righteousness and integrity in all his actions; and last of all the justice of God
rewarding the worthiness of his deserts with the crown of eternal glory" (*Laws* I.xvi.5).

faith unquestioning, God's justice or at least his beneficence grants man super-natural life. Perhaps in strict justice even original man did not deserve such a reward. The oldest Adam may have been subject to God's bountifulness, subject to the Master's reward. Erring man is unqualifiedly subject. He is utterly sub-ordinate to God's mercy, to a "mystical and supernatural" way requiring of men the "supernatural virtues" of Faith, Hope, and Charity. There follows a distinc-tive tenor of dutiful resignation to the laws of reason and of men. According to Hooker, providential rule is always perfectly just, in an important sense. Ac-cording to Aristotle, political rule is so rarely just in practice that its stature in principle becomes questionable. Generally rulers are not the best men, and jus-tice in the generality of regimes calls for conduct inferior to that of which the best men are capable. Hooker's treatment of human justice, however, is condi-tioned by the perfection of divine justice. Evil laws and rulers are somehow dictated by the law of God—if only by His first and unknowable eternal law. A passage from Calvin illustrates this point with un-Hookerian bluntness:

> Every man of understanding deems it most absurd to submit to un-just and tyrannical domination, provided it can by any means be thrown off, and there is but one opinion prevailing among men, that it is the part of an abject and servile mind to bear it patiently, the part of an honourable and high-spirited mind to rise up against it. Indeed, the revenge of injuries is not regarded by philosophers as a vice. But the Lord, condemning this too lofty spirit, prescribes to His people that patience which mankind deem infamous.[36]

**External Goods**

Like Aristotle, Hooker speaks of goods external to the soul (unlike the virtues and philosophy) and nevertheless good because required for happiness. Both writers include friends, wealth, success in what we take in hand, children, health, a full span of years. Hooker omits three that Aristotle includes: political power, good birth (for its worldly advantages), and beauty (for inducing admi-ration, friendship, and love). He adds one, quietness. The two accounts differ also in interpretation. Hooker allows external goods as good only where they are aids to virtue and the acquiring of knowledge; Aristotle is not so strict, although he acknowledges them to be bad where they contribute to vice.[37] Ar-istotle shows a tolerance from the heights with respect to the various pleasures of men, even as to lower pleasures that are the only pleasures for many.[38] Also, Hooker prefers as much moderation in such goods as wealth as is compatible with a man's "station and place." Also, Aristotle's complicated hedging about the consequences for happiness of the afterlife finds no parallel in Hooker; the afterlife involves not fortune but virtue and grace. Despite his Aristotelian dis-dain for the Stoics, in short, Hooker looks down somewhat on all external goods

---

36. *Institutes* IV.xx.16, quoted by Duncan Forrester in Strauss and Cropsey, *History of Political Philosophy*, p. 321.
37. *Laws* V.lxxvi.5; *Nich. Ethics*, 1099ᵃ 31–1099ᵇ 8.
38. *Laws* V.lxxvi.4, 5; *Nich. Ethics*, 1154ᵃ 7–1154ᵇ 21.

(which he usually calls temporal goods). The true and Christian soul will triumph over all temporal obstacles. Aristotle could not say: "In a word not to whom no calamity falleth, but whom neither misery nor prosperity is able to move from a right mind, them we may truly pronounce fortunate." Aristotle does say:

> No activity is perfect when it is impeded, and happiness is a perfect thing; this is why the happy man needs the goods of the body and external goods, i.e., those of fortune, in order that he may not be impeded in these ways. Those who say that the victim on the rack or the man who falls into great misfortune is happy if he is good, are intentionally or unintentionally saying nothing.[39]

To recapitulate: Hooker's ethics follows from his Christian understanding of man as a spiritual animal, not simply a rational and political animal. Its focus on a law of reason, its religious content and strict legality, reflect an all-powerful deity's command of the means needful for salvation. Philosophy and moral virtue are reduced in importance, subordinated to supernatural virtues and in general to God's various laws; politics, pleasure, and friendship are more radically demoted. And the urbane tenor of Aristotle's moral excellences is reshaped in light of the humility, sober awareness of sin and guilt, and apolitical righteousness that befit justice not human but divine.

39. *Nich. Ethics*, 1153ᵇ 16–22; *Laws* V.lxxvi.5.

# 6

# Knowing What Is Good:

## The Role of Desire

A curious paradox in Hooker's account of morality has attracted comment. While his ethics seems to depend on divinely revealed law, he maintains that the basic duties toward God and man are known naturally, "without the help of Revelation supernatural and divine." He cites profusely the pagan philosophers and seems to reason on the same basis, that is, from human inclination alone. "A law of reason," he sums up his teaching, is a rule "whereunto by the light of reason men find themselves bound in that they are men."[1]

In this chapter and the next we take up the manner in which laws and virtues become known, illuminating Hooker's views by extended comparison with Aristotle's. Underlying the particulars is the relation between nature and supernature, reason and grace, that we considered at the end of Part I. The moral nub is this: our nature discovers—but nature of the sort that Christian revelation reveals to be under God's perfect providence. Reason finds its laws—but reason unspotted by the original sin which revelation reveals. Whatever the appearance of simple reason and simple reliance upon the pagans, Hooker's true understanding shows itself as Book I of the *Laws* deduces the law of reason. In chapter 7 he would not be understood to say that man's natural understanding can "rightly perform its function as oft as we cause God in his justice to withdraw"; Chapter 8 is decisive:

> For whatsoever we have hitherto taught, or shall hereafter, concerning the force of man's natural understanding, this we always desire withal to be understood; that there is no kind of faculty or power in

1. *Laws* I.xvi.1; I.vii.9.

man or any other creature, which can rightly perform the functions allotted to it, without perpetual aid and concurrence of that Supreme Cause of all things.[2]

The reason that knows truly is the reason aided by grace. Hooker openly determines by scripture doubtful precepts of reason when he reaches the later sections of Book I.

Hooker's account of moral knowledge follows a clear order. In chapter 5 man is said to be in possibility what he is not in act, and therefore to desire a variety of perfections, especially those arising "externally" from what he learns. Chapter 6 sets forth the way man rises to knowledge through sensation and particularly through proper reasoning. Chapter 7 dwells on the propriety of the will, desire for that which reason dictates, distinguished from appetite, desire for sensible goods. The long chapter 8 sums up the chief laws and how they are known, superficially through signs, fundamentally by discourse of reason. Chapter 9 discusses the way counsels of reason are known to be divinely enforced, and hence to be laws as well as counsel. Chapter 11 recapitulates, concluding that supernatural and mysterious means are needed now that man has disabled his rational nature. We clarify this moral epistemology by discussing in turn the direction given by desire, reason, and will.

Chapter 5 distinguishes three basic sorts of human desire, interpreted as three different ways of imitating the divine. Like other creatures, first, man seeks to be like God in being always, if only by "offspring and propagation." Like other living creatures, second, he covets semblance with God "in the constancy and excellency of these operations which belong unto their kinds." Finally, he seeks perfections "not expressly desired unless they be first known, or such as are not for any other cause than for knowledge itself desired: . . . by proceeding in the knowledge of truth, and by growing in the exercise of virtue, man amongst the creatures of this inferior world aspireth to the greatest conformity with God."

Hooker describes the most basic desire as a striving for immortality, obtained in this world through children. This is distinctive. In equivalent portions of the *Ethics* Aristotle spoke of fear of death, to be moderated by the virtue of courage, and desire for sexual pleasure, to be moderated (together with hunger and thirst) by the virtue of moderation. In writings lacking a distinctively ethical perspective, however, he made a different and perhaps deeper suggestion. *On the Soul* maintains that all things yearn after participation in the eternal and divine. Since perishables cannot be immortal, each tries to persist in "a representative which is specifically, not numerically, one with it."[3] Yet this inclination to reproduce is obscured in humans by unmoderated sexual desire; the pleasures of sex can fill one's mind. Commenting upon the generality of men Aristotle remarks in the *Ethics* that "it is possible that they in truth do not pursue the

2. *Laws* I.viii.11.

3. Aristotle, *De Anima*, trans. W. S. Hett (London and Cambridge, Mass., 1957), 415[a] 28–415[b] 7.

pleasure which they think and would say they do, but all the same pleasure; for nature has implanted in things something divine."[4] The divine spark determines neither what men generally think, nor what their desires generally *are*. What is true of most men would be true of all, were it not for the fine character of some. Hence the importance of virtue, not desire as such.

The *Nicomachean Ethics* had begun by weighing various familiar arts, activities, and opinions, not with a psychology of desire or any account of human nature. "Every art and every inquiry, and similarly every practical action and pursuit, seems to aim at some good," and every subordinate good serves a higher good and those finally a chief good. About this good almost all men agree in name: "happiness." They agree only in name, however. Most people identify happiness with something obvious like pleasure, wealth, or honor, and indeed vary in their opinion with circumstance; when sick, a man says health is the most valuable of goods, when poor, wealth. Or, feeling their ignorance, men admire those propounding something grand and above them. Judging from their ways of life, Aristotle concludes that men divide chiefly into those favoring lives of pleasure or enjoyment, of honor, politics, or virtue, of contemplation—and of moneymaking.

Why did Aristotle begin with the obvious variety of clashing practices, activities and views, rather than with a more definite basis such as Hooker's? Aristotle begins with the obvious, however inconclusive, rather than with the conclusive, which unfortunately is not obvious. Whatever may be knowable in itself, as Aristotle puts it, we must begin from what is known to us, and hence from the various views believed to be known. One cannot deduce correct conduct from true desire until one has weighed the conflicting views about what is truly desirable. Book I of the *Ethics* is a treatise on happiness, rising dialectically by considering the worth of opinions that seem worth considering.

Hooker feels no such need. He knows the knowable in itself, or as he phrases it, the *cause* of what we see and believe to see. He begins by promising to penetrate to the roots of the particular laws disputed by his opponents. Deepest is God's eternal law, "which giveth life unto all the rest." This confident knowledge allows the theologian to dispense with Aristotle's winnowing of opinions. He can deduce the tendencies of man from the attributes of all things other than God, and the object of those tendencies from their relation to God. He attends not only to the kinds of things, the beginning and in a way the end of wisdom according to Aristotle, but also to that law "which doth assign unto each thing the kind."[5]

Similarly, Hooker's delineation of a desire for "absolute exactness" in the operations of "his kind," the second of his trilogy, also presupposes nature's subservience to divine law.[6] For evidence of this desire Hooker relies upon axioms which assert that "the works of nature do always aim at that which cannot be bettered"; he cites two remarks of Aristotle. Both passages append the qualification "so far as possible," however. Both are said to be from Aristotle's *On*

4. *Nich. Ethics*, 1153[b] 30–33.
5. *Laws* I.viii.3; I.ii.1.
6. *Laws* I.v.2.

*the Heavens*; the motions of heavenly bodies lack the imperfection and mortality of human affairs. Finally, the one remark I have located is stated only conditionally in the original (prefaced with an "if"). It occurs in the context of an argument, as to the reason for the direction of heavenly motion, whose scientific status has just been questioned.[7] On even such matters Aristotle does not evince Hooker's certainty as to nature's perfection. Hooker remarks that the "defect in things natural" was "observed often by the heathen." The true cause, "divine malediction" on account of "the sin of man," they could not have known.[8]

Hooker's description of the second desire has other implications. These exact operations are identified with the human kind, with no saving mention of philosophy or virtuous action, *the* activities befitting the human kind according to Aristotle. What this peculiarity signifies is not clear (no example appears), and yet Hooker's procedure is clearly peculiar in even the tradition of Christian Aristotelianism. Consider the corresponding views of St. Thomas Aquinas.

The *Summa Theologica* also elaborates a threefold division of the natural inclinations. There is the desire to continue in being (shared by all things), the things like sexual intercourse and education of children (which nature has taught all animals), and finally an inclination to good according to the nature of reason (which is proper to man). Man wishes "to know the truth about God, and to live in society."[9]

Hooker's changes amount to these: he includes "offspring and propagation" as object of the basic desire to continue in being. Thomas puts this with his second inclination. Hooker's second inclination is for "constancy and excellency" in operations, about which Thomas says nothing. Thomas reserves remarks about man's kind to his third inclination, toward inquiry and life in society. Probably Hooker's difference as to desire number two is owing to the character of his number three. While of his kind, virtue and knowledge are means to a perfection above his kind, and from that good they obtain their distinguishing character. Perhaps only necessary tasks, arts, and duties, merely instrumental to life, are operations peculiar to man's kind.

The full character of the third basic desire hardly appears from Hooker's first brief account, but one peculiarity foreshadows others that eventually appear. This desire is said to grow "externally." Virtue and knowledge are perfections "not expressly desired unless they be first known, or such as are not for any other cause than for knowledge itself desired."[10] The emphasis upon express knowledge externally obtained is distinctive. True, the *Nicomachean Ethics* had insisted upon the crucial role of parents, customs, and laws in inculcating moral virtue; yet these external forces nourish an internal seed. The virtues preserve and cultivate vague, hardly conscious inklings of the noble and the fair, which Aristotle implies to be natural to developed intelligence and to be manifest in a

---

7. Aristotle, *De Caelo*, trans. W. K. C. Guthrie (London and Cambridge, Mass., 1960), 288ᵃ 2–4.

8. *Laws* I.iii.3.

9. Aquinas, *Summa Theologica*, trans. Anton C. Pegis (New York, 1944) I, II, Qu. 94, Art. 2.

10. *Laws* I.v.3.

fine man's or woman's opinions. In any event parents and polity are in a sense natural; man is both a pairing and a political animal. According to Hooker, however, the immortal life ultimately desired is external to our nature, at least to our fallen nature. Knowledge of this end, and of the means God requires, presupposes elaborate investigations of man's dependence on God. All this becomes clear during the second account of the desires, in the second and supernatural portion of Book I. The human perfections externally acquired are divided into those sought for use and those sought for their own sake.[11] Virtue and knowledge are lumped with health as good in themselves and yet not principally so, not the last mark at which we aim. While man's desire for good is infinite, virtue and knowledge provide only a finite good.[12] Hooker sums up:

> Man doth seek a triple perfection: first a sensual, consisting in those things which very life itself requireth either as necessary supplements, or as beauties and ornaments thereof; then an intellectual, consisting in those things which none underneath man is either capable of or acquainted with; lastly a spiritual and divine, consisting in those things whereunto we tend by supernatural means here, but cannot here attain unto them.[13]

This final end of men is "better than themselves" and

> doth neither depend upon the nature of the thing itself, nor proceed from any natural necessity that our souls should so exercise themselves for ever in beholding and loving God, but from the will of God, which doth both freely perfect our nature in so high a degree, and continue it so perfected.[14]

All important peculiarities of Hooker's ethics are traceable to this final end external to man as he knows himself. Man reaches for something above not merely his lower nature, but his nature as he can know it.

Earlier we remarked a difficulty that can now be confronted. How is this end above nature nonetheless natural and knowable by natural reason? Hooker makes two arguments, one from the very process of desire and the other from general opinion. Desire seeks something above vital use, and even

> somewhat above capacity of reason, somewhat divine and heavenly, which with hidden exultation it rather surmiseth than conceiveth; somewhat it seeketh, and what that is directly it knoweth not, yet very intentive desire thereof doth so incite it, that all other known delights and pleasures are laid aside, they give place to the search of this but only suspected desire.

Hooker points beyond definite objects of the understanding to an infinite object beyond understanding. The argument turns not on our grasp of the end, but

11. *Laws* I.xi.1.
12. *Laws* I.xi.2–3.
13. *Laws* I.xi.4.
14. *Laws* I.xi.3.

upon our desire for an end beyond what we grasp. What man "coveteth as good in itself, towards that his desire is ever infinite." Unless the final good sought be infinite, we go amiss, and since "no good is infinite but only God; therefore he our felicity and bliss."[15]

Still, we are said to know definitely of an infinite God, or a God whose capacities are infinite. There *is* guidance by knowledge, and knowledge definite enough to understand God and infinity. Is this knowledge possible without revelation, however? Hooker urges a maxim borrowed from Thomas's commentary on Aristotle's *Metaphysics*: It is an axiom of nature that "natural desire cannot utterly be frustrate." The conclusion does not follow from the premises stated, however. Suppose natural desire may not be utterly frustrate. It may be somewhat frustrate. Perhaps desire must rest content with a qualified happiness not fully satisfying the best desires of man's composite nature. That is Aristotle's opinion.[16] Moreover, should an object be shown to be impossible, desire may not be frustrated. "Let Reason teach impossibility in any thing, and the Will of man doth let it go." The soul's life after death has rarely been discovered by unassisted reason—and the body's salvation, never.[17]

Hooker's other key argument infers divine reward and punishment from the universal belief that secret actions are rewarded and punished: "The general and perpetual voice of men is as the sentence of God himself."[18] Yet he shows himself aware that "multitudes," "the greatest part," even "whole nations," have been ignorant "even of principal moral duties," and that some "godless" have been ignorant of God's providence.[19] His inference from universal belief may remind the reader of Aristotle's starting-point in accepted opinion. Yet Aristotle and his predecessors Socrates and Plato had confronted the variety of accepted opinions; Aristotle, in a relevant context near the beginning of his *Nicomachean Ethics*, had noted also the deference of men (conscious of their ignorance) to something grand and above themselves. Aristotle weighs only views widely prevalent and arguable and concludes by selecting these from the lives men lead, rather than from their opinions as such. After noting the manner in which all except the wise believe happiness the supreme good, Aristotle does not present any opinion as one which all men have at all times learned until Book VII, and then the object of agreement is pleasure. Apart from this common denominator, common even to brute and man, Aristotle seems not much to credit universal opinion. He introduces an obscure phrase from the poet Hesiod to testify that "no voice is wholly lost put forth by many peoples." In the original, however, the poet is cautioning men to avoid not only vengeance of the gods but also the evil rumors, perhaps of divine vengeance, set by men. No rumor dies fully away which many peoples spread abroad; rumor is itself a sort of goddess.[20] This does not much strengthen the authority of men's opinions; one

15. *Laws* I.xi.2,4; I.ii.2.
16. *Nich. Ethics* 1154$^b$ 20–31, 1170$^a$ 6; *De Anima*, 406$^b$ 3.
17. *Laws* I.xii.2; I.vii.5; III.viii.8.
18. *Laws* I.viii.3.
19. *Laws* V.ii.1; I.viii.11; I.x.11; I.xii.2.
20. Hesiod, *Works and Days*, trans. J. Banks (London, 1889), p. 463.

would not identify Aristotle with the view *vox populi, vox dei*, except in an unorthodox way.

Aristotle should not be accused, however, of contradicting the opinion of many as to God's rewards and punishments. In the *Nicomachean Ethics*, at any rate, the first and last references to the gods speak of their care for the happiness of men. It is true that both are hypothetical, and the second in the form, "If, as is generally believed, the gods exercise some superintendence over human affairs."[21] These references are not essential to the argument, and intermediate remarks gradually move from a notion of eventual personal immortality as the result of divine favor, to that of personal participation here in a divine and timeless activity. Book I avoids circumspectly the obscuring implications of a life hereafter. A remark that the gods must be above praise indicates a remoteness further developed; beings so superior are above virtue and friendship as well; the impossibility of personal immortality is allowed to slip out in an offhand manner. Book VIII interprets religious association as arising from pleasure in association and in relaxation, and as a part of the polity. Book X suggests contemplation to be the only activity of god. The best men endeavor through philosophy and contemplation to live up to the divine in them, or to actualize it. Finally, the gods' providence is said to consist in their love and benevolence to the wise.[22] Aristotle urbanely moderates and modifies common beliefs, with a view to the good life. In the *Metaphysics* a further explanation is given: the belief in gods with human capacities makes the multitude more politically docile, and men generally more lawabiding.[23]

Although *Ethics* VII maintains that pleasure, which all brutes and men pursue, is somehow the chief good, Aristotle also remarks there that men pursue diverse pleasures. In fact the bodily pleasures have appropriated the name (at least in most men's minds); most men are to that extent misled by their opinions. To orient the *Ethics* by what men universally think good would foster vulgar pleasure-seeking. Finally, Book X does say that "what everyone opines, that we say to be so. For he who subverts our trust in the opinion of mankind, will not lead us to trust his own."[24] The opinion in question is the goodness of pleasure. No longer bound by the effort of Books II through VII to properly master and frame the lower desires, Aristotle can admit the goodness of what all animals (including intelligent ones) desire. That deep desire originates the opinion of intelligent animals as to the goodness of pleasure. Even in his discussion of philosophy Aristotle does not decide "whether we desire life for the sake of pleasure or pleasure for the sake of life."[25]

We have remarked that Hooker's special knowledge enables him to look through the various pleasures to see the purport of the desires, their function in drawing man to God. This procedure is a distinct variation upon the Aristotelian

21. *Nich. Ethics*, 1179ᵃ 25–27.

22. *Nich. Ethics*, 1179ᵃ 27–32, 1099ᵇ 11–14, 1100ᵃ 10–32, 1101ᵃ 22–1101ᵇ 9, 1101ᵇ 19–24, 1158ᵇ 35–1159ᵃ 6, 1111ᵇ 22–23, 1160ᵃ 18–25, 1198ᵇ 22–24.

23. *Nich. Ethics*, 1074ᵇ 1–9.

24. *Nich. Ethics*, 1173ᵃ 1–3.

25. *Nich. Ethics*, 1175ᵃ 17–19.

original. The *Ethics* supposes that desire is for the apparent good and that *the* apparent good desired is pleasure: "Desire has regard to the object as pleasurable or painful, choice has not."[26] An account of the irrational part of the soul, divided into appetitive and desiring parts (*epithumetikon, orektikon*), remains very much in the background. Aristotle attends instead to the particular desires relevant to the various deeds and virtues he treats, and especially to the particular pleasures. Moral virtue has to do with pleasures and pains, we are told early and often, and the discourses on friendship and the philosophic life are each preceded by a reconsideration of pleasure. Nothing parallel occurs with respect to desire. Finally he says: "The pleasures involved in activities are more proper to them than the desires (*orekseis*); for the latter are separated both in time and in nature, while the former are close to the activities."[27]

Aristotle had come closest to Hooker's disparagement of pleasure in his discussion of practical virtue and continence, almost the whole of Books I through VII. The first mention of pleasure is deprecatory—"that pursued by men generally and the vulgar"—and Book I dwells not on following desire but on subjecting it to reason. So greatly is reason's direction emphasized that Book I remains undecided whether to call the soul's parts rational and irrational, or to call both *logos* and *pathos* rational, the last participating by obeying. The very term *pathos* connotes a suffering, an impulsion by something foreign to the true self. With occasional exceptions that foreshadow the restoration of pleasure to favor at the end of Book VII, right reason and the moral virtues are celebrated in the first seven books, pleasure warned against.[28] Pleasure connotes all too often the obvious and visible goods of the body; these arise earlier and more by nature, and are all too easily ingrained in our second nature during growth. Moreover, the intellect hardly exists in some few men (morons, some of the bestial), has slight influence on the young, and rarely comes to rule without sound upbringing. The young tend to be moved by desire for the most obvious pleasures, and only by adults to the activities that are necessary and appropriate.[29] Moral dispositions may govern in adults, however, as parents or tutors govern well-brought-up children. From the moral virtues, not from desire or pleasure, we seem to obtain the ends of practical life; at the least, "vice perverts us and causes us to err as to the first principles (*archai*) of action."[30]

Still, the *Ethics*'s initial subjection of pleasure and desire to moral virtue is not the whole story. The moral virtues are ways of governing desire—as in our term "manners"—and forms of desire, dispositions. They obtain their character in part from what they govern. "Gentleness is the mean with respect to anger," courage with respect to fear, moderation as to the cruder bodily pleasures—and so in a more complicated way with liberality, magnanimity, and ambition. The mean is not an absence of satisfaction and pleasure, but an ap-

26. *Nich. Ethics*, 1111ᵇ 17–18; see also *De Anima*, 413ᵇ 21–24, 414ᵇ 4–5.
27. *Nich. Ethics*, 1175ᵇ 30–33.
28. *Nich. Ethics*, 1109ᵇ 8–12, 1095ᵃ 22–24, 1097ᵇ 29–1098ᵃ 20, 1102ᵇ 12–1103ᵃ 4, 1104ᵇ 10–24, 1113ᵃ 35–1113ᵇ 2. But see 1101ᵇ 27–32.
29. *Nich. Ethics*, 1119ᵇ 6–16, 1153ᵇ 33–35.
30. *Nich. Ethics*, 1144ᵃ 34–35, 1114ᵇ 23–25, 1103ᵃ 31–33, 24–26.

propriate amount. Despite Book III's characteristic antithesis between desire on the one hand, and nobility and deliberation on the other, Aristotle observes there that noble and good acts may be done out of desire or anger, and that (contrary to Hooker's opinion) "the irrational passions are thought to be no less human" than reason.[31] Aristotle displays toward the common preoccupation with low pleasure a humane tolerance, albeit a tolerance from the heights, a tolerance that condescends to tolerate despite its awareness of the dignity befitting men. From the heights of Book X Aristotle allows gravely that mankind is subject to many corruptions, many weaknesses. While discussing in Book VII most men's vacillation between indulgence and continence, however, he offers an urbane and gentling explanation. Violent bodily pleasures counteract the harsh pains inseparable from most lives, and they attract people unable to enjoy finer pleasures. Desirous of sensation, lacking better tastes, or wishing to erase strong pains, the animal nature seeks pleasures obvious and strong.[32]

Now Hooker too had questioned the inclinations of most men. Recall that "the greatest part of the world are better able by sense to discern the wants of this present life, than by spiritual capacity to apprehend things above sense, which tend to their happiness in the world to come." Yet he understands the cause to lie not in unalterable or inevitable disposition but in "lewd and wicked custom" spreading from a first fall. Choice being responsible, all men are to be encouraged and indeed required to choose better, to aim above sensible pleasures at an end beyond any pleasures we know. "For which cause the Apostle, who knew right well that the weariness of the flesh is an heavy clog to the Will, striketh mightily upon this key, 'Awake thou that sleepest; Cast off all which presseth down; Watch; Labour; Strive to go forward, and to grow in knowledge.'"[33] Nevertheless, to allow for spotted nature the moralist must forgive sins and sinners: virtue is beyond fallen man's powers. Rigor in rule, mercy in enforcement: the perpetual extremes of ecclesiastical polities, the considered theme of Shakespeare's *Measure for Measure*.

Eventually Aristotle praises pleasure and natural activity in a manner simply alien to Hooker's Aristotelianism. Pleasure comes to be called, remarkably, "in some sense the supreme good."[34] Our scarlet woman is now addressed in worshipful tones as worthy queen; all the arguments defend her rule, or at least rebut some churl's opinion that pleasure is not good or the best of goods. While these excesses are retracted in Book X, and the claim to royalty is challenged, specific pleasures are there admitted to be good as the unbought grace accompanying the best activities. Meanwhile, Books VIII and IX on friendship move from pleasures associated with friendship of the noble—a sort of mutual if cool esteem for one another's characters and deeds—to warmer pleasures of those living together in mutual conversation and delight as to one another's deeds, qualities, and thoughts.

According to Hooker, this orientation by pleasures and pleasurable activ-

31. *Nich. Ethics*, 1111$^b$ 1–2.
32. *Nich. Ethics*, 1154$^a$ 27–1154$^b$ 16, 1133$^a$ 21–23, 1135$^b$ 20–23.
33. *Laws* I.vii.7; I.viii.11; V.xxxv.2.
34. *Nich. Ethics*, 1153$^b$ 7–8.

ities, however graded in quality, attends to the earthly and misses the one thing most needful. For our end is spiritual, beyond pleasures here and pleasure in one's own, even beyond our nature and natural activities as we know them.

> But of one thing we must have special care, as being a matter of no small moment; and that is, how the Will, properly and strictly taken, as it is of things which are referred unto the end that man desireth, differeth greatly from that inferior natural desire which we call Appetite. The object of Appetite is whatsoever sensible good may be wished for; the object of Will is that good which Reason doth lead us to seek.[35]

Hooker concentrates more ascetically on desire, foregoing pleasure; on desire rather than love, since love involves satisfaction of desire as one takes pleasure in the thing loved; and on need and pain rather than fruition and pleasure, since desire is for what is lacking and is thereby painful. Yet he promises an eventual end less qualified by pain and need, an end more divine.

35. *Laws* I.vii.3.

# 7

# Knowing What Is Good:

## Rational Deduction
## and Rational Will

### The Prominence of Reason

From desire for infinite life and bliss Hooker deduces the principal moral duties, and his deduction by reason is no less singular than his orientation by desire. That the Christian Aristotelian Hooker relies more on calculation than the philosopher Aristotle will appear peculiar. The cause we have touched. Hooker claims that reason's discourse discovers an end above nature. This claim extends radically the scope of reason's guidance and lessens its subordination to custom and necessity—and to pleasure, other things naturally desired, the virtues, and even judgment and intellect itself.

What custom and law, upbringing, character, and the pleasures of friends and thought are to Aristotle, the search for knowledge and the discovery of the good are to Hooker. "Want of knowledge of God is the cause of all iniquity amongst men, as contrariwise the very ground of all our happiness." Knowledge enough must be gained "as sufficeth to make [a man] capable of those Laws, whereby he is then bound to guide his actions."[1] The Christian soul makes its own way to God, according to Hooker's reformed teaching, and must search out the path. The search is conducted by reason, according to Hooker's revision of reformed teaching, even by speculative enquiry employing deduction above all. At some ripeness of years a man can reach "higher than unto sensible things." If he joins earlier and cruder conceits of things more obvious to "the

---

1. *Laws* I.vi.5; I.v.3; V.xviii.1.

right helps of true art and learning"—"Aristotelical Demonstration"—he can discern the laws henceforth to guide him.[2]

Hooker's reliance upon Aristotelian demonstration is curious. In the *Nichomachean Ethics* Aristotle sets forth deliberation and then prudence as the sorts of thinking relevant to practical conduct. We deliberate, he suggests, about things within our power and attainable by action, in particular by our own action. We do not deliberate about things fully settled by some science, as spelling of words has been settled by orthography.[3] Demonstration in the strict sense is reserved for science, in which the premises are settled and unchanging. Aristotle reserves to his *Metaphysics* demonstrations about things not sensibly perceived.

From Aristotle's point of view, Hooker makes moral conduct a matter of exact science and even of metaphysics. He expects from men generally a theoretical acuteness that Aristotle had expected only from the philosophic few. If men would use Aristotle's method, writes Hooker, they would differ from men now as men differ from mental defectives. He dwells far more on instruction (precept) as opposed to education (use or practice) than does Aristotle. "For the possession of the virtues knowledge is of little or no weight," Aristotle had remarked;[4] habituation by repeated practice is crucial. While the importance he later attributes to prudence tempers this judgment, a basic point remains: moral virtue guides the prudent man's judgment. Right reason as such guides the continent or self-restrained man, who must contain desires that are morally ill-attuned. Aristotle might describe Hooker's Christian as in a condition similar to continence; he measures himself by a duty above his inclination.

Hooker appears to begin with moral phenomena as commonly grasped. He distinguishes knowledge of the causes of goodness from observation of "signs or tokens": "which being the worse in itself, is notwithstanding now by reason of common imbecility the fitter and likelier to be brooked."[5] Of these signs, the most certain is the general persuasion of all men which "nature herself must needs have taught." Hooker lists some principles that enjoy common consent, such as "the greater good is to be chosen before the less," "God to be worshipped," "parents to be honored," "others to be used by us as we ourselves would be by them."[6] The procedure might call to mind Aristotle's. It also differs. Hooker treats such opinions as crude indications of something different, more basic, and otherwise known, not as a crude inkling of the human good otherwise unknown. He follows common opinions only initially.

Abruptly his account turns from signs to causes, from opinion to speculative inquiry. The common principles that are signs of the good are but decayed remnants of prior inquiry. They were "at the first found out by discourse, and drawn from out of the very bowels of heaven and earth." Knowledge of every thing in the whole world, we learn, serves as "mother of all those principles" in the law of reason. Hooker spells out the process of birth. Having observed that

2. *Laws* I.vi.3.
3. *Nich. Ethics*, 1112ᵃ 18–1112ᵇ 30.
4. *Nich. Ethics*, 1105ᵇ 2–3; *Laws* I.vi.3, 5.
5. *Laws* I.viii.2.
6. *Laws* I.viii.5.

the best things produce the best operations, and that the best thing in us is our soul and especially its diviner part, "the soul then ought to conduct the body, and the spirit of our minds the soul." This first and preliminary law establishes the rule of soul and of spirit—and in turn depends upon axioms not argued. Hooker then deduces laws of reason in the substantive sense, the "several grand mandates" imposed by our mind or spirit (its superiority now established). Here, in chapter 7, Hooker expressly "presupposes" the argument spelled out in chapters 9 and 11 whereby "the minds even of mere natural men" have grasped the dependence of human action upon God's commands. From this presupposition the first law, directing honor, worship, and prayer to God, has arisen. Similarly, "my desire to be loved of my equals in nature as much as possible may be" imposes upon me a reciprocal duty.[7]

These thoughts are distinctive in the tradition of Christian Aristotelianism; at least they differ markedly from those of St. Thomas Aquinas.[8] Thomas's views about the place of speculative reason in moral reflection are subtle and difficult to plumb. His obvious teaching holds, nevertheless, that practical reason is self-sufficient, without need of speculative inquiry. It is guided by naturally known principles of practical conduct, from which other precepts of the natural law may be deduced. These basic principles are grasped by a natural faculty of practical principles, *synderesis*, which corresponds to the speculative intellect that grasps the natures or ideas of things.[9] Conscience is the application to specific instances of the practical principles grasped by *synderesis*. Simply put, Thomas holds that a natural conscience imposes basic principles of conduct upon man's reason.

Hooker supposes no such natural faculty of right principle, no *synderesis* or conscience in Thomas's sense. The term *synderesis* is absent from Hooker's works, I believe; it is not in Keble's index. More to the point, nothing in Hooker's teaching corresponds to *synderesis*. Indeed, some language reminds of Thomas's doctrine and seems to have misled even so close a student as J. W. Allen.[10] Occasionally Hooker will speak of "conscience," or of "that law which is written in all men's hearts," or of "an infallible knowledge imprinted in the minds of all the children of men. . . ."[11] Hooker seems to use the words "heart" and "conscience" metaphorically, however, only to refer to what we call emo-

---

7. *Laws* I.viii.7.

8. I have not attempted to compare Hooker with St. Augustine, no doubt a revealing project. Consider Father Ernest Fortin's remark on the difficulty that, "although conscience is presented by Augustine as a universal human phenomenon, any true knowledge of it is predicated on the acceptance of important speculative truths which are prior to it and hence not simply known through it." See also Fortin's solution, in "The Political Implications of St. Augustine's Theory of Conscience," *Augustinian Studies* 1 (1970):150–51.

9. Aquinas, *Summa Theologica*, trans. Anton C. Pegis (New York, 1944) I, II, Qu. 94, Art. 2, 3; Qu. 90, Art. 3, ad 3, 4 ad 1; Qu. 91, Art. 2, ad 2, 3, ad 2; Qu. 51, Art. 1, 2; Qu. 63, Art. 1, 2, ad 3; Qu. 100, Art. 2; cf. I, Qu. 79, Art. 11; Aquinas, *Truth*, trans. J. V. McGlynn (Chicago, 1953), Qu. XI, 1.

10. J. W. Allen, *A History of Political Thought in the Sixteenth Century* (London and New York, 1964), pp. 188–98; F. J. Shirley, *Richard Hooker and Contemporary Political Ideas* (London, 1949), p. 80.

11. *Laws* II.viii.6; III.vii.2.

tions and he called affections. The persuasion of hearts and consciences, he says, ought to depend upon probable or necessary reasons. If he does refer to certain seeds of Godliness, they are of a kind "*sown* in the hearts of many thousands" by religious feasts.[12] Finally, Hooker speaks of the imprinting of knowledge in two senses, neither of which implies any grasp by a practical intellect of nature's precepts. Usually, imprinting refers to the inquiry by which reason obtains knowledge. "The soul of man being therefore at the first as a book, wherein nothing is and yet all things may be imprinted; we are to search by what steps and degrees it riseth unto perfection of knowledge."[13] The term also indicates God's impression upon man of the natural faculties, reason especially. Only the *faculty* of reason is the "infallible knowledge imprinted in the minds of all the children of men, whereby both general principles for directing of human actions are comprehended and conclusions derived from them." The Law of Reason is imprinted only as reason, by whose discourse the law's precepts may be discovered.[14] Perhaps Hooker's distrust of anything like the reformers' internal light made him avoid *synderesis*.

The singular prominence of discursive reason gives a singularly calculating cast to Hooker's ethics. Moral duties serve a private or personal good above family, friends, and citizens. They are deduced from each man's desire to obtain all good, coupled with a calculation that no goods will issue from God or neighbor unless he treats each rightly. "My desire to be loved of my equals in Nature as much as possible may be, imposeth upon me a natural duty of bearing to them-ward fully the like affection."[15] Also all earthly goods are chiefly instrumental, but means to bring us to another life. "We labor to eat, and we eat to live, and the good we do is as seed sown with reference to a future harvest." Hooker has distressed his closest admirers with the refrain that divine happiness comes as reward for "such duties performed as are rewardable."[16]

The calculating cast of the law of reason is due fundamentally, however, to another cause: the law's intelligibility to common souls. The few who love fine things for their own sake, who come nearest to God's perfection in their own understanding and will, need hardly calculate their duties. They desire divine things almost spontaneously. But, again, "the greatest part of the world" is "better able by sense to discern the wants of this present life, than by spiritual capacity to apprehend things above sense, which tend to their happiness in the world to come."[17] The law of reason must cater to the greatest part. Now one might lead common men to an uncommon end without dwelling on the usefulness of duties here to another life there. Thomas had supposed all men spontaneously guided by naturally known principles to the most necessary duties.

12. *Laws* V.lxxi.2. Cf. *Summa Theologica*, I, II, Qu. 63, Art. 1, 2 ad 3; Qu. 51, Art. 1; *Laws* Preface.i.3; Preface.vi.6, 3; Sermon III, in *Works* III, 613.

13. *Laws* I.vi.1.

14. *Laws* II.viii.6; see I.viii.3.

15. *Laws* I.viii.7.

16. *Laws* I.xi.5. See I.x.6, *Works* III, 598 f., 609, and editor's notes 626–27, 641. R. W. Church notes that "the doubtful explanation of the *shortest and easiest way* is a favorite one with Hooker" (*Of the Laws of Ecclesiastical Polity, Book I* [Oxford, 1905], p. 121).

17. *Laws* V.xxxv.2.

Hooker rejected this doctrine of natural conscience. Instead he deduced the law of reason from man's desires. Unable to deduce this law from the better desires restricted to few, he deduced it instead from a reliable desire characteristic of all. "It is the demand of nature itself 'What shall we do to have eternal life?' The desire of immortality and the knowledge of that whereby it may be attained, is so natural unto all men, that even they which are not persuaded that they shall, do notwithstanding wish that they might, know a way how to see no end of life." "That sovereign good, which is the eternal fruition of all good, being our last and chiefest felicity, there is no desperate despiser of God and godliness living which doth not wish for it. The difference between right and crooked minds, is in the means which the one or the other do eschew or follow." [18]

Hooker's attempt to find a solid basis for the minimal duties resembles the effort of Thomas Hobbes to find the most solid basis and minimal duties possible. Searching for a doctrine of obedience that might be effective universally, Hobbes founded men's duties on the strongest and steadiest natural passion, the fear of death and especially of violent death. Hooker neither grounds his ethics on repulsion from pain, nor his politics on minimal duties alone. The analogy is useful nevertheless. Searching for a morality universally appealing, Hooker bases the most necessary duties to God on a desire common even to the most "desperate despiser of God and godliness living."

Both this basis and the elaborate calculations that follow distinguish Hooker's Christian Aristotelianism from Aristotle's account of moral knowledge. True, the *Nicomachean Ethics* began by agreeing with a common formula for right conduct: "To act according to right reason (*orthos logos*)." [19] This formula follows from the definition of the human function developed in Book I: active exercise of the soul's virtues, or the best of them, according to reason. Having agreed as to the formula, however, Aristotle insists again on the imprecision of moral matters, and then expounds, as the measure of correct action, his famously imprecise notion of "the mean."

Aristotle's account differs from Hooker's in the following ways: (1) it attends chiefly to dispositions to a mean (rather than deductions from a supreme will); (2) it indicates the dependence of dispositions upon parents and customs and laws (rather than upon one's calculations simply); (3) it points toward inklings or divinations of what is noble or fair (rather than laws, in words, dictating specific actions); (4) it yields to political law and justice a primary place in formulating actions and to prudence a crowning place; (5) it is obscure about the principles (*archai*) of practical conduct and therefore about the goodness of good conduct. The worth of conducting the soul according to reason, as opposed to exercising the intellect in knowing, remains hazy and is eventually questioned. We discuss briefly these particular contrasts.

18. Sermon II, 23, in *Works* III, 511; Sermon III, ii, in *Works* III, 599, 615. "There never was that man so carelessly affected towards the safety of his own soul, but knowing what salvation and life doth mean, though his own ways were the very paths of endless destruction, yet his secret natural desire must needs be, not to perish but to live."

19. *Nich. Ethics*, 1103$^b$ 32–35.

To begin with, Aristotle establishes the title of reason to guide the soul, and not that of the "spirit of the mind," which Hooker equates with reason and finally interprets as manifesting God's providential spirit. Also, the title of reason is from the beginning obscure or tarnished. The stature of practical reason is established by a discussion concentrating upon the practical work of man, and equivocating as to whether the practical work (*ergon*) is the same as the proper activity (*energeia*). Correspondingly, at first reason (*logos*) is prominent and intellect (*nous*) is called but "that having reason."[20]

Aristotle elaborates the formula "to act according to right reason" by clarifying the mean in action and the various dispositions to a mean that are the moral virtues. Since moral virtue is a kind of habit produced by the practicing of appropriate acts, training is crucial to proper dispositions, and a hierarchy of family and political relations to proper training. Aristotle insists that a man's choices usually control his particular actions and to some extent his dispositions. Yet the dependence of character and thus of choice upon circumstance, family, and polity is in the background and often in the foreground of his discussion. This is not true of Hooker's account.[21]

Moreover, the moral knowledge which the virtues provide is not principally a set of definite and necessary duties. Aristotle does list certain general prohibitions (e.g., never commit theft or adultery); in the sequel he also gently doubts the truth of generalities as applied to conduct. He discusses chiefly the virtues, and these are dispositions to a mean. This famous formula connotes the fitting rather than the legal, the suitable rather than the obligatory. Varying with the different virtues (courage, for example, aims at what is noble, magnanimity at what is grand, justice at what is proportionate), the mean in conduct is characterized by its end (nobility, or splendor, or grandeur, or the appropriate, or the equal), its form (the sort of disposition or action that suits the situation), and its relation to external goods like property (the proportionate).

The mean as to justice specially illuminates the way Hooker holds the law of reason to be known. The *Nicomachean Ethics* treats of the virtue of justice, and of law only as related to justice. The mean as to justice, however, proves more complicated than the mean of the other virtues, precisely because justice in the obvious sense is not a virtue but what (one's country's) law commands. Equivocal meanings of justice are remarked from the start, and the gravest complication attends the most obvious equivocation: we call just both the lawful and the fair. To the extent that just action originates in an external and common command, a habit of lawabidingness seems the appropriate virtue, and specific duties replace the vaguer sense of what is appropriate. We are reminded of Hooker's attention to law, duty, and dutifulness. The relation of law to the mean as heretofore described by Aristotle is problematic. Without pretending to exhaust these complexities, the following points illuminate Hooker's views.

20. *Nich. Ethics*, 1097[b] 21–1097[a] 1.
21. See Robert K. Faulkner, "Spontaneity, Justice and Coercion," in John Chapman and J. Roland Pennock, eds., *Coercion* (New York, 1972), pp. 81–106; *Nich. Ethics*, 1105[b] 2–5, 1103[b] 24–25; see 1095[b] 5–7.

(1) At first Aristotle tells us that law at its best prescribes all the acts of moral virtue, and our problem seems no problem. Aristotle repeats a proverb: "In law is all virtue found in sum."[22] The vague divination of what is noble, appropriate, and proportionate heretofore discussed seems amplified and defined by the definite commands of law. The words of law seem to fulfill the obvious formula for correct conduct, the rule of right reason.

Even if this were simply true, Aristotle's account differs from Hooker's. Knowledge of public law arises almost naturally from parental and public upbringing or schooling, combined with the ordinary attentiveness expected of a citizen: "Ignorance of the law is no excuse."[23] Nothing like speculative inquiry is needed, neither by all men nor by any. The prescriptions of natural justice in particular involve nothing more than the judiciousness of politically active men—a rudimentary statesmanship, a knowing calculation of the political necessities. Perhaps the Averroist Marsilius of Padua illustrates the Aristotelian spirit: natural right is perceived "not as a result of prolonged inquiry, but solely by the common dictate of reason and a certain duty of human society."[24]

(2) Besides justice in general, what the laws prescribe, there is justice in the special sense, the apportionment of proper shares of things generally regarded as good. Officials distribute honors, offices, privileges, and franchises; judges weigh damages and punishments. This kind of justice tends toward the mean only as related to the mean: it aims not at the appropriate in itself, but at such an apportionment of things that a man receives his appropriate share. Justice requires knowledge of what is fitting, but only as a basis for distributing or dividing: the mean of just acting is not the fitting, but the equal in the sense of the proportionate.[25] In the background of particular distributions and divisions, however, is the law of one's polity. It determines what traits are regarded as deserving (merit in an aristocracy, wealth in an oligarchy, freedom and equality in a democracy, etc.), what kinds of gains or losses deserve punishment or redress, and what particular acts are just or unjust. The law is the authoritative measure of a proportionate relation between citizens, and knowledge of the law is to some extent knowledge of justice in the particular sense.

(3) Since law reflects the demands of a community, however, the mean as heretofore presented is clouded. Oriented to the com-

---

22. *Nich. Ethics*, 1129[b] 28–30.

23. *Nich. Ethics*, 1113[b] 30–1114[a] 3. See Faulkner, "Spontaneity, Justice and Coercion," pp. 85–88, 93–94.

24. Marsilius of Padua, *Defensor Pacis*, trans. Alan Gewirth, vol. 2 of Gewirth's *Marsilius of Padua, Defender of Peace* (New York, 1956), I.iii.4; I.xix.30.

25. *Nich. Ethics*, 1131[a] 25, 10, 1131[b] 34 f.

mon good, law attends more to what serves the community than to what is good in itself. Aristotle's correlation of law with perfect virtue partakes of poetic license or the cloudiness of proverbs. Besides, the good man generally differs from the good citizen, if only because citizen duties vary with the laws, which are rarely framed by the best men.[26] Little wonder, then, that Book V on justice concludes with various allusions to the distinctions between law and act, and between act and disposition; to the several kinds of acts injurious whatever the motive; to the fact that an unjust act does not necessarily mean an unjust or base disposition; and to acts that are incidentally just (moved by a passion such as fear or vengeance or righteous indignation). Aristotle finally characterizes the acts prescribed by law as merely accidentally just.[27]

(4) Such a questioning of the relationship between law and virtue, or even between law and justice, affects the way we are said to know what is just. To know the law is not enough. Actions prescribed by law are appropriate only in the appropriate circumstances, and if done in the proper manner. Judgment and a fair disposition are needed. How to act or to distribute is harder to know than the doctor's art, Aristotle finally says,[28] and this for many reasons. Justice concerns not merely the agent's good, but the apportionment of goods according to desert or relative merit. Furthermore, the laws govern in a way all goods, not just health; apportionment requires an assessment of priority. Besides, the inevitable intrusion of expediency compounds complexity. Finally, law is inherently faulty in its generality (however good in its intention), due to the variable materials of conduct. Hence we praise equity, a rectification of law's generality in accord with fairness, or with the legislator's intention, or even with the priority of nobler things. The complications of just action thus call for the judiciousness of judges, touched in Book V, and the more comprehensive judgment of statesmen, treated in VI. In addition, a country's laws and customs may need to be renewed, or revised, or ignored, or even, at a time of founding or refounding, framed. The deeper art of the lawgiver is also treated in Book VI. The true mean as to justice calls for a crucial role in practical life for prudence, and for the lawgiver's comprehensive prudence.

To sum up these particulars: obedience to what we calculate to be God's commands is the theme of Hooker's account of moral knowledge, action according to what we judge appropriate, of Aristotle's. Hooker provides a set of clear basic principles, from which the chief commands to love God and neighbor may be deduced. Aristotle speaks first of a vague intuition (of what is right or appropriate), focuses on dispositions that produce or preserve an eye for

---

26. *Nich. Ethics*, 1135$^a$ 3–6, 1130$^b$ 26–29, 1134$^a$ 25–30, 1134$^b$ 8–17, 1132$^b$ 32–1133$^a$ 3.
27. *Nich. Ethics*, 1135$^a$ 6–1136$^a$ 5, 1136$^b$ 33–1137$^a$ 17, 1136$^a$ 10–1136$^b$ 15.
28. *Nich. Ethics*, 1137$^a$ 12–17.

things, indicates the importance of custom and law in defining propriety, and discusses the crowning importance of prudence, especially uncommon prudence.

Aristotelian moral knowledge involves deliberation, and yet so informed by a vision of appropriate acts that it is not mere calculation. The fine man is in part moved by a vision of what is fine, ultimately a vision of a fine kind of man.[29] This vision is the contribution of *nous* or intellect, that which grasps the kinds or definitions of things. Moral choice involves both *nous*'s vision and reason's calculations as to means. One "sees" what a situation "calls for," "in the light of," for the sake of, what is noble or right, *i.e.*, what a true man should do. There is a difficulty, however. In itself, as St. Thomas puts it, *nous* "thinks nothing practical, . . . says nothing about what is to be avoided or pursued."[30] It grasps kinds of natural things, the defining form of a tree or man, for example. To act for the sake of being some sort of man, then, is to act for the sake of something beyond action.[31] A contrast or even abyss yawns between Hooker and Aristotle: for Aristotle, one could almost say that there are no first principles (*archai*) of action. Conduct points to a vision not concerned with conduct. Actually, the *Ethics* and the *Politics* repeatedly mention first principles of conduct. Examples of these are notable by their absence, however. Perhaps they amount only to the sense of the noble that guides the gentleman. In Book VII of the *Politics* Aristotle remarks laconically that "the first principle" even of "all things" is that "leisure is to be spent nobly."[32] So far, then, is Aristotle's ethics from a basis in law that it seems to lack basic principles, strictly speaking. There can be no strict deduction from a fundamental command. Morality's status is dark. Perhaps this is why Aristotle's account of prudence, in *Ethics* VI, is less than clear and distinct. A series of near-repetitions of the disjunction between scientific knowing and practical judgment concludes with a terse comparison between the grasping of ultimate definitions and the grasping of ultimate particular acts.[33] Perhaps one's grasp of particular moral principles comes chiefly from repeated practice of particular appropriate acts—acts of courage, moderation, and so forth.

To a dim extent, then, our end is known by nature, as Book III's treatment of wish intimates darkly in suggesting some moral vision by nature.[34] More obviously, however, our ends depend upon our dispositions and our efforts. Since we do not do the noble as such, we must have knowledge otherwise obtained of the various acts we should do. The motives for acting are as many as the necessities and desires of men, and all differ from the mere seeing of the fine or the true. It follows that our moral dispositions do more than preserve our

29. *Nich. Ethics*, 1113ᵃ 31–34.

30. *Commentary of St. Thomas Aquinas*, trans. Kenelm Foster and Silvester Humphries (New Haven, 1959) III.ix.312. Aristotle, *De Anima*, trans. W. S. Hett (London and Cambridge, Mass., 1957), 432ᵇ 27–32; cf. *Nich. Ethics*, 1178ᵃ 22–24.

31. *Nich. Ethics*, 1177ᵇ 7–18.

32. *Politics*, 1337ᵇ 3–4, 1325ᵇ 21–22, 1323ᵇ 32, 1326ᵇ 30–33, 1328ᵇ 40–1329ᵃ 3, 1333ᵃ 31–37; hereafter, *Pol.*, 1337ᵇ 3–4, etc.

33. *Nich. Ethics*, 1094ᵇ 35–1095ᵃ 12, 1095ᵇ 5–9, 1103ᵃ 31–1103ᵇ 25.

34. *Nich. Ethics*, 1114ᵇ 7–8.

knowledge of first principles; they contain knowledgeable tendencies toward all sorts of appropriate particular actions. A child is habituated, for example, to the manners of the table, to respect for his elders, to sturdiness in fearful situations; only to a limited extent (more as his judgment develops) can he himself discern and choose these acts in their appropriate form. By the accretion of particular knowledge of such acts as befit a man, he becomes educated to a general grasp of what is fitting. "No more in ethics than in mathematics are the first principles imparted by process of reasoning, but by virtue (*arete*), whether natural or acquired by training in right opinion as to the first principle."[35] We see why Aristotle begins his *Ethics* by considering men's opinions as to the good: the opinions of well-brought-up men are *the* medium of the noble and just. And we see why custom, law, and judgment are of such importance. What action best fits the situation, what means best suit the end, is hard to discern, especially as one rises from the application of the conventional wisdom embodied in custom and law to the decisions of the equitable man or judge, statesman, or founder.

In Hooker's attention now and then to the virtues, he is aware that "the constant habit of well doing is not gotten without the custom of doing well, neither can virtue be made perfect but by the manifold works of virtue often practised," and aware also that virtue is a "mean between" two extremes of vice.[36] Yet this understanding of moral knowledge and the virtues themselves fade in significance before the preeminent importance of knowing and following God's path to salvation.

### Will and Choice

Desire for good and knowledge of good lead to choice of the good, or, as Hooker puts it, the "will." Aristotle himself had spoken of desire, wish, choice, but not of will. Will connotes an ability less to choose than to carry out one's choice. In ordinary usage the term still implies the control exercised by deliberate purpose over impulse, particularly desire. It thus implies a contrariety of reason and desire, or duty and interest, with the will-power to assure that right will prevail. In Hooker's usage will befits man's orientation to an end above human nature, requiring means, less spontaneous than calculated, imposed upon nature. "To choose," says Hooker, "is to will one thing before another. And to will is to bend our souls to the having or doing of that which they see to be good."[37] He emphasizes bending the soul to good, not deliberating on the means that a particular situation calls for. Deliberation is played down, because reason's demands are basic, clear, and unqualified. Controlling the soul is played up, because reason demands from all that to which few are drawn.

Hooker is reminiscent of Aristotle when he remarks that "besides . . . fitness for use, there is also in rectitude, beauty"; hence "the Grecians most divinely have given to the active perfection of men a name expressing both beauty and goodness (citing *kalokagathia* and not *kalon*)."[38] Still, the attractive-

---

35. *Nich. Ethics*, 1151$^a$ 16–19; cf. 1095$^b$ 5–8, 1142$^a$ 12–24, 1098$^b$ 2–4.
36. *Laws* V.lxv.20; V.xxi.2.
37. *Laws* I.vii.2.
38. *Laws* I.viii.1.

ness of the good is nevertheless subordinate to rectitude and ultimately to use. Amiability as well as profit may accompany goodness, but it is only a sign of goodness: our duties are discerned fundamentally by the speculations discussed. Again, Hooker instructs us especially to observe that

> Will, properly and strictly taken, as it is of things which are referred unto the end that man desireth, differeth greatly from that inferior natural desire which we call Appetite. The object of Appetite is whatsoever sensible good may be wished for; the object of Will is that good which Reason doth lead us to seek.[39]

Little wonder that the noble and the beautiful play a negligible role. "The last premise which originates action," Aristotle had remarked, "is an opinion as to some object of sense."[40] In pointing to a spirit above even intelligence, however, Hooker points beyond beauty and nobility. Hooker more stringently disapproves of the appetites. Aristotle looks down on the lower bodily pleasures, counseling moderate indulgence; Hooker criticizes sensible things rather than pleasures, and all sensible things, not merely the baser ones. He even celebrates the mastery of nature by spirit. Aristotle says that a gentleman can never become miserable out of moral degradation; he could not say that "true felicity consisteth in the highest operations of that nobler part of man which showeth sometime greatest perfection not in using the benefits which delight nature but in suffering what nature can hardliest endure."[41]

Hooker acknowledges that "Sensible Goodness" is most apparent and near. Moreover, among the many things to be done, "there are so few, the goodness whereof Reason" can discover.[42] Nevertheless, men must try to perform their duties. Sinners could do better if only they would try: "There is not that good which concerneth us, but it hath evidence enough for itself, if Reason were diligent to search it out." Aristotle had thought only rare natures, fortunate in upbringing or education, to be ruled by the desire to know. That most or all men are deterred by the pain and labor of reasoning is admitted by Hooker himself. Yet he blames this on man's own sin, "the root thereof, divine malediction; whereby the instruments being weakened wherewithal the soul (especially in reasoning) doth work, it preferreth rest in ignorance before wearisome labour to know." Man must struggle against his own and fallen nature—and yet this is consistent with his true and original nature: "The Apostle, who knew right well that the weariness of the flesh is an heavy clog to the Will, striketh mightily upon this key, 'Awake thou that sleepest; Cast off all which presseth down; Watch; Labour; Strive to go forward, and to grow in knowledge.'"[43]

While Hooker's discussion of will emphasizes bending the soul to what reason dictates, Aristotle's discussion of choice attends chiefly to deliberation about particular means. The gentleman's actions are less willed than sponta-

---

39. *Laws* I.viii.3.
40. *Nich. Ethics*, 1147$^b$ 10–11; *De Anima*, 431$^a$ 16–17.
41. *Laws* V.lxxvi.6; cf. V.lxxii.16.
42. *Laws* I.vii.6; I.viii.11.
43. *Laws* I.vii.7.

neous; the fundamental bending of the soul has already occurred (as his dispositions were formed through habituation and because his soul is naturally drawn to what is admirable and correct). Aristotle's discussion of choice centers upon deliberation and not will. While choice involves reasoning, however, it need not be governed by reasoning. Aristotle's initial definition of choice includes voluntary action that follows deliberation, even if in the true and precise sense choice is governed by deliberation.[44] His procedure thus defers to common usage, and thereby to the power of the desires. Hooker's rigid separation of rational will from appetite is absent from Aristotle's more tolerant view. Aristotle can say that most or all men wish for the noble, but choose the profitable.[45] While discussing justice, acts of which are often dictated by common demands and standards, he recurs to the less demanding definition of choice: spontaneous action preceded by deliberation.[46]

Hooker's very conception of voluntary conduct is singular. Aristotle had distinguished choice from voluntary action as one kind of voluntary action, that preceded by deliberation. Actually, voluntary is not a particularly good translation of *hekousion*, which refers to action a man wishes to do or which any animal does readily or spontaneously. Spontaneous action, as we may call it, need not involve choice. Animals, children, and men acting out of passion or desire act readily (neither under compulsion nor in ignorance of relevant circumstances), and yet not after deliberation.[47] Hooker's view differs. Choice is not a species of spontaneous action, but instead *is* voluntary action. For Hooker, to choose is to will, and actions done by will are those done voluntarily (itself connoting willfulness). He distinguishes sharply between the natural action of animals and the voluntary action of men. "Those things are termed most properly natural agents, which keep the law of their kind unwittingly, (and) we give unto intellectual natures the name of *Voluntary* agents. . . ."[48] The reason seems this: the distinguishing mark of any creature is obedience to God's law, and men do this through bending their nature to follow reason. Their distinctive obedience follows from their will, not from animal instinct or nature, and hence their action as men is voluntary, not spontaneous.

Hooker defends a freedom of the will that contrasts sharply with Aristotle's outlook. Virtue has complicated preconditions; since Aristotle does not presume providence's provision, he is less sanguine about the efficacy of individual effort. Actually, he gives three different opinions: (1) the habits in which one is brought up make "a very great difference, or rather all the difference"; (2) from their vision of the good men can form their own dispositions; (3) "we are ourselves somehow partly" responsible for our dispositions.[49]

These equivocations follow from Aristotle's adoption of the perspective of someone choosing. Such a person sees the forces about him as but conditions

44. Cf. *Nich. Ethics*, 1112ᵃ 15–18, with 1113ᵇ 9–13.
45. *Nich. Ethics*, 1162ᵇ 34–36.
46. *Nich. Ethics*, 1135ᵇ 8–11.
47. Faulkner, "Spontaneity, Justice and Coercion," pp. 82–84.
48. *Laws* I.iii.2.
49. *Nich. Ethics*, 1114ᵇ 6–9, 22–25; 1103ᵇ 23–25.

circumscribing his freedom to act as he wishes. So Aristotle's narration of these forces. At first he counts as conduct involuntary or unspontaneous only that compelled by a force from without, or that done inadvertently (in ignorance of some important circumstance). Such issues Hooker need not take up, since the dutiful or righteous heart obtains its reward whatever its success. Goodness rules, external circumstance has its assigned place, if only in God's inscrutable plan. Still, even the practical viewpoint adopted by Aristotle proves optimistic. Attuned to what is open to accomplishment, it fails to perceive the deeper limits that border choice, especially the limits in the agent's own character, customs, and nature. Faithful at first to the actor's outlook, Aristotle gradually and gently brings out a whole web of circumscribing conditions: first, external force and ignorance of circumstance; then the desires and passions, pleasures and pains; natural necessities such as climate; property or its absence; some vision of the good; other goods such as friendship and philosophy; the polity under whose laws, conventions, and religion one lives; and, finally, the differences of body, desire, and intelligence that nature bestows.[50]

At first Aristotle suggests that the proper attitude toward the forces confronting one is an austere moral strength extending to heroism. "Some acts perhaps we cannot be forced to do, but ought rather to face death after the most fearful sufferings." Conversely, to excuse as compelled actions done for pleasure is to call compulsory all acts.[51] These first statements contain some overstatement, soon revised. Discussing courage Aristotle says without qualification that some terrors are thought to be beyond human endurance; later he asserts that pain can upset and even alter the sufferer's nature; later still that passions such as sexual desire can alter the body's state and even cause madness, and that there is nothing wondrous or disgraceful if a man is defeated by violent pleasures and pains—we are ready to pardon if only he has resisted.[52] A bodily limit exists to the claims of the good.

Similar difficulties confront our ability to know what is good. Apart from inadvertence and natural differences in intelligence, there is the problem of bad parents and of the diverse quality of customs and laws. Aristotle intimates that gentlemen, like all men, depend for most knowledge upon their country; they are aware of what is customary, lawful, and sacred, are acquainted with its arms, machines, and arts, and are guided by its horizons and priorities. A citizen is informed by his country's laws and by the regime that forms and sustains the law; he is even an instrument of the law. Aristotle might think cruelly rigorous and rather ineffective Hooker's insistence upon private diligence. The philosopher's toleration extends beyond the necessities of man's animal nature to an inevitable diversity of customs and thus, to some extent, of morals.[53] Aristotle's toleration of the alternatives is not without a ranking of the alternatives. There is lacking from the *Ethics* both Hooker's disinterest in political regimes, and his

50. Faulkner, "Spontaneity, Justice and Coercion," pp. 85–91.

51. *Nich. Ethics*, 1110$^b$ 9–10; 1110$^a$ 26–28.

52. *Nich. Ethics*, 1115$^b$ 6–7, 1119$^a$ 23–24, 1147$^a$ 15–20, 1150$^b$ 5.

53. *Nich. Ethics*, 1111$^a$ 8–21, 1134$^a$ 18–1136$^a$ 9. Faulkner, "Spontaneity, Justice, and Coercion," pp. 97–98, 102–4.

insistence that any polity enforce the laws of reason. Aristotle cannot demand of all men an heroic overcoming through will or diligence of their lower nature. Hooker can suppose this possible, because his ethics is oriented to man's perfect nature, before the fall, and he can suppose it necessary because the law of reason is *the* natural means to *the* good. Aristotle concludes his account of justice and law by diminishing justice, as dealing with rather common things, and law, as inherently faulty. Hooker insists upon the scrupulous performance of the saint or martyr. Although he diminishes politics and political prudence, his moral expectations prepare a stringent polity. While presuming "the will of man to be inwardly obstinate, rebellious, and averse from all obedience unto the sacred laws of his nature," the statesman is to impose "such laws of government as serve to guide even nature depraved to a right end."[54]

54. *Laws* I.x.2.

# Part III

## Christian Politics

# 8

## The Laws of
## Christian Politics

That politics of some sort is central to the *Laws of Ecclesiastical Polity* has been obvious to almost all commentators. An occasional scholar may call Hooker's work essentially one of theology or of the inner life, in reaction to the more common misinterpretation of Hooker as merely political or partisan. These extremes of interpretation, however, slight Hooker's thematic effort to defend (and introduce) judicious governance in the English religious situation of his time. In this conjunction Hooker makes his most massive assault upon "our reformers'" tendency to divorce an otherworldly gospel from this world's requirements, devotion from prudence. As the sober guide of his flock, Hooker tries to unite the two in a Christian political prudence, "the wisdom of serpents tempered with the innocent meekness of doves," for "the public and common good of all."[1] There are consequences for the prudence that he assimilates, as well as for the Christianity that he supplements. Just as the account of human inclinations in chapter 5 of Book I presupposes supernatural aspirations later introduced, so the account of political life in chapter 10 presupposes that society "most excellent" later discussed, the church. Christian salvation displaces things political from their Aristotelian position. It generates the distinctive general features of Hooker's account (discussed in this and the next chapter): primacy of law as God's order, depreciation of politics in favor of dutiful obedience, insistence upon individual consent as source of political authority, and primacy beneath law of ecclesiastical arrangements and rulers. Applied to the English politico-religious situation, this Christian Aristotelianism made up Hooker's practical

1. *Laws* V.Dedication.9.

policy (discussed in chapters 10 and 11). Hooker defends Elizabeth's temperate Christianity and her monarchy moderated by law and aristocracy. At the same time he tries to further moderate the monarchy by religious law, and to restore the bishops to primacy within the aristocracy. By restoring what might be called a church state, he would reverse the Elizabethan tendency toward a state church. Nevertheless, England had to be Christian in character without a theocratic state strictly speaking, without a priest as head of state—or even as head of church. Hooker presses for the restoration in many respects of the old English church prior to Henry VIII's reforms, even as he defends, or rather acquiesces in, Henry's settlement putting state above church. To understand Hooker's reinterpretation of what he defends, together with his defense, is to understand the gist of his practical solution. We will begin in chapters 8 and 9 as he does, however, with premises or "generalities." For Hooker's politics, like his ethics, is distinctive in its subordination to higher laws.

## Rule or Devotion?

Hooker refutes the English reformers not by denying God's rule and the primacy of Scripture, but by pointing out the various ways in which God rules and the consequent boundaries of Scriptural authority. "No doubt if men had been willing to learn how many laws their actions in this life are subject unto, and what the true force of each law is, all these controversies might have died the very day they were first brought forth."[2] Within this variety Hooker gives special prominence (after the law of reason) to so-called human laws: laws of public regiment and laws of nations. Hooker opens a sphere for political choice and for statesmanlike discretion. The sphere is nevertheless limited, in comparison with its Aristotelian original, at least. Politics like ethics is circumscribed by the laws of reason and God. Aristotle treated ethics as in some sense a branch of politics, and at the beginning of the *Politics* made his famous if difficult remark that man is by nature a political animal.[3]

On its face Hooker's doctrine differs. The "merely" human laws of polity are set apart in Book I from the laws that reason, nature, and God dictate. They are but secondary and instrumental, to be sharply distinguished from those dealing with the excellence of man. "The law of nature and the law of God are sufficient" to declare "what belongeth unto each man separately"; they show "plainly and fully whatsoever God doth require by way of necessary introduction unto the state of everlasting bliss." "Men by that which is proper are severed, united they are by that which is common."[4]

Although political life is not natural in the Aristotelian or Thomistic sense, *social* life is. Among the foundations which bear up public societies is a "natural inclination whereby all men desire sociable life and fellowship."[5] Hooker has little or nothing in common with the enlightened philosophers of individualism before and since, chiefly Machiavelli, Bacon, Hobbes, and Locke. They inter-

2. *Laws* I.xvi.5.
3. *Pol.*, 1253ᵃ 3–4.
4. *Laws* VIII.ii.18; cf. VIII.i.6.
5. *Laws* I.x.1.

pret man as essentially an individual, as naturally separated from justice and his kind by passions only for private goods, for his own safety and profit and glory. While Hooker acknowledges society's provision for bodily needs, he acknowledges also that the exercise of speech or reason requires society; the species is to that extent communal. In this moral and political orientation by speech Hooker follows Aristotle. Society involves the good life, activity of the higher portions of the soul; it is more than an instrument of the secure life accompanied by bodily pleasures and perpetuated by the glory of one's name. Yet Hooker understands distinctively the difficult relationship between society and rationality, in accord with the relation of reason to conduct discussed in the last chapter.

Through mutual speech and reasoning we come mutually to know. "The chiefest instrument of human communion therefore is speech, because thereby we impart mutually one to another the conceits of our reasonable understanding." Our pleasure in society follows upon communication, because there "mutual participation is so much larger than otherwise."[6] In attending to mutual knowledge as such, Hooker tacitly ignores the *Politics*'s concentration on practical judgment, on guiding actions. While other animals possess mere voice, Aristotle wrote, men alone possess speech capable of indicating the "advantageous and inexpedient, the just and unjust, and the like." This crucial passage speaks only of "that part of language which is concerned with our moral ideas," as Jowett rightly if loosely observes.[7] Politics concerns practice rather than speculation, action rather than knowing as such, and speech in politics yields the light by which we admire and together pursue worthy actions. "The political fellowship," Aristotle writes, "must therefore be deemed to exist for the sake of noble actions, not merely for living in common."[8] Loosely put, Aristotle's political peak, noble deeds in common, is replaced by Hooker with mutual discourse.

In the *Ethics* Aristotle eventually praised philosophic life in preference to practical life. Is Hooker, then, not Aristotelian when he suggests, with Socrates as witness, that the inclination to know leads men to covet a fellowship with all mankind?[9] Or is he not disguising his difference from the ancient political philosophers, who thought human society necessarily practical, particular, and political?

In his *Politics* Aristotle praises most a small, homogeneous, and aristocratically governed *polis* or city. He does not encourage a city or its rulers to provide directly for philosophy, although he intimates that rulers should be somewhat guided by philosophers and should look up to them. Aristotle the philosopher visibly intervenes repeatedly in the *Politics*. He sets forth in Book III the priority of virtue among the common claims to rule, for example. He seeks in Book VII to guide noble ambition away from mastery of the world and toward what serves a good community. He sets forth in Book VIII a best regime oriented at its peak to education for leisure rather than for ruling. That peak of

---

6. *Laws* I.x.12.
7. *The Politics of Aristotle*, ed. B. Jowett (Oxford, 1885), I.xviii. *Pol.*, 1253$^a$ 10–18.
8. *Pol.*, 1280$^b$ 40–1281$^a$ 4. Cf. 1280$^a$ 31–4.
9. *Laws* I.x.12.

education is presented as music. While thus is encouraged a disposition appreciative of what we may call the liberal arts, such an education disposes the emotions rather than cultivating the intellect as such. The *Politics* concludes or breaks off without saying more. It seems that the few fitted for philosophy are above politics because in simply intellectual activity they are above humanity: like gods, the *Ethics* put it. Hooker universalizes this suprahuman possibility. "Nature doth presume that how many men there are in the world, so many gods as it were there are, or at leastwise such they should be towards men."[10] Still, Hooker would not attribute philosophic capacity to all men in their fallen state, that is, as we know them. And a life supposed to be devoted merely to speculation or belief unfits most men for the actions politically noble and necessary. Might not a depreciation of noble actions in favor of discourse encourage a certain wordy and hypocritical servility, men subpolitical and not suprapolitical? From Hooker's point of view, however, the contemplation that unfits for man's work is required by a divine end above man. The means to salvation can be naturally "drawn from out of the bowels of heaven and earth" only by "discourse." After the instance of universal fellowship involving Socrates, Hooker adduces the visit to Solomon by the Queen of Sheba.[11]

For Aristotle, on the other hand, *polis* is prior to individual. It forms him. More, it is the self-sufficient community that provides, in citizenship and rule, opportunity for the activity that is his practical end. Newman only exaggerates a little: the *polis*

> produces virtue and develops virtuous action in those who are not yet virtuous, but its end is to afford the virtuous and happy a field for the exercise of their virtue and happiness. It comes into being "for the sake of life," but exists "for the sake of good life"; or, if this is an end common to it with other things, it exists for the sake of "life perfect and complete in itself." As the Christian is said to be "complete in Christ," so the individual is said by Aristotle to be complete in the *polis*.[12]

In short, Hooker's reinterpretation of human sociality removes the political culmination of Aristotle's version: the exercise of virtue in ruling. A warrant is afforded for sociable life and fellowship, but not for ruling and being ruled. Gough was incorrect in saying that "political life, then, in Hooker's view, is in accordance with nature."[13] Hooker concedes a "foundation" which "bears up" public societies, but not an inclination that makes political rule natural. Hooker ignores Aristotle's words as to the city's self-sufficiency. His public regiment is not the culmination of household and village, nor does Hooker even distinguish between village, city, and nation. None of these is capable of self-sufficiency, in his sense, and village and nation are equally possessed of his kind of civic regiment.

10. *Laws* I.x.12.
11. *Laws* I.x.12; I.viii.5.
12. W. L. Newman, *The Politics of Aristotle*, 4 vols. (Oxford, 1887), I, 68.
13. J. W. Gough, *The Social Contract* (Oxford, 1967), p. 72.

Biblical universality points to universal fellowship under God's rule, not to particular polities under human rule. While this tendency is qualified by Hooker's insistence upon a particular people's "consent," it is nevertheless incompatible with Burkean or conservative views, or with those of Aristotle.[14] Hooker treats the relationship between speech and community as he discusses the laws of nations—a topic never touched by Aristotle. He proceeds to agree with two ancient churchmen in their criticism of Sparta, a closed city admired somewhat by philosophers as late as Rousseau. By forbidding all access of strangers to their coasts, the Spartans were "enemies to that hospitality which for common humanity's sake all the nations on earth should embrace."[15] If political excellence requires a parochial polity it must yield before the humanity and gospel of Christ. Aristotle had preferred the small *polis*. A polity should be large enough to supply its various needs, but small enough to permit the rulers' pervasive acquaintance with the ruled. Hooker's difference as to the importance of good rulers leads to a different opinion as to size. If any size is implicitly commended, it is a universal Christian empire; the gospel must be spread throughout God's people. In Book VIII of the *Laws* Hooker acknowledges that the causes of Christ's choosing to "divide his kingdom into many portions, and to place many heads over it," are difficult to discern; "the power which each hath in particular with restraint, might illustrate the greatness of his unlimited authority."[16] At best, the particularity of political rule intimates by its imperfection the perfect and universal rule of God.

Indeed, rule is so far separable from virtue that it is unnatural or at least non-natural. There is "no impossibility in nature considered by itself, but that men might have lived without any public regiment. Howbeit, the corruption of our nature being presupposed, we may not deny but that the Law of Nature doth now require of necessity some kind of regiment." Political rule is required only by the fall. On the point politically decisive among Christians Hooker follows Augustine, not Aquinas. Governance arises from "deliberate advice, consultation, and composition between men, judging it convenient and behoveful." Despite the opinion of some very great and judicious men that there is "a kind of natural right in the noble, wise, and virtuous, to govern them which are of servile disposition" (Hooker cites Books III and IV of the *Politics*), the right to rule issues only from "common consent."[17]

Aristotle's account occurs in Book I of the *Politics*. "Ruling and being ruled are conditions not only inevitable but advantageous." Ruling and subjection exist in every composite thing in which a plurality of parts combines to make a common whole. Animals are composites of body and soul, Aristotle argues, the soul by nature ruling in the best or more natural state. Among men in particular, "it is natural and expedient for the body to be governed by the soul and for the passionate (*pathetiko*) part of the soul to be governed by the intel-

14. Compare Sheldon Wolin, "Richard Hooker and English Conservatism," *Western Political Quarterly* 6 (1953): 28–47.

15. *Laws* I.x.13.

16. *Laws* VIII.iv.7. Cf. *Pol.*, 1326ª 8–1326ᵇ 23.

17. *Laws* I.x.4.

lect (*nous*)."[18] As prudence and moral virtue should govern the man, prudent and virtuous men should govern the political composite. The polity at its best is a partnership in the best qualities and deeds, and the best men should set the tone and lay down the law. From this follows Aristotle's preference, however muted and qualified as the *Politics* proceeds from Book III through Book VI, for a kind of aristocracy[19] or, in very rare circumstances, for monarchy.

According to Hooker, however, the whole of nature is one composite governed by God's law, in its original form perfectly governed. He dwells less upon self-government of creatures inclined to their natural ends, than upon their correct operating according to the law of their creator. "Operating" or "working" are characteristic Hookerian words. Both signify a regular activity that fits an expected pattern, in this case the order expected of men by God. Before their fall men could fulfill by themselves the tasks set by God's law. Law is natural in the best sense, in short, politics not so.

Nonetheless, political rule is necessary, if not in accord with the best in man, natural in a secondary sense, if not in the primary sense. Secondary laws of nature, such as laws of war, now supplement those for mutual intercourse and commerce. "Men always knew that when force and injury was offered" they might defend themselves, that self-seeking by injuring others was not to be suffered but withstood, and that because of human partiality no man might determine his own right. Hence the establishment of public regiment by general agreement. "Nature findeth out such laws of government as serve to direct even nature depraved to a right end." Government is not a manifestation of virtue, but removes impediments to virtue. Although fallen man is presumed almost a beast, laws should frame "outward actions" so they not hinder the common good.[20] Politics concerns outward actions, because it concerns the public, sharply distinguished from the inner and spiritual proper to man. We can now understand Hooker's term "public regiment." It lacks the connotation of city or community in Aristotle's "politics," while implying a sharp distinction of public from proper, and a stringent discipline. More of this after we have discussed the necessities that call forth government.

### Rule in the Christian Household

*Slaves and Serfs*    According to Hooker, the first of natural necessities is economic and the second pedagogical; both are met chiefly by the family association. God assigned man maintenance of life and then expected him to obey His law. Want and penury must first be overcome. Implements and mechanical arts are necessary, just as wisdom, virtue, and religion are "things of greatest dignity."[21] The ensuing paragraph on public regiment begins: "But neither that which we learn for ourselves nor that which others teach us can prevail, where wickedness and malice have taken deep root." Wickedness interrupts education

18. *Pol.*, 1254[b] 7–9, 1254[a] 22–24.
19. *Pol.*, 1254[b], cf. 1260[a] 10 f.
20. *Laws* I.x.1, 4, 13.
21. *Laws* I.x.2.

in God's ways, and calls for association beyond the family. Quarrels and murder tore even the first family and grew with the multiplication of families. Agreement upon political rule was thus needed where paternal rule could not reach: over "a whole grand multitude having no such dependancy upon any one, and consisting of so many families as every politic society in the world doth."[22]

The Aristotelian original differs. The primacy of economic necessity is there: Book I of the *Politics* is largely given up to the subject. Yet economic needs do not explain the distinctive shape of the household: the combination of husband and wife, parents and children, and (among the wealthier) slaves. There are other and prior forces. The beginning of Book I counts two associations as basic, resulting from two different necessities. There must be a union of those "who cannot exist without each other; namely, of male and female, that the race may continue . . . , and of natural ruler and subject, that both may be preserved."[23] Hooker mentions neither the pairing of the sexes, nor the rule and subordination for survival that leads to slavery and government. He shrinks also from a harsher point. Among some barbarians (that is, among people closest to nature in one sense) "the female and slave have the same rank," and among the very poor this relation is sometimes necessary.[24]

The *Politics*'s discussion of slavery has difficulties, as the best commentators have noted. A distinction between natural and conventional slavery, conspicuous at the beginning of Book I, becomes obscured and (as it were) forgotten in later remarks. No longer is slavery restricted to "men that differ as widely as the soul does from the body and the human being from the lower animal";[25] it seems taken for granted. Just as Aristotle progressively lowers his sights from monarchy or aristocracy toward a democratic or oligarchic republic (prior to Books VII and VIII), he also comes to overlook the unjust character of slavery in most places and times. Yet this particular injustice seems to serve a higher justice—the provision of sufficient leisure that the activity of politics (occasionally music and philosophy are also mentioned) may be pursued. Economic necessity prevents perfect justice, and slavery of some is a precondition of leisure for others.

Slave-owners treat their subjects as living tools (as Aristotle puts it), whereas by nature (as Hooker thinks) men should be as gods to one another. Despite the Old Testament's accounts, Hooker fails to mention slavery as a form of human association, let alone a defensible form, and he speaks of family rather than household. Moral causes connected with religion have been called the chief agent in the disappearance of the English sort of slavery, the old villenage,[26] and Hooker manifests Christianity's antipathy toward slavery. The opportunity of some for leisure and nobility pales toward insignificance before the opportunity of all for union with God, and before the common sin of pride

22. *Laws* I.x.4.
23. *Pol.*, 1252ᵃ 26–31.
24. *Pol.*, 1252ᵇ 5–7.
25. *Pol.*, 1254ᵇ 16–21.
26. Thomas Babington Macaulay, *History of England* (New York, n.d.) I, 31–33.

against God. Cultivation of virtue cannot, it seems, be given priority over the opportunity of all men for spiritual instruction. Whether this doctrine might not encourage *de facto* serfdom is another question.

It was a question touched by a statesman and diplomat better known to Hooker's contemporaries, Sir Thomas Smith. In *De Republica Anglorum* (1583), an influential commentary on England and its laws, Smith discusses the origin of serfdom. "Necessity and want of bondmen," he concluded of his time, "hath made men to use free men as bondmen to all servile services, but yet more liberally and freely and with a more equality and moderation."[27] Christianity had ended the system of bondage whereby villains were bound to person or manor. "The change of religion to a more gentle, humane, and more equal sort (as the Christian religion as in respects of the Gentiles) caused this old kind of servile servitude and slavery" to be moderated. But a need or wish for service and rule persisted among the powerful, despite the obligation to regard one another as Christian brethren. Hence the custom developed that "not the men, but the land" was to be bound—and service went with the land. While persons and bodies were free, they were annexed as a condition to the land, and this served as a means of bringing "owners and possessions thereof into a certain servitude." The resulting serfdom was less rigorous than slavery. It was also, however, but part of a certain servitude pervading the whole order. For all land was held either by church or by prince—and by tenants only in "trust and confidence," in "faith" and thus "feudum." Smith links feudalism with Christianity, in England at least, although he speaks most explicitly of serfs alone. He intimates that the actual results included excessive dominance by churchmen and king, as well as real oppression of the Jews.[28] The deprecation of political ambition and rule, out of concern for Christian equality, engenders a certain general servility before the rulers who uphold Christian order.

**Husband and Wife, Parent and Child**   In discussing the relation of husband and wife Aristotle describes the use and excellence intrinsic to marriage, whereas, not unexpectedly, Hooker attends to the family's smoothing of the path to God. According to the *Nicomachean Ethics* and the *Politics*, the marital relation generally combines pleasure with utility. The sexes associate to reproduce, and also to supply through division of labor one another's wants. In the best case marriage may be more: "Based on virtue, if the partners be of noble character; for either sex has its particular excellence, and this may be the ground of attraction."[29] Since the husband's traits better fit him to command (Aristotle intimates that there are exceptions), he is to rule, aristocratically (as the *Ethics* suggests), or in republican fashion by agreement although without rotation of roles (as the *Politics* suggests while speaking of families in general).[30] More likely, however, are the relationships characteristic of oligarchies, where wives

27. Thomas Smith, *De Republica Anglorum* (London, 1583, repr. 1970), p. 115.
28. Smith, *De Republica Anglorum*, pp. 108–13.
29. *Nich. Ethics*, 1162[a] 25–27.
30. *Pol.*, 1259[b] 1–10, *Nich. Ethics*, 1160[b] 32–35.

and children of the rich are indulged, and of democracies, where weak character in the men permits wives and children to dominate.[31]

While Aristotle indicates that family relations vary with the political regime, Hooker discusses them in the light of religious law. Although "single life be a thing more angelical and divine," Hooker nevertheless concedes rather gracefully that "the replenishing of earth" with blessed inhabitants and of heaven with saints "did depend upon conjunction of man and woman." Woman is created unequivocally for man's sake, to be his helper in the "having and the bringing up of children," and her subordination follows from man's superior "excellency." Hooker nonetheless manages a warm acknowledgment of "that kind of love which is the perfectest ground of wedlock": woman was indeed "but inferior in excellency . . . unto man, howbeit in so due and sweet proportion as being presented before our eyes, might be sooner perceived than defined."[32] Still, the subordination of marriage to reproduction of the blessed occasions a certain strictness. Man and woman were "of necessity to be linked with some strait and insoluble knot."[33] Aristotle himself never discusses divorce. Also, Hooker treats husbands fundamentally as fathers, with a right to monarchic rule, to be "lords and lawful kings in their own houses." Book I's account of the family concludes with three quotations from the Old Testament, and the last of these indicates the connection between theological law and strict fatherly rule: "Abraham will command his sons and his household after him, that they keep the way of the Lord."[34] The Lord's rule over nature is somehow model for the father, who creates his children and instructs in the Heavenly Father's way.

Near the beginning of the *Politics* Aristotle suggests a monarchic rule of father over children, and yet his account differs from Hooker's. "It is as natural for a father to rule his children, and forefathers those descended from them, as for a king to rule his subjects."[35] The kingly analogy is singular, and indicates a certain favor of strict order in the family. Yet this indication is subsequently eroded. In Book III a king's right to rule turns out to depend on his devotion to the common good, his judgment, and his character—coupled with the absence of other men so fitted. It is likely, I suspect, that such a disparity between one man and his fellows exists only as a superior man leads clans or villages out of barbarism to civilized political life. The rule of father or eldest over his adult descendants would not, then, be generally just in civilized communities. Indeed, patriarchy of this sort appears to derive from a precivilized time when the father was seen as godlike, a source of life and of all its benefits. The rule of the oldest is the most obvious form of the rule of the traditional, which understands the older as the better, and engenders the sort of reverence for fathers that ends in ancestor worship. Aristotle characteristically couples remarks about

31. *Pol.*, 1310ᵃ 22, 1373ᵇ 32 f. Cf. Newman's remarks in his edition of the *Politics* I, 170.
32. *Laws* V.lxxiii.2.
33. *Laws* V.lxxiii.3. Newman, in his edition of the *Politics* I, 180.
34. *Laws* I.x.2.
35. *Pol.*, 1259ᵇ 10–15, 1255ᵇ 18–21.

the father's royal rule with references to Zeus and citations from the poets (especially Homer). The passage as to royal rule over children continues: "For the male parent is the ruler in virtue both of affection and of seniority, which is characteristic of kingship (and therefore Homer nobly calls Zeus 'father of men and gods,' as the king of them all)." A passage of the *Ethics* criticizes those who desire too much even of good things, and the example given, that of Satyrus "the filial," involves a king who deified his father.[36]

Aristotle does suggest that children owe filial gratitude for the greatest of benefits: existence and nurture. In a civilized family in which rule is to some extent mutual, however, the debt will be owed in part to the mother. Besides, what if the nurture is not well provided? Persian fathers evidently enslaved their children;[37] in the same context Aristotle mentions a democratic father who neglects disciplining his children. Generally, filial love and honor issue partly and rightfully from a realization of benefits received, and are rightfully proportionate to those benefits. "Honor thy father and thy mother" is conditioned by what is fitting in each particular case, although the benefit of existence yields a presumption in favor of some honor. Besides, existence comes in a way by nature, the parents as man and woman being drawn together (at best) by desire to leave behind something like themselves, the children being loved the more as they are the more surely theirs, as more trouble has been expended in their care,[38] and (one would think, although Aristotle does not mention it) as the child is more lovable or admirable.

In short, Aristotle treats the relation between parent and child, as between husband and wife, as a special kind of association or friendship. By attending to the intrinsically different kinds of associations, Aristotle is compelled to distinguish sharply among different kinds of rule—master-slave, husband-wife, parent-child.[39] Still, there is a ranking of these associations. One should not "give a father the preference in everything, as one does not sacrifice everything to Zeus."[40] One must provide food for parents above all others (perhaps in accord with parents' distinctive provision of existence and daily needs), "and honor too one should give to one's parents as one does to the gods, but not any and every honor." One should not "give them the honor due to a philosopher or to a general."[41] Honor is due a philosopher and a protecting *polis* above (but not exclusive of) the family. Hence education of women and children should vary with the different regimes and, perhaps, with the philosopher's prescription.[42] In the *Laws of Ecclesiastical Polity*, on the other hand, paternal rule is called for by God's natural and universal order, and political regiment provides merely the enforcement now needful.

36. *Nich. Ethics*, 1148[b] 1. See J. Burnet's comment on this passage in *Ethica Nicomachea*, ed. W. D. Ross (Oxford, 1915).

37. *Nich. Ethics*, 1160[b] 28.

38. *Nich. Ethics*, 1168[a] 25–27, 1161[b] 18–20.

39. *Pol.*, 1255[b] 17 f., *Nich. Ethics*, 1160[b] 33.

40. *Nich. Ethics*, 1165[a] 15–16.

41. *Nich. Ethics*, 1165[a] 24–27. Cf. 1163[b] 15–17.

42. *Pol.*, 1260[b] 8–21.

## The Divine Authority of Public Regiment

If merely necessary, public regiment is nevertheless unqualifiedly divine. God's regular and hierarchical arrangements, the lowest knit to the highest, are repeatedly celebrated by Hooker; "this order of things and persons in public societies is the work of polity, and the proper instrument thereof in every degree is power. . . ." Whether men conquer political power, obtain it by agreement of other men, or get it directly by word of God, it is of God:

> Of what kind soever the means be whereby governors are lawfully advanced unto their seats, as we by the law of God stand bound meekly to acknowledge them for God's lieutenants, and to confess their power his, so they by the same law are both authorized and required to use that power as far as it may be in any sort available to his honour.[43]

Aristotle does not lightly question the authority of rulers, and yet they are by no means simply lieutenants of Providence. The title to rule is excellence of rule, and political excellence is qualified by political necessity in the best of cases. Slavery is not the only smudge on the quality of political life. The economic problem thus doubtfully solved works its influence in other ways. By the end of *Politics* IV, Aristotle shows that the basic political division is between rich and poor, oligarch and democrat, rather than between noble and base or just and unjust. Most citizens distinguish among their fellows according to wealth or the lack of it. This problem is more than economic. For wealth is prized by most men because it is *the* means to the low pleasures most prize above all. Rich or poor, most men are not and cannot be nobly disposed. Also, political possibility is constrained by prepolitical institutions other than economic, such as family, region, religion, and village. One theme dominates Book II's discussion of the best regimes suggested by preceding thinkers: none (and least of all communism) comes to grips with the intractable problems caused by slaves, women, and, above all, property and the multitude. Book III proceeds, then, by taking very seriously the claims of rich and poor to rule in virtue of their wealth and freedom respectively. First setting forth the common claims of the *demos*, Aristotle seems to back only reluctantly if necessarily up the mountain toward the best claim, of the best. According to that authority on philosophic sobriety, John Locke, Aristotle was "the soberest of the philosophers"; the beacon of the noble and aristocratic, which had illuminated the *Ethics*, appears for most of the *Politics* only through clouds and haze, is continually dimmed as the more practical Books IV through VI proceed, and is finally allowed to shine only after this trip through sobering practicalities. The student of politics should know of the rarity of gentlemen, the voraciousness and power of the rich and the poor, and the massive danger that, given the chance, either will overbear and be at the other's throat. Proceeding in the middle books through ever milder oligarchies Aristotle finally inclines toward a democratic

43. *Laws* VIII.ii.6, 2, 3.

republic, although in rare circumstances something nobler might exist (as Churchill ruled Britain in our times only because of extraordinary peril, and De Gaulle France). If some equality in power exists between rich and poor, each may be kept from tyrannizing, especially through administrative or legal arrangements (as they might deceptively appear), and through inquests and other devices that hem in officials. All such devices are difficult to institute and rarely achieved. The political problem tends to be insoluble.

A deeper root is uncovered in Book VII. Aristotle intimates that no one besides philosophers thinks empire unjust; the desire to tyrannize is inherent in politics.[44] It is inherent, perhaps, not only in the passion for gain, or for freedom to indulge in every pleasure, but even in the noble disposition itself. Gentlemen are all too rare; nowhere do there exist one hundred men well born and good, Aristotle declares, whereas rich men are everywhere.[45] That is one problem, but there is another. For even the political man great of soul seeks deeds great in extent as well as in quality. The great-souled man inclines to be an imperialist. Churchill and De Gaulle were imperialists, even if compelled by circumstance to retrench. The tension between magnanimity and justice, resolved in principle by the *Ethics* and *Politics* in favor of the *polis* and justice, is resolved in practice by statesmen as well as most men in favor of empire and injustice.[46] To allow justice to dominate requires that one rank the claims of others equal to one's own. But the great-souled man claims the best for himself. When Aristotle himself turns from practical polities to define in Book VII a great polity, he defines greatness as that which performs its function or work.[47] Does it take the philosophic temper, disposed to contemplate the various natures and their working, to be content with excellence of working for its own sake? In any event, Book VII discusses the best regime of gentlemen under the (impossible) supposition of no *demos*, only after the sluggish weight present in all (possible) politics has been revealed, and only as a beacon of principle that would have to be dimmed in practice. Elsewhere Aristotle suggests friendship as in some ways superior to political office (the gentleman can pretty much pick his friends), music as recreation from politics and consolation for the frustrations of politics, and, not least, family as the sphere in which a man may cultivate his character and rule in a manner worthy of himself. So far do the necessities of politics dilute its possibilities, and thus its claims.

## Consent

The unnaturalness of politics, combined with its unequivocal necessity, occasions Hooker's famous doctrine of consent. The fame is from reflected light; Hooker's was thought to anticipate Locke's doctrine of consent. This thought was shared by Michaelis, Gough in the original edition of his *Social Contract*, and many others, and has been correctly challenged by Allen, Bull, and d'Entrèves. D'Entrèves and (more recently) Cargill Thompson have instruc-

44. *Pol.*, 1324ª 13–1324ᵇ 37.
45. *Pol.*, 1301ᵇ 35–1302ª 3, 1283ᵇ 10–11, 1295ª 28–31.
46. *Pol.*, 1325ª 35–42.
47. *Pol.*, 1326ª 12–17.

tively reviewed Hooker's doctrine. We will add only an account of the way its peculiarities reflect political fundamentals already discussed. Some say that Hooker's doctrine of consent is "the most important principle of his theory of government."[48] It is truer to say that Hooker's doctrine is basically derivative from the law of reason, primary and secondary. Men consent to governance because they must.

"Two foundations" bear up public societies, Hooker tells us: (1) a natural inclination, (2) "an order expressly or secretly agreed upon touching the manner of their union in living together." The first joins men in fellowship but not in a mode of governing; the second alone provides for governance.[49] "Men always knew" that no man may "in reason take upon him to determine his own right" and proceed thereby, "inasmuch as every man is towards himself and them whom he greatly affecteth partial; and therefore that strifes and troubles would be endless, except they gave their common consent all to be ordered by some whom they should agree upon: without which consent there were no reason that one man should take upon him to be lord or judge over another. . . ."[50] Aristotle had urged the natural right of the naturally fit. Hooker urges every man's partiality toward his own. Aristotle admitted such preference for the self, but argued that certain better selves seek noble action, great deeds involved in conducting honorably the affairs of their fellow men. Hooker, however, thinks just this political virtue a partiality that conflicts with a due subordination to God and His order. Ambition for great tasks leads inevitably to contests for power, to strife and faction, in extreme cases to rebellion, and in any case to disruptions of "order." The *Laws* repeats and repeats two themes: our God is a God of peace, not of confusion; men must leave off ambitious and proud strivings that endanger the peace of God's order. Hooker never denies the existence of different abilities to rule. "Nevertheless, for manifestation of this their right, and men's more peaceable contentment on both sides, the assent of them who are to be governed seemeth necessary."[51]

Still, government is now unequivocally, in a sense naturally, necessary. "The Law of Nature doth now require of necessity some kind of Regiment, so that to bring things unto the first course they were in, and utterly to take away all kind of public government in the world, were apparently to overturn the whole world." While choice originates government, it is a choice moved by necessity, and Hooker's doctrine of consent follows thereby. For example: "Nature hath appointed that there should be in a civil society power to make laws; but the consent of the people (which are that society) hath instituted [in England] the Prince's person to be the subject wherein supremacy of that power shall

48. W. D. J. Cargill Thompson, "The Philosopher of the Politic Society," in W. Speed Hill, ed., *Studies in Richard Hooker* (Cleveland and London, 1972), p. 38; Alexander Passerin d'Entrèves, *The Medieval Contribution to Political Thought* (New York, 1959), pp. 127–33; Gottfried Michaelis, *Richard Hooker als politischer Denker* (Berlin, 1933); George Bull "What Did Locke Borrow from Hooker?" *Thought* 7 (1932): 122–35.

49. *Laws* I.x.1.
50. *Laws* I.x.4.
51. *Laws* I.x.4.

reside." Allen understandably called Hooker's a doctrine of recognition rather than of consent.[52]

Consent is acquiescence in the public regiment that necessity itself calls for, and regiment being once established, consent is to be presumed. Indeed, a man "is born lord of himself." "All things natural have in them naturally more or less the power of providing for their own safety: and as each particular man hath this power, so every politic society of men must needs have the same."[53] But each man is to be guided by reason, and the secondary laws of reason prescribe regiment. As men are presumed rational so any man is presumed to be part of his political order and thereby to have consented. This thought underlies Hooker's well-known puzzles: "To be commanded we do consent, when that society whereof we are part hath at any time before consented, without revoking the same after by the like universal agreement." "The act of a public society of men done five hundred years since standeth as theirs who presently are of the same societies, because corporations are immortal; we were then alive in our predecessors, and they in their successors do live still."[54] True, what universal agreement can put up it can put down. It can "revoke" its acquiescence. But only agreement that is universal will do. The consent of rulers to their own demotion may be presumed rare, despite Hooker's bland assurances to the Puritans that supreme governors will not be "stiff" on such occasions.[55] It follows that consent is presumed to the acts of rulers, "as in parliaments, councils, and the like assemblies," and even "when an absolute monarch commandeth his subjects that which seemeth good in his own discretion. . . ." We are held to have consented to subjection by force—as "they who being subdued are fain to submit their necks unto what yoke it pleaseth their conquerors to lay upon them." Hooker pushes very far this presumption of acquiescence.

> Conquerors by just and lawful wars do hold their power over such multitudes as a thing descending unto them, divine providence itself so disposing. For it is God who giveth victory in the day of war. And unto whom dominion in this sort is derived, the same they enjoy according unto that law of nations, which law authorizeth conquerors to reign as absolute lords over them whom they vanquish.[56]

Hooker dilutes consent to acquiescence in an absolute lord, whose conquest is presumed to reflect the true Lord's wish, and thus to the "absolute subordination" of "whole multitudes."

This strange outcome we have brushed against before. Once natural necessity calls (in God's name) for rule, an original nature neutral to rule tends to condone any rule between utter freedom and perfect slavery. Just as Hooker's natural ethics vacillates from a rigid stringency fitting perfect nature to an ex-

52. J. W. Allen, *A History of Political Thought in the Sixteenth Century* (London, 1964), p. 190; *Laws* VIII.vi.3; I.x.4.

53. *Laws* VII.xiv.3; VIII.ii.5.

54. *Laws* I.x.8.

55. *Laws* VIII.ii.10.

56. *Laws* VIII.ii.5; I.x.8.

cessive flexibility appropriate to the weaknesses of fallen nature, so his politics moves between perfect freedom and absolute subjection. It tends principally toward stringency in action and domination in rule, both to abide by God's order. Hooker interprets consent as calling for acquiescence to a ruler who has subjected one's multitude. It becomes a question whether any society, undergoing civil strife or otherwise tending toward a multitude, is not fair game for a conqueror imposing order—and is not thus fair prey for something approaching servility if not slavery. This teaching is more and more principled than merely the conservative distrust of fundamental change with which some, squinting at Burke, have credited Hooker.

Indeed, precisely the principles that underlie Hooker's doctrine of consent also limit its toleration of absolutism; they contribute to limits heretofore ignored. Hooker argues in accord with old Christian teachings that even kings by conquest are bound by "the law of God and nature."[57] Our God is a God of peace—but of *this* peace, the peace that passeth all understanding. Hooker admits and even insists that obedience is not obliged if there be necessary reason against it.

Here we confront, however, a characteristic endeavor by Hooker. The essentials of a Christian order are to be observed, but Hooker reduces these to the minimum necessities. Since such necessities do not involve matters merely political, his tendency to eliminate grounds for disobedience applies to political grounds *a fortiori*. Throughout his *Laws* Hooker argues with the English reformers in roughly this way: "You don't like our institutions. Fine, but you must have reasons. Now, are your reasons necessary or merely probable? Do they show that our ways are against the very essentials of natural right or of scripture, or are they merely concerned with matters probable, that is, things on which salvation does not hang? If the former, then we agree: out with unnatural or sinful ways. But mind you, the necessary tenets are very few and minimal indeed." Seeking a Christian politics humbly obedient to his church and finally to his God, the cautious Hooker would extract controversy from politics and especially from Christian politics. Apart from God's minimal requirements for salvation, on which (he says) all Christians can agree, men are to defer to what public authority, itself authorized by God, has determined. In merely probable matters, private reason defers to public, and public matters in themselves are merely probable. Politics and its quarrels over rule are put like Satan behind us.

Nothing in Aristotle's views corresponds very precisely to Hooker's doctrine of consent. The *Ethics* does remark that the *polis* is founded "as it were on a definite compact."[58] Agreement on a way of life, partnership in a certain justice, is needed to link citizens, whereas family and friends associate more from natural inclination, or at least from pleasures and necessities intrinsic to the association. This sort of agreement is not to the inception of government, however. It is rather a sharing in one's regime or form of government. Less "fundamental" than Hooker's doctrine, because not concerned with the foundation

57. *Laws* VIII.ii.11.
58. *Nich. Ethics*, 1161$^b$ 12–15.

of government, Aristotle describes something more active, being a sharing and not a mere acquiescing. Aristotle's compact is a common participation in common ways and customs, a partnership in justice. Far from being something men always knew, such agreements have to be made. Aristotle praises to the skies the founder or lawgiver; "the man who first united people in such a partnership was the greatest of benefactors."[59] Hooker's doctrine of rational beginnings would seem politically naive to Aristotle, and did to later critics of Christian politics such as Machiavelli, Hobbes, and Locke. Before cities succeeded families, villages, and tribes, men were primitive and base, sundered from law and justice. Hooker presumes the providential role of a divine legislator. He presumes also a divine spark shedding light enough for each to see and all to see alike; consent is a universal agreement by all members of a human fellowship. Aristotle's partnership of citizens, however, implies a certain loyalty to a certain regime. An American who is a fascist or communist is not a good American, for America is a liberal democracy. Yet liberal democracy is understood differently by the unions and the entrepreneurs. Citizen loyalty is both particular and controversial, then, varying somewhat with the customs and classes to which one adheres or belongs. Not so for Hooker and his doctrine of consent. Politics is but a facilitating means, political justice but secondary or probable, aristocracy but an ornament. Aristotle's distinction between the politically necessary and the politically noble is replaced by Hooker's distinction between laws necessary and probable.

### The Rule of Law

Hooker's political science is a Christian jurisprudence or even a cosmic jurisprudence, and this form marks the connection between the importance of law and its source in divine command. At first Hooker defines law as but a "directive rule of goodness"; he stresses its origin in human reason. With humankind's fall taken into account, however, divine rule enters the foreground of reason's directions; by chapter 9 of Book I, Hooker is quick to exhibit God's rewards and punishments. So also in his treatment of human laws. He first says they are discovered naturally. Chapter 10's task is to "consider how nature findeth out such laws of government as serve to direct even nature depraved to a right end"; it suggests that "wise men" should make the laws.[60] Hooker quickly modifies this suggestion: however made, rulers' commands partake of divine authority.

> Howbeit laws do not take their constraining force from the quality
> of such as devise them, but from that power which doth give them
> the strength of laws. That which we spake before concerning the
> power of government must here be applied unto the power of making
> laws whereby to govern; which power God hath over all.

Hooker's singular doctrine of consent shows itself in the ruler's laws. They are manifestations of reason commanded (albeit indirectly) by God the supreme

59. *Pol.*, 1253ᵃ 30.
60. *Laws* I.x.1, 7.

lawgiver. Law is therefore "the very soul of a politic body."[61] Law is *the* political touchstone, supplanting the regime central to Aristotle's political science.

In both natural and supernatural parts of Book I Hooker attends extensively to human laws. They are needed in both civic and religious communities, church as well as state (as we would say). Since both communities have the Christian's life and afterlife as their end, no clear distinction between them can be drawn. Indeed, Hooker tries in Book VIII of the *Laws* to integrate into a true ecclesiastical polity what Christian theology (especially of the reformers) had tended to sunder. Still, he too distinguishes means natural from those revealed, and among human laws those civic from those ecclesiastical. Here we examine briefly Hooker's general treatment of law, especially civic law, before turning in the next chapter to the church and its laws, and in the final two chapters to his practical policy: the renovation of English ecclesiastical polity.

Hooker distinguishes merely human laws, which deal with probable matters, from those "mixedly" human, which clarify and enforce the necessary precepts of reason. Theft is naturally punishable, for example, but the kind of punishment is positive, and "such lawful as men shall think with discretion convenient by law to appoint." Laws human must be made according to the general laws of nature, and without contradiction to any positive law in Scripture. "That which is natural bindeth universally," that merely positive does not, and with his doctrinaire opponents no doubt in mind Hooker dwells on the way that variety and changeableness in the matter treated by law call in turn for diversity of laws. Hardly arguable. He fails to suggest another cause of diversity, however: the variety of opinions as to what is fair, especially in the distribution of office and privileges. It seems that opinions about justice involve fixed laws of God, and opinions about political justice involve things merely probable and secondary: another merely probable matter that the Christian lawmaker can manipulate for his purposes. Under this heading, incidentally, Hooker includes a lawmaker's republican device: balancing a ruling few of the wealthiest in some circumstances and a ruling multitude in others.[62]

For Aristotle, on the other hand, law is of secondary political importance since "the laws should be laid down, and all people lay them down, to suit the regime."[63] All the laws of which the Greek philosopher speaks seem to be made by men. The *Rhetoric* alone speaks of laws made by gods, and only in tidbits taken from poets. True, the *Politics* does distinguish written from unwritten laws, praising more the latter. These seem but customs, however, old and settled opinions accepted as authoritative. They too are called finally the product of a lawgiver.[64] In short, human laws are not "merely" human. They follow less from a higher law than from the justice for which men wish. Hence the priority of equity to law, and, above all, of rule by the best man or men. When the *Politics* edges away from monarchy and aristocracy toward more moderate political solutions, however, its praise of law increases. Laws "regulate how the

---

61. *Laws* I.x.1, 8.
62. *Laws* I.x.9, 6–11.
63. *Pol.*, 1289ᵃ 13–20, 1282ᵇ 10; cf. *Nich. Ethics*, 1181ᵇ 23–4.
64. *Pol.*, 1319ᵇ 38.

magistrates are to govern and . . . guard against those who transgress them."[65]
The less reliable the magistrates, the more needful regulation by law. When
Aristotle discusses moderate democracy he remarks that "where the laws do not
govern there is no regime, as the law ought to govern all things while the magistrates control particulars."[66] Besides true royalty and aristocracy, the more
acceptable regimes are those monarchies, oligarchies, and democracies which
are tempered by written and unwritten law. A crude form of reasonableness and
prudence is thus provided, a restraint absent from the narrow dynasties and
demagogic democracies that verge on tyranny. For even this purpose, however,
law is somewhat defective. Laws that moderate require the support of a moderate regime; unchecked rulers take the law into their own hands. One should
restrict citizenship in democracies to those with some property, oppose a narrow
property qualification in oligarchies, and rely in both on citizens of middling
property, should a middle class exist.[67] Moderate politics calls for a moderate
arrangement of classes and above all for a moderate distribution of property.

Hooker is well aware of the dependence of law upon regime. Yet his emphasis differs. He dwells on keeping rulers observant of law. Hence he attends
chiefly to such institutions as courts and assemblies rather than to property distribution and the ruling classes. Since the laws of nature and God rule men's
souls, Hooker can treat the political regime as Aristotle does law—as secondary
and instrumental. Nevertheless he knows of the difficulty in obtaining in practice the subordination of rulers to higher law. In practice men who understand
true law should rule human law. "Most requisite therefore it is," Hooker says,
"that to devise laws which all men shall be forced to obey none but wise men
shall be admitted."[68] The place Hooker gives to knowledge in governing men
makes him place in knowledgeable men responsibility for human laws. Book
VIII defends control by ecclesiastics over the essentials of English religious law.
Although God's law supersedes any human regime, men of God are to lay down
the fundamentals of human law. An ecclesiastical polity calls for the predominance in ecclesiastical matters of ecclesiastical men, courts, and convocations.

## Laws of Ecclesiastical Polity: A Transition

Hooker's discussions of church politics cannot be said to receive much illumination from Aristotle's political science. In chapter 6 we failed to find in the
*Nicomachean Ethics* a consistent account of the bearing of religion upon conduct. The *Politics* does not seem much more satisfactory. It treats religious
guilds or clubs as but partial and secondary, in light of the more comprehensive
good sought by the *polis*, and it includes priests (*hierateiai*) among the officials
necessary in all polities, not among those peculiar to polities more leisured,
prosperous, and concerned with virtue.[69] It remarks also that men's views of the

---

65. *Pol.*, 1289ᵃ 17–20.
66. *Pol.*, 1292ᵃ 32–34; cf. 1287ᵃ 18–28.
67. *Pol.*, 1295ᵇ 1–1296ᵇ 2.
68. *Laws* I.x.7; VIII.vi.11: "The most natural and religious course in making of laws is,
that the matter of them be taken from the judgment of the wisest in those things which they are to
concern."
69. *Pol.*, 1328ᵇ 11–22; *Nich. Ethics*, 1095ᵃ 25–27.

gods follow from their own experience. The *Politics* does insist that seemly provision be made for worship. Perhaps this recommendation is not without political purport. Tyrants are advised to show exceptional zeal in religious observances, to reassure their subjects and discourage the rebellious, although a ruler should not indulge in "foolish religiosity." The priesthood at best might be composed of older citizens, already distinguished, of the ruling class;[70] thus stature is lent to nobility and prudence.

Aristotle knew that political dangers as well as benefits accompany religion, although Locke seems to think that the pagan philosophers (without experience of the revealed religions) were not sufficiently apprehensive.[71] We have noted the *Ethics*'s efforts to temper the indignant moralism sometimes accompanying religious zeal. The *Politics* seems to advise blending worship with the needs of the polity. All painting, statuary, and tales told to children should be seemly and approved by public authority. The place of worship should be common land, and worship itself ought encourage friendship and unity among citizens. Aristotle notes the connection between holy days and seasonal festivals, and the wisdom of linking in a single honored *agora* religious observance and common dining. Two final remarks seem to link worship of gods with that of heroes (a connection that the *Ethics* intimates to be necessary to a polity's existence).[72] Religion seems one way of obtruding politically salutary opinions, not least the noble examples that inspire loyalty to the best things that citizens have in common. Not much more concerning what might be called political religion is expounded by Aristotle, except for an indication that the olympic religion "established by law" in Greece might be rendered a little less licentious. He seems to have supposed that statesmen have to act largely within the particular customs of their polity. Or perhaps religion is but a secondary mode of civic education. Aristotle did not trouble himself with details of worship,[73] and yet he devotes a whole book of the *Politics* to education, chiefly by music. Hooker treats music briefly although generously as a part of the divine worship to which his longest book is devoted. Aristotle thinks that appropriate music moves the soul appropriately. It helps to develop fitting character in the young, as well as to occupy the leisure of the old and to purge the frustrations of practical life. This attention to character, action, and in general to the lower parts of the soul cannot satisfy Hooker. The peculiarly theoretical tone we have traced throughout Hooker's ethics appears again in his displacement of music and action by belief, of political education by instruction in true doctrine, and of religion as part of the polity by a supernaturally directed Christianity governed by "the most glorious" of human communities, the church.

70. *Pol.*, 1329[a] 27, 1328[b] 11, 22, 1314[b] 39–1315[a] 4.

71. *Pol.*, 1331[b] 16–17, 1332[b] 17–18, cf. 1342[a] 8–10. John Locke, *The Reasonableness of Christianity as Delivered in the Scriptures*, in *The Works of John Locke*, 9 vols. (London, 1824), VI, 136–37.

72. *Pol.*, 1336[a] 31–32, cf. 1342[a] 8–10, 1330[a] 8, 1322[b] 18, 1335[a] 20–22, 1335[b] 14–16, 1331[a] 24, 1336[b] 10–20.

73. *Pol.*, 1331[b] 18–19.

# 9

## The Church and True Religion:

### How to Understand the Faith Judiciously

The political generalities thus far discussed prepare us for Hooker's understanding of church polity and of English church polity in particular. This brief chapter reviews one more generality, his interpretation of the faith and sacraments that make of a community a church and that thus inform all churches. Many scholars and intellectuals resident in liberal and social democracies will find alien Hooker's endeavor to mix faith with politics. To them he seems to introduce things merely worldly into the spiritual realm or to reintroduce an old tyranny of dogma. We will shortly consider the argument that the Word of God is too pure to mix with the things of Caesar. To those who would separate church from state for the sake of individual liberty, we will simply address A. S. McGrade's curiously disregarded defense of "public religion."[1]

McGrade contends that the modern separation of church from state has in effect separated religion from most human affairs and them from religion. It has led to an impoverished religious experience and an irreligious social and political life, to a "lack of a religious dimension of any depth in the activities we do engage in." Hooker's public religion, McGrade argues, avoids the contemporary tendencies to dilute the faith and to substitute for the faith a secular life or a faith in reform. Hooker sought both the "Christianizing of the public domain

1. Arthur S. McGrade, "The Public and the Religious in Hooker's Polity," *Church History* 37 (1969): 404–22, esp. 415–21, from which the remarks that follow in my text are drawn.

and the publicizing of Christianity." The *Laws* was intended to give a Christian tone to his community's self-understanding (Books I–IV), to its common and ordinary affairs (Book V), and to its laws, hierarchies, and politics (Books VI–VIII). Hooker provided for family, economy, and recreation an appropriate place within Christian concern. His mixture of Christianity with community affairs "is not intended as an alternative to inwardness, but as an appropriate expression of it." It is not the chief expression, worship, but one appropriate to activities other than worship, especially to the political activity that shapes many others.

## True Religion

According to Hooker, a church is like other politic societies in its two foundations, natural inclination and common agreement, but is radically distinguished by the divine origin of a part of its common agreement. The care of religion may be common "unto all societies politic," but only "such societies as do embrace the true religion have the name of the Church."[2] With the new dispensation comes a new problem, however. How can a community so definitely governed by God be governed by men? "Part of the bond of their association which belong to the Church of God must be a law supernatural, which God himself hath revealed concerning that kind of worship which his people shall do unto him."[3] How does one govern judiciously a society so bound by truths above human judgment? This was not a new problem, having been with Christians since Christ. But it was a problem newly critical with the Reformation's turn or return to faith alone in the crucial respect. Hooker's reforming opponents, Cartwright and Travers, made "Christ to be the King and law giver of the Church . . . God the Author of Discipline (whereupon it followeth that we have to fetch the rules thereof from no other fountaines but from the holie scriptures)."[4]

Hooker's reply begins with an old distinction between the invisible church of Christ, his "body mystical," and the visible church, a body politic on earth. The former is a "supernatural community" known only to God, comprising "God, angels, and holy people" who are chosen receptacles of God's grace. The visible church is constituted by the performance of a Christian's duties rather than by reception of Christ's benefits, by the fellowship of actions proper to a politic society rather than by the spiritual union of the invisible church. By this distinction Hooker cuts the unequivocal link between true Christians and any earthly church. The former are truly known only to "God, who seeth their hearts and understandeth all their secret cogitations";[5] the latter are known and governed by their earthly churches. Hooker cultivates the possibility of politic discretion in the earthly churches. Still, he agrees that the visible church is united "in outward profession of those things, which supernaturally appertain to the

---

2. *Laws* VIII.i.2.

3. *Laws* I.xv.2.

4. *A full and Plaine Declaration of Ecclesiastical Discipline and of the word of God and of the teaching of the Church of England from the same* (n.p., 1574), p. 7. See the account by Ronald Bayne, ed., *Of the Laws of Ecclesiastical Polity: The Fifth Book* (London, 1902), pp. 1–2, n.2.

5. *Laws* III.i.2; I.xv.

very essence of Christianity, and are necessarily required in any Christian man."
Christian prudence cannot be separated from a prudent understanding of
Christian faith and sacraments. Hooker's rather undogmatic but faithful treatment of the problem posed by faithful dogmatism has two parts: he limits orthodoxy to "the few essential articles of Christian belief," and he sharply distinguishes orthodox essentials from matters of polity.

Hooker's ecumenicism, his attempt to turn the Christian West to unity and
to common fundamentals, appears in his very manner of elaborating the
Christian creed. Although terse remarks on essential points occur in the earlier
books, little discussion occurs prior to the complicated interstices of Book V.
He is visibly reticent as to the theological issues in heated dispute. His writing
appears to presume that all good Christians can be brought to agree about essentials, that judgment and the judicious should govern where disputes happen to
arise, and that, in any event, dutiful acquiescence is preferable to quarrelsome
dissension. His tone is that of a Christian doctor binding up the wounded faith,
urging clemency and caution in place of zeal and rigor. Some commentator
sardonically noted Hooker's willingness to let his adversaries give up, for the
sake of peace, doctrines they would die to witness. Not for him a slashing attack
on corrupted Papism or zealous fanaticism. Inevitably Hooker is compelled to
define the faith and thus to set himself off from reformers and Romanists; he
does this quietly and without rancor, after appropriating any common ground
and explaining his departure. His manner is the more cool as he finds himself in
the hotter areas, such as the place of faith in justification, or the character of the
eucharist. Above all he discourages "sharpness of wit," the hot disputatiousness
that occupies itself in argument instead of devotion, theological quarrelsome-
ness instead of a duly humble piety. "Curious and inflamed speculations," he
writes of the paper wars over the transformation of bread and wine into Christ's
body and blood, "do hinder, they abate, they quench such inflamed motions
of delight and joy as divine graces use to raise when extraordinarily they are
present."[6]

In interpreting the faith, Hooker seeks to carve out a Christian core on
which the various schools must agree, and to exhibit as secondary accessory
matters on which they might agree to disagree. Again Hooker fixes on the "necessary" as opposed to what he here calls the "accessory." Some beliefs and
observances are necessary to salvation; others may vary without jeopardizing
salvation.[7] Like the reformers, Hooker takes his Christian bearings from Scripture, disdaining the traditions insisted upon by Rome. Yet he disdains also the
reformers' biblicism, their tendency to guide every jot and tittle of godly conduct by Scripture. He interprets the Bible according to its "main drift," of the
Old Testament that the "holy Scriptures are able to make thee wise unto salvation," of the New, "that ye might believe that Jesus is Christ the Son of God,

---

6. *Laws* V.lxvii.3, 4, 5. Compare W. D. J. Cargill Thompson, "The Philosopher of the
Politic Society" in W. Speed Hill, ed., *Studies in Richard Hooker* (Cleveland and London, 1972),
pp. 13–14.

7. *Laws* V.i.2.

and that in believing ye might have life through his name."[8] One tenet is alone unequivocally necessary. "The foundation of our faith" is the acknowledgment of Jesus as Christ or savior.[9] Christ acknowledged, a man or church is Christian. Only "direct denial" constitutes apostasy; mere denial "by consequent," by failure to hold a necessary implication, does not make a non-Christian. "Whole Christian churches" have so erred and are yet Christian.[10] To follow another argument of Hooker's: what distinguishes Christianity from other religions is its belief in Christ as savior. Besides that, all else is secondary. When his opponents cry that the foundation of the faith is that Christ saves by faith alone, Hooker reminds them of the tenet that Christ saves. All who hold to that tenet are members (if not necessarily the best members) of the visible church. Hooker draws the obvious conclusions, de-emphasizing heresy and, most enraging of all to the reformers, allowing that followers of Rome might be saved. "We must acknowledge even heretics themselves to be, though a maimed part, yet a part of the visible Church."[11]

Still, Hooker went farther. It is not enough to return to essentials when the essentials themselves are controverted. "Believe and ye shall be saved," indeed, and yet the belief to be held and propagated must be true belief. As by a providential fiat believers tend to dispute what each other must believe, and this tendency, endemic to the religion of the true and jealous God, was exacerbated by reformers' insistence on the priesthood of all believers. Hooker tries to restore devotion to the savior while reducing contention over how he saves. Oh, "that men would more give themselves to meditate with silence what we have by the sacrament, and less to dispute of the manner how." This requests belief without specifying much of its object, a type of request repugnant to the spirited and intelligent, however satisfying to many. Little wonder that Hooker had to match his obvious warnings against speculation with enough inconspicuous speculation to guide preachers in interpreting the Christian creed. He enters upon a field in battle and always potentially so. It is not safe to neglect

> them, who desiring to serve God as they ought, but being not so skilful as in every point to unwind themselves where the snares of glosing speech do lie to entangle them, are in mind not a little troubled, when they hear so bitter invectives against that which this church hath taught them to reverence as holy, to approve as lawful, and to observe as behoveful for the exercise of Christian duty.[12]

Hooker provides no easy and dangerous checklist of tenets to be believed and ceremonies to be performed. Only from scattered remarks can his thoughts on the marks of the true Christian be compiled.[13] He mentions such beliefs as

8. *Laws* I.xiv.4.
9. Sermon II, 23, in *Works* III, 513.
10. Sermon II, 25, in *Works* III, 515.
11. *Laws* III.i.11; V.lxviii.6.
12. *Laws* V.iv.2; V.lxvii.3.
13. Consider the pained remark of one student of Hooker: "With most writers one could strike a balance based on a choice of quotations, but of no author in this study can it be said with

unity of God, Trinity of Persons, salvation by Christ, resurrection of the body, life everlasting, and a last judgment. Not all of these are simply scriptural. Scripture contains everything needful for salvation—but only in the sense that reason can derive all necessary beliefs from its key tenets. Things not contained yet true include "our belief in the Trinity, the co-eternity of the Son of God with his Father, the proceeding of the Spirit from the Father and the Son, the duty of baptizing infants."[14]

Hooker attends less to belief than to the few principal ceremonies of Christianity, the sacraments. These involve directly the dilemmas resulting from a God made man and from the action on man of God's grace. Both the visible ceremony and "somewhat else more secret" are present, and because of this "mixed nature" the sacraments "are more diversely interpreted and disputed of than any other part of religion besides."[15] Some seven ceremonies had been considered by Rome to be sacraments required for salvation: ordination (the investment of the priest with holy orders or with the authority of Christ), marriage, baptism (the introduction of the soul into the fellowship of Christ), confirmation (the affirmation of the last), penance (the church's acceptance through confession of satisfaction for sin), the eucharist (participation in God through Christ's body and blood), and finally, extreme unction (the priest's commendation to God of the dying man). The Reformation churches, suspicious of earthly mediators and earthly ceremony, reduced the sacraments in both number and importance. The Church of England, in particular, had eventually settled upon baptism and the eucharist as alone sacraments.

Hooker provides no such bald accounting of the dispute as he found it. In the course of Book V he simply defends ceremony after ceremony as practiced by his church, rebutting particular attacks by English reformers and only occasionally engaging the bigger batteries of Rome, Geneva, and Germany. He carves out a coherent Christian service without needlessly heating the controversy he wishes to cool. Baptism and the eucharist are alone named expressly as sacraments. Extreme unction is not mentioned, and a lengthy discourse on penitence denies expressly that penance is, as the Catholics say, a sacrament.[16] Confirmation and marriage, however, should be regarded as "sacred," to emphasize the occasion's solemnity if for no other reason. Hooker goes farther with respect to ordination. Although he·"does not make ordination a sacrament he endows it with all the characteristics of a sacrament," as we have remarked before. The bestowal of Holy Orders coincides with a real reception of "the presence of the Holy Ghost," and thus ordains forever a priest with spiritual "authority a part whereof consisteth in power to permit and retain sins."[17] So far

greater truth that even a carefully selected choice of quotations will fail to illustrate his teaching" (E. T. Davies, *Episcopacy and the Royal Supremacy in the Church of England in the XVI Century* [Oxford, 1950], p. 41).

14. *Laws* I.xiv.2.

15. *Laws* V.lvii.2; V.i.3, 2.

16. *Laws* VI.iv.3; Sermon II, 5, in *Works* III, 486.

17. *Laws* V.lxxvii.7. John S. Marshall, *Hooker and the Anglican Tradition* (Sewanee, Tenn., 1963) p. 117.

does Hooker go in reestablishing the power and dignity implied by Christ's bestowal of the keys, in countering the priesthood of all believers, and in restoring a Christian basis for governance of the Christian ministry by Christian churchmen.

Hooker is occasionally described as mediating between Rome and Reformation, and his interpretation of the sacraments is an example. He begins treatment of the wretchedly disputed eucharist, in particular, by a characteristic survey of opinion. The various parties have in fact arrived at "a general agreement concerning that which alone is material, namely the *real participation* of Christ and of life in his body and blood *by means of this sacrament*; wherefore should the world continue still distracted and rent with so manifold contentions, when there remaineth now no controversy saving only about the subject *where* Christ is?"[18] If the camps do not really differ as to fundamentals, however, they will fight over what Hooker supposes to be accessories. Here enters a level of argument beyond mediation. He insists that no argument of reason can fully account for the secondary deductions from Christian fundamentals; he then cautions the various camps as to the pointlessness of further controversy. Inquiry should halt before piety. A mysterious and revealed beginning makes what follows to some extent irretrievably mysterious and beyond reason. God in man and as man, the eternal in the perishable: intellect alone cannot plumb these mysteries. Hooker the watchful guide sets forth the chief things to be believed and done, deduces what can be deduced to the satisfaction of the major disputants, and then warns men back from "curious and intricate speculations" seeking to define the indefinable:

> Seeing in this point as well Lutheran as Papists agree with us, which only point conteineth the benefit wee have of the Sacrament, it is but needles and unprofitable for them to stand, the one upon consubstantiation, and upon transubstantiation the other, which doctrines they neither can prove nor are forced by any necessity to maintain, but might very well surcease to urge them, if they did hartily affect peace, and seeke the quietnes of the Church.[19]

The judicious Hooker seeks with respect to belief or theory the mean, that middle but fitting path, which Aristotle had thought restricted to practical conduct. These Christian speculations are not for the sake of speculative knowledge, however; they originate in commands and point to salvation. Christian wisdom is a kind of practical wisdom. Surely J. W. Allen is correct in judging Hooker "never quite the complete philosopher," a writer who passes over "difficulties for which he had no solution," who refrains from asking questions "he was wise enough to know he could not answer." Precisely this defect in the Christian Hooker is owing to a kind of wisdom, however, one that finally ranks prudence ahead of a simply theoretical wisdom. "Judiciousness" is not then "the

18. Darwell Stone, *History of the Doctrine of the Holy Eucharist* (London, 1909) II, 239–49.

19. MS note reprinted by Keble at *Laws* V.lxvii.6 (*Works* II, 354); *Laws* V.lxii.12; V.lii.1.

almost ludicrously inadequate epithet" that Allen suggests.[20] It may be the perfect epitome of Hooker's qualities, so long as one appreciates the theoretical wisdom involved in Christian judiciousness. The Christian believer needs a kind of theoretical wisdom even to be prudent, and great prudence to warn against imprudent theory. Reason that serves faith warns the faithful from reasoning that interferes with judicious faithfulness. Hooker refrains from disturbing the simple, educates their teachers in a horizon of sober Christian doctrine, and educates their church governors to politic governance whereby the visible church can preserve the faith in an unpromising world.

## Church Polity

To be Christian is to believe, to believe we need instruction, and the visible church is our instructor. The church teaches the knowledge that saves. "For preservation of Christianity, there is not any thing more needful, than that such as are of the visible Church have mutual fellowship and society one with another." Hence the importance of what sustains fellowship and society: "public regiment."[21]

In general, the visible church undertakes the duties prescribed by God's Word in a manner, a "polity," subject to some human discretion.

> The matters wherein Church polity is conversant are the public religious duties of the Church, as the administration of the word and sacraments, prayers, spiritual censures, and the like. To these the Church standeth always bound. Laws of polity, are laws which appoint in what manner these duties shall be performed.[22]

Hooker divides ecclesiastical authority into two, "order," ministering to fallen man the word and sacraments that are God's spiritual ordering, and "spiritual jurisdiction," judging and releasing sins of the penitent, ordaining to the special powers of Christ, and governing the affairs of the church. Only jurisdiction involves governing in Hooker's sense of the word, governing of men by men, and only the last sort of jurisdiction, governing the affairs of the church, is by mere men, men unendowed with supernatural capacities. This last is alone polity in Hooker's sense, although it supervises all of ecclesiastical authority. We see how extensively the church is shaped by the faith, and how subordinate are political arrangements within the church. Nevertheless, Hooker's problem lay with those who challenged human discretion within the narrow sphere of church polity just described.

Hooker's general defense of politic discretion in church governance dwells on the way polities must vary with circumstance, thus preparing his particular defense of English church polity in English circumstances. The reformers had forgotten that laws look not only to their general end, but also to their particular subject. Besides, the intractability of a given matter might require what would

20. J. W. Allen, *A History of Political Thought in the Sixteenth Century* (London, 1964), p. 186.

21. *Laws* III.i.14; V.viii.1–4.

22. *Laws* III.xi.20.

otherwise not be preferred: "half-a-loaf." "In civil affairs to declare what sway necessity hath ever been accustomed to bear, were labour infinite. . . . Should then only the Church shew itself inhuman and stern, without relaxation or exception what necessity soever happen?"[23] Among intractable necessities that afflict any earthly society Hooker significantly puts public utility. When later he indicts church robbers who commit sacrilege on religion's worldly sustenance, he is careful circumspectly to acknowledge circumstances, perhaps involving the commonwealth's defense, that permit some confiscation. Also, antiquity alone is reason enough for a law where no "known weighty inconvenience" appears. Not the prejudice of novelty but the more common prejudice in favor of the old is to be preferred. Is there present in all this that trust in history supposed to underlie Burke's conservatism, as some have suggested? I don't think so. Burke's crucial skepticism of reason is absent from Hooker's account, and Hooker's crucial Christianity is absent from Burke's. Hooker's outlook seems a Christian intensification of the old Aristotelian reluctance to disturb lawabiding habits. Christian essentials are few enough to be more or less present in every Christian polity and essential enough to be rendered permanent. "Change of laws, especially concerning matter of religion, must be warily proceeded in."[24] Also, a Christian regime finds political or social improvement of small importance, and fears change and disorder that might compete for attention with worship.

Necessity, utility, stability: these reasons for variety in laws support also the first and familiar string on which Hooker harps most often—Christian consent, deference to Christian authority established as by the edict of the Lord. The authority of a particular church is the public reason of a Christian society to which private reason must defer on all matters probable or accessory. It alone "may give so much credit to her own laws, as to make their sentence touching fitness and convenience weightier than any vain and naked conceit to the contrary."[25]

23. *Laws* V.ix.1.
24. *Laws* V.vii.3.
25. *Laws* V.viii.5.

# 10

## English Church Polity:
### The Rhetoric and Discipline of the Faith

Richard Hooker defends his English church as defensible, not as the best expression of the generalities we have now discussed. One is tempted to say that he defends it as legitimate, but the temptation should be resisted. Rousseau originated the modern notion of legitimacy, and he insisted on popular government in a manner differing sharply from Hooker's requirement of consent. Hooker inculcates not the rights of man, and the general will as rightful governor, but the duties of men before established rulers, especially established churchmen. Under the laws of God and reason, peoples have broad discretion in submitting themselves to ecclesiastical rulers, and such rulers have broad discretion in ruling peoples.

The *Laws* begins by phrasing its defense of the English Church thus: "Surely the present form of church-government which the laws of this land have established is such, as no law of God nor reason of man hath hitherto been alleged of force sufficient to prove they do ill, who to the uttermost of their power withstand the alteration thereof."[1] One must take this precisely. Hooker does not defend his church as a necessary deduction from his Christian and political fundamentals.[2] Nor does he defend it as best. As I shall argue in chapter 11, he thought its royal headship a second-best arrangement. He inclined

1. *Laws* Preface.i.2.
2. Arthur S. McGrade, "The Coherence of Hooker's Polity: The Books on Power," *Journal of the History of Ideas* 24 (1963): 163–82; McGrade, "Hooker's *Polity* and the Establishment of the English Church," in *Of the Laws of Ecclesiastical Polity*, ed. McGrade and Brian Vickers (London, 1975), pp. 28–30, 34.

toward a more theocratic regime, such as that of the archbishops of Mainz and Cologne, who were "both archbishops and princes."[3]

In any event, visible speculations about his church's inferiority would only have interfered with Hooker's task. He had to show that the English church was acceptable, a task in itself. That is the burden of the last four books of the *Laws*, after the new foundation of Book I, and the rebuttal of the reformers' generalities in Books II, III, and IV. Book V defends and reinterprets his church's ordering of ceremonies and ministry. Book VI, sadly mutilated as we have it, evidently rebutted the reformers' insistence on a church governed solely by elders, and defended English church government at levels lower than the bishops. Book VII considers the bishops, and VIII defends after a fashion the monarch's supremacy over the church. The spirit of all this: "When the best things are not possible, the best may be made of those that are."[4] That could mean putting the best light on doubtful things. Hooker does some of that in repelling the reformers. It also means making the best use of the material given; Hooker points the church toward something better than it is. His defense is also a reform, as most commentators have in one way or another noted, and as we will have occasion to develop.

## English Ceremonies

Hooker fixed on the term *polity*, he tells us, because "it containeth both government and also whatsoever besides belongeth to the ordering of the Church in public."[5] That "whatsoever besides" is principally a certain administration of Word and sacraments. The English manner of ministering is the topic of Book V, which became a kind of Anglican handbook. After an introduction to the civic utility of religion and of Christianity in particular, Book V treats in turn of churches and their fashion, preaching and recitation, prayers of various kinds, sacraments and their ministration, other ceremonies such as festival days and the rites of burial, and, finally, the ministry's quality and arrangement and the church's finances.

In all of this Hooker dwells on the "outward form of administration" of English religious practices, in a manner contrary to the reformers' occupation with the inner light. Christian ceremonies should bespeak the Christian spirit and thereby instruct in it. "That which inwardly each man should be, the Church outwardly ought to testify. And therefore the duties of our religion which are seen must be such as that affection which is unseen ought to be." Natural excellence being complementary (if subordinate) to Christian grace, these ceremonies should be naturally as well as religiously fitting. Book V seems designed to show the simpler sort of preacher how to celebrate generously and prudently the Christian mysteries. It is particularly opposed to an "almost barbarous" hardness of heart that often accompanied the reformers' singular zeal. "Goodness of nature itself more inclineth to clemency than rigour."[6] In particular, baptism of

3. *Laws* VII.xv.5.
4. *Laws* V.ix.1.
5. *Laws* III.i.14.
6. *Laws* V.lxxvii.4; V.lxviii.7.

the young into the way of salvation should be understood according to "natural equity," and the state of unbaptized infants according to "clemency." Hooker is at pains to expound a more generous interpretation of God's will than the Calvinist predestination of untold numbers, whatever their efforts or innocence, to damnation.[7]

That ceremonies should be politic, as well as appropriate and generous, is a more prominent theme. The political task of the church is spreading the Word to new believers and strengthening its sway over old. Rites should be edifying, then, propagandistic in the old-fashioned sense of propagating the faith. The importance of this is as grave as the church's task.

> We bring not the knowledge of God with us into the world. And the less our own opportunity or ability is that way, the more we need the help of other men's judgments to be our direction herein. Nor doth any man believe, into whom the doctrine of belief is not instilled by instruction some way received at the first from others.[8]

The church ministers the wisdom unto salvation to which men only in a way, and only to an extent, incline. Christianity (we have observed repeatedly) is peculiarly spiritual in its requirements and in its salvation, whereas the multitude seem little able to "apprehend things above sense, which tend to their happiness in the world to come." Perhaps even the prominent incline insufficiently to the spirit. "Devotion and the feeling sense of religion are not usual in the noblest, wisest, and chiefest personages of state, by reason their wits are so much employed another way, and their minds so seldom conversant in heavenly things."[9] To be propagated in Hooker's circumstances, Christianity had to be propagated shrewdly. Book V sets forth a Christian rhetoric of rites, a part of Hooker's various efforts at shrewd propagation.

Chapters 2 and 4, above, discuss Hooker's concealment of his differences from philosophers and theologians influential during his time; he made them appear to support his Christian Aristotelianism. This was a Christian rhetoric for those somewhat concerned with premises, or at least for clergy and those classically educated. There is also a rhetoric for the ruling class that chapter 2 touches only slightly: to be loved for its true religion, the church is also to be supported for its political use. This argument opens Book V and is freshly expounded in aid of the embattled clergy. "So at this present," Hooker says of the ministry, "we must again call to mind how the very worldly peace and prosperity, the secular happiness, the temporal and natural good estate both of all men and of all dominions hangeth chiefly upon religion," and thus how "the priest is a pillar of that commonwealth wherein he faithfully serveth God."[10] Hooker then exhibits for pages how all worldly goods depend on a religiously disposed soul, and how it is important to exhibit this dependence to the laity. It is a revealing discussion. Although he will "confess with St. Augustine most will-

---

7. *Laws* V.lxiv.3, 4, 5.
8. *Laws* V.xxi.3.
9. *Laws* VII.xxiv.15; V.xxxv.2.
10. *Laws* V.lxxvi.1; see also V.lxxii.17.

ingly" that the chiefest happiness of Christian kings is found not in external goods but in virtuous reigning, "nevertheless considering what force there is even in outward blessings to comfort the minds of the best disposed," the heavenly and earthly being twined, "let it not seem to any man a needless and superfluous waste of labour that there hath been thus much spoken" to show how religion "either giveth honours, promotions, and wealth, or else more benefit by wanting them than if we had them at will."[11] Hooker uses similar tactics while discussing the wealth of the maligned bishops. First he argues at length that these possessions are God's and hence sacrosanct. Then he contends that, in any event, the public can extract more revenue from church lands than from other owners.

> Let any politician living make it appear, that by confiscation of bishops' livings, and their utter dissolution at once, the commonwealth shall ever have half that relief and ease which it receiveth by their continuance as now they are, and it shall give us some cause to think, that albeit we see they are impiously and irreligiously minded, yet we may esteem them at least to be tolerable commonwealth's-men.[12]

Finally he distinguishes sharply the present churchmen from the monasteries and nunneries that the Tudors had ravaged.

The rhetoric of rites and ceremonies in particular has to appeal to most men, not specifically to "worldly superiors" or the educated. Men generally follow their desires, and the desire to live forever is most basic of all. The church should take advantage of its unique attraction. Hooker observes casually that ministers are dear for their power to remit sins, sometime after he had remarked that Rome had capitalized sufficiently to convert "a pretended sacrament into a true revenue."[13] "The promise of eternal life is the seed of the Church of God," and his own sermons do not neglect this theme. "To our own safety, our own sedulity is required. And then blessed for ever and ever be that mother's child whose faith hath made him the child of God."[14] Nor does Hooker neglect other worldly inclinations. He refuses to condemn a certain ambition for ecclesiastical preferment: "Hardness of things in themselves most excellent cooleth the fervency of men's desires unless there be somewhat naturally acceptable to incite labor."[15]

The most engaging example of lower things used as inducements for higher involves prayer, as one might guess. Certain reformers had totted up the English church's set prayers and found fully one-third concerned with earthly benefits. To their indignant protests Hooker gently replies that God is not above helping "the weaker sort, which are by so great odds great in number," in the not unworthy things they want for daily life. By relying upon God in small

11. *Laws* V.lxxvi.8.
12. *Laws* VII.xxiv.23.
13. *Laws* VI.v.9; VI.vi.5.
14. Sermon I, in *Works* III, 481; *Laws* V.lxiii.1.
15. *Laws* V.lxxvii.14.

matters men are habituated by a "heavenly fraud" to rely simply on God: "These multiplied petitions of worldly things in prayer have therefore, besides their direct use, a service, whereby the Church underhand, through a kind of heavenly fraud, taketh therewith the souls of men as with certain baits."[16]

Christian rhetoric is better exemplified in shrewd appeals for spiritual goods, however, than in the turning to spiritual account of our desires, as Hooker would say, for those merely natural. The mysteries of Christ are unfathomable by nature; their propagation cannot proceed fundamentally by appeal to nature. Yet a supernatural call can be made in a manner most appealing to nature, and this means not to spiritual or even rational capacity chiefly. Hooker rebukes the reformers for singling out preaching as the sole means of spreading the Word. Such a practice is unscriptural; furthermore, it reaches "just to the weaker auricale." For edification of the church,

> not only speech but sundry sensible means besides have always been thought necessary, and especially those means which being object to the eye, the liveliest and the most apprehensive sense of all other,

16. *Laws* V.xxxv.2.

> Touching prayers for things earthly, we ought not to think that the Church hath set down so many of them without cause. They peradventure, which find this fault, are of the same affection with Salomon, so that if God should offer to grant them whatsoever they ask, they would neither crave riches, nor length of days, nor yet victory over their enemies, but only an understanding heart: for which cause themselves having eagles' wings, are offended to see others fly so near the ground. But the tender kindness of the Church of God it very well beseemeth to help the weaker sort, which are by so great odds more in number, although some few of the perfecter and stronger may be therewith for a time displeased.
>
> Ignorant we are not, that of such as resorted to our Savior Christ being present on earth, there came not any unto him with better success for the benefit of their souls' everlasting happiness, than they whose bodily necessities gave them the first occasion to seek relief, where they saw willingness and ability of doing every way good unto all.
>
> The graces of the Spirit are much more precious than worldly benefits; our ghostly evils of greater importance than any harm which the body feeleth. Therefore our desires to heavenward should both in measure and number no less exceed than their glorious object doth every way excel in value. These things are true and plain in the eye of a perfect judgment. But yet it must be withal considered, that the greatest part of the world are they which be farthest from perfection. Such being better able by sense to discern the wants of this present life, than by spiritual capacity to apprehend things above sense, which tend to their happiness in the world to come, are in that respect the more apt to apply their minds even with hearty affection and zeal at the least unto those branches of public prayer, wherein their own particular is moved. And by this mean there stealeth upon them a double benefit: first because that good affection, which things of smaller account have once set on work, is by so much the more easily raised higher; and secondly in that the very custom of seeking so particular aid and relief at the hands of God, doth by a secret contradiction withdraw them from endeavouring to help themselves by those wicked shifts which they know can never have his allowance, whose assistance their prayer seeketh. (*Laws* V.xxxv.3).

have in that respect seemed the fittest to make a deep and strong impression.[17]

The creed should be made vivid and memorable through sensible representations and especially through visible signs. In a most uncalvinist manner Hooker defends the sign of the cross in baptism. For such a custom his church had been charged with idolatry and worship of things not prescribed by God's Word. Hooker acknowledges the danger. Nevertheless he defends these various images, not as things worshipped but as symbols useful in confirming our worship. The mind of men does nothing without relying upon imagination; thoughts always betray themselves "through the crevices of that wall wherewith nature hath compassed the cells and closets of fancy." An unhardened mind considering a sinful act will find shame or ignominy rising to counter it, and this barrier is strengthened by images like the sign of the cross, "a most effectual though a silent teacher to avoid whatsoever may deservedly procure shame."[18]

The benefit is obtained only when such images have been embedded by habituation. Hooker dwells on the impact of habit: "Ceremonies have more in weight than in sight, they work by commonness of use much, although in the several acts of their usage we scarcely discern any good they do." For the same reasons holy days and festival days should be regular: "By repetition they enlarge, strengthen, and confirm the habits of all virtue."[19]

In general, public worship should be well considered and beautiful. To "solemn actions of royalty and justice their suitable ornaments are a beauty. Are they only in religion a stain?"[20] Services should be sufficiently long, lest the world "deem that the thing itself is but little accounted of, wherein but little time is bestowed." Nor should one insist, with some Puritans, upon apostolic simplicity and poverty. Where wealth exists, it is fitting that men honor God by "pomp and statelyness" in building magnificent churches. The very majesty and fearsomeness of places, articles, furniture, and dress serves "as a sensible help to stir up devotion."[21] Most notable are Hooker's remarks on music, as he adapts to his own purposes some ancient discussions. Music expresses and represents the very standing, rising, and falling "of all passions whereunto the mind is subject." As music can imitate, it can evoke. Some harmonies are then pestilent, others "nothing more strong and potent unto good." Music, when it "fitly suiteth with matter altogether sounding to the praise of God," edifies "if not the understanding because it teacheth not, yet surely the affection, because therein it worketh much." Although the church has left the more simple and plain music typical at the first, the reason is defensible: "The custom which we now use was not instituted so much for their cause which are spiritual, as to the end that into grosser and heavier minds, whom bare words do not easily move, the sweetness of melody might make some entrance for good things." He quotes St. Basil: "O

17. *Laws* IV.i.3.; V.xviii.3.
18. *Laws* V.lxv.7; V.xx.9.
19. *Laws* V.lxxi.2; V.lxv.4, 5, 7.
20. *Laws* V.xxix.1; V.xvi.2.
21. *Laws* V.xvi.2; V.xv.4; V.xxxii.2.

the wise conceit of that heavenly Teacher, which hath by His skill, found out a way, that doing those things wherein we delight, we may also learn that whereby we profit." [22]

Still, all the baits and sweeteners that lead toward faith are but preparatory; faith itself must be grasped, Christ believed and followed. Even this can to an extent be imaged forth. Hooker defends public worship of saints and martyrs, heroes of the church so to speak, as profitable notably for weaker minds. [23] He sets forth other arts of propagating the creed, especially by thorough catechism of the young. Belief being crucial, education is essentially habituation to correct belief, not habituation to correct dispositions. The English draw the substance of Christian belief into few and short articles "according to the weak and slender capacity of young beginners." Neither Hooker nor his Christian opponents thought "that the church should hazard so many souls by letting them run on till they come to ripeness of understanding." Hooker never urges the corrosive teaching of Locke: the right of each individual to arrive at his own "inward and full persuasion of the mind." [24] Indeed, the "first thing whereof we have occasion to take notice is, how much hath been done already to our great good, although without our knowledge." [25] Thus the benefit of repeating psalms and set prayers.

The outward form of ceremonies, then, should be fitting and edifying, politic in its appeal to imagination and its reliance on habit—and it should generally be public. On this Hooker dwells. Worship should occur in a public place and be conducted by publicly approved ministers according to a publicly defined form of prayer and reading. Part of the cause is simple appropriateness; the service which is public seems more worthy, "as a whole society of such condition exceedeth the worth of any one." Also, a salutary instruction accompanies joint worship. Where we pray publicly, "the alacrity and fervour of others serveth as a present spur." Besides, the whole church is bettered "by our good example." Finally—the point most pressing in the Elizabethan situation—private worship easily disintegrates into new fancies and sects, "heresies" and "dangerous practices": just what enlightened proponents of the rights of private conscience, such as Locke, expected and planned. "If men were wholly left to their own voluntary meditations in their closets, and not drawn by laws and orders unto the open assemblies of the Church that there they may join with others in prayer, it may be soon conjectured what Christian devotion that way would come unto in a short time." [26]

### English Regiment: Ministry and Discipline

Although a church by its care of Word and sacraments is unlike other societies, it must have the governance needed by any society—or go under. That is the

22. *Laws* V.xxxviii.3, 1.

23. *Laws* V.xx.9; V.xiii.3, 1.

24. John Locke, *A Letter Concerning Toleration*, ed. Mario Montuori (The Hague, 1963), p. 17.

25. *Laws* V.lxiv.1.

26. *Laws* V.lxxii.13; V.xxiv.2; V.xii.2. See Locke, *A Letter Concerning Toleration*, pp. 99–103.

great message of Hooker's whole work, a message he supposed especially needed in his own time. Disputes over a peculiarly theoretical and incomprehensible faith had been transmitted into great politico-religious divisions among the faithful, divisions the more terrible as the faithful were more zealous. European Christianity was "flaming at all points at once," and Hooker portrays his English church as a polity racked by civil war. These internal struggles weakened the church before threats from Elizabeth's monarchy and council, from the avarice, jealousy, and disdain of old peers and a rising lesser gentry already enfurbished with ecclesiastical spoils, and from an increasingly influential secular learning, ancient and modern. The war between established church and reformers might well open a way, as our Part I suggested, for "an enemy who will dance in the ashes of them both."[27] Luther had said that the true Christian could "give up the world to who wants it." Thus could the world be given up, Hooker suggests, to dreadful wars over Christian truth, to ignorance of Christian truth, or even to those who would (subtly or brutally) exterminate Christian truth.

If the church avoids judicious governing, in short, it will be governed by someone else, and according to their priorities. So Hooker's insistence on church governance, and his constant instruction in politic governance. Lessons were evidently needed. "It is not safe for the Church of Christ, when bishops learn what belongeth unto government as empirics learn physic by killing of the sick."[28] Hooker is a doctor of the church also in the ancient sense of statesman, or teacher of statesmen.

Hooker's discussion of English church governance follows the traditional distinction between the power of order, which ministers the faith and sacraments and is not directly involved in governance, and that of jurisdiction, which disciplines the sinning faithful.[29] Two considerations dominate Hooker's discussion of the English ministry. This holy task is to be regulated by the visible church, and the ministering clergy are beset with blots that reflect both episcopal laxity and a more dangerous enmity in the civil powers.

Hooker differs from the reformers in including within the power of order "contemplation," which helps the "principal work" of the ministry, as well as ministry itself; he differs more conspicuously in insisting upon governance by church authorities. Here on earth ministry is not only *the* holy work but, in a sense, the political work of holiness. "Religion without the help of spiritual ministry is unable to plant itself, the fruits thereof not possible to grow of their own accord." Thus ministers come to have a kind of ruling power, albeit "such power as neither prince nor potentate, king nor Caesar on earth can give."[30] As Hooker had insisted that the manner of worship be public, so he insists that the ministry of worship be publicly regulated.[31] The ordinary clergy is not to think itself constituted merely by an inner call or by a congregation's laying on of

27. "Answer to Travers," in *Works* III, 596.

28. *Laws* VII.xxiv.5.

29. Sir David Lindsay Keir, *The Constitutional History of Modern Britain since 1485* (London, 1961), p. 66; G. R. Elton, *The Tudor Constitution* (Cambridge, Eng., 1960), p. 336.

30. *Laws* V.lxxvii.5, 10.

31. *Laws* V.lxxvii.1; cf. I.xiv.3; Sermon V, 3–5, in *Works* III, 661–65.

hands. The minister's power is given only at the visible church's ceremony of ordination, a ceremony, it will be recalled, that Hooker practically restores to a sacrament. As for extraordinary ministry of a prophet, Hooker insists that such deeds of divinity by mortal men are no more. No natural man can reach to divine knowledge and, as to men inspired by God,

> His surceasing to speak to the world, since the publishing of the Gospel of Jesus Christ and the delivery of the same in writing, is unto us a manifest token that the way of salvation is now sufficiently opened, and that we need no other means for our full instruction than God hath already furnished us withal.[32]

This defense of ecclesiastical authority over the ministry, however, was accompanied by an unsparing diagnosis of illnesses besetting the English ministry on account of the English authorities. The ministry should be the cutting edge of the church, but the English ministry was a very dull blade indeed. In chapter 1 we noted Hooker's expatiation upon the "eyesores and blemishes," "the scum and refuse of this whole land," who had crept into the church to extract a pittance. There too we observed his defense, which is more excuse than defense, and his subdued but powerful indictment of the hierarchy in church and state that would tolerate or even encourage such a condition.

It is true that he rebuts at the end of Book V the Puritans' demand that every minister be a preacher, chosen with the acquiescence of a particular flock to which he is then irretrievably linked. The reformers forget the need of the "two great universities," for the "ripening of such as be raw," and hence of the liberty of non-residence for clergy who teach. More important, the reformers forget those grounds of public utility that require clergy to reside in the families of bishops, or in the families of noblemen or in princes' courts. In an aristocratic and monarchic regime the ordinary ministry must attend on the higher powers. "Whoever doth well observe how much all inferior things depend upon the orderly courses and notions of those greater orbs," will not think absence from an ordinary cure without due recompense.

> For we are not to dream in this case of any platform which bringing equally high and low unto parish churches, nor of any constraint to maintain at their own charge men sufficient for that purpose; the one so repugnant to the majesty and greatness of English nobility, the other so implausible and unlikely to take effect that they which mention either or both seem not indeed to have conceived what either is.[33]

The church ministers specially to the higher powers to obtain their esteem and hence the benefit of their power.

The church's deference must extend far, to what appears the crucial case. Against his opponents Hooker defends selection of ministers by lay patronage.

32. *Laws* I.xiv.3; V.lxxviii.6, 3.
33. *Laws* V.lxxxi.6, 7, 5.

The reason is politic necessity: the power over the clergy of laity in general and of landowners in particular. The ministry of the land must obtain consent of the owners of the land, in a somewhat feudal country where much governance goes with land, or there will be no ministry. We quote a considerable example of Hooker's judiciousness:

> Is it not manifest that in this realm, and so in other the like domin-
> ions, where the tenure of lands is altogether grounded on military
> laws, and held as in fee under princes which are not made heads of
> the people by force of voluntary election, but born the sovereign
> lords of those whole and entire territories, which territories their fa-
> mous progenitors obtaining by way of conquest retained what they
> would in their own hands and divided the rest to others with reser-
> vation of sovereignty and capital interest, the building of churches
> and consequently the assigning of either parishes or benefices was a
> thing impossible without consent of such as were principal owners
> of land; in which consideration for their more encouragement here-
> unto they which did so far benefit the Church had by common con-
> sent granted (as great equity and reason was) a right for them and
> their heirs till the world's end to nominate in those benefices men
> whose quality the bishop allowing might admit them thereunto?[34]

The necessities of English rule require that the laity be admitted so far into the church as to choose those endowed with "holy and ghostly power." Suppose, however, that the oligarchic voice politically necessary proved to be religiously deadly? We come near the root of the danger graver than the reformers: how to assure the primacy of Christianity in an England in which the church no longer had a certain primacy of rule. This general problem underlay the ministry's particular problems. Of all the faults which the reformers indict, Hooker admits that "the greatest is that threefold blot or blemish of notable ignorance, uncon-scionable absence from the cures whereof men have taken charge, and unsa-tiable hunting after spiritual preferment without either care or conscience of the public good." The causes are various, but one is poverty. Learned clergy and more clergy the church wants but cannot afford; the miserable pittance afforded by many church livings cause the miserable quality of many clergy and their unseemly scrabbling to provide for themselves. In chapter 1 we showed how blame rested chiefly with the gentry, nobility, and crown, who among them-selves bestowed five-sixths of the church's livings. To clarify the problem of lay power over the ministry, however, we must first consider the various levels of church government above the ministry: ecclesiastical courts, bishops, and mon-arch.

The second kind of ecclesiastical power, that of jurisdiction, involves the visible church's enforcement of church law. We are thus brought to the subject concluding Hooker's *Laws*, English church government in the precise sense. If

34. *Laws* V.lxxx.11.

disputes about ceremonies were "the silliest" that ever troubled the church, those over "jurisdiction, dignity [episcopal prerogatives], and Dominion Ecclesiastical [the royal supremacy]," were the "weightiest remains" of the cause. Unfortunately, the text of the *Laws* is most doubtful and apparently abused on just these subjects, and most doubtful and abused as to jurisdiction in particular. Various editors incline to agree that we have Book VII on episcopal authority in a finished form, and, in a quite unfinished form, much of the crucial Book VIII on the royal supremacy. They also agree, however, that we lack all of the long essay on jurisdiction, the original Book VI as evidenced in some extended comments by Hooker's young friends, Edwin Sandys and George Cranmer—a great loss to us and to any student of English church history. The extant Book VI comprises a long and involved treatise on penitence. It seems of Hooker's pen and is indeed relevant, as C. J. Sisson has urged,[35] to the topic announced by Hooker, "The power of Jurisdiction, which the reformed platform claimeth unto lay-elders, with others." Yet its length and detail, and the lack of a clear and explicit connection with the announced topic, persuade me that Keble was correct in judging the piece not intended for the *Laws*. Keble has endeavored to reconstruct from the notes of Sandys and Cranmer the topics treated in the missing essay. These indicate the scope of ecclesiastical jurisdiction. Evidently the original Book VI discussed in turn the relation between order and jurisdiction, the distinction between causes ecclesiastical and civil, the character of ecclesiastical courts, their sanction of "anathema" as manifest in excommunication, the offenses calling for excommunication, its effects, the effects of mere presbyterian authority (especially as it impinged upon the king's authority), and, finally, the precedent of the Jewish polity.[36]

The connection between order and jurisdiction, between the ministry of Word and sacraments and the ecclesiastical enforcement of church law, is most apparent in the discipline of repentance. To be saved one must obey God's law and keep His faith, but sin makes perfect obedience impossible. What can be required is a striving to obey, together with an unfeigned regret for one's sins and a wholehearted desire for forgiveness. Hence moral introspection, preoccupation with the soul as such, humility, and penitence before our Maker and Ruler.[37] This last fruit is cultivated by the pastor's ministry of God's forgiveness to the repentant believer. Yet the sin may require more. Repentance must "proceed to the private contentation of men, if the sin be a crime injurious; but also further, where the wholesome discipline of God's Church exacteth a more exemplary and open satisfaction." The satisfaction of private men is called by Hooker the virtue of repentance, of the church, the discipline of repentance. "The Lord Himself hath promised to ratify" the church's judgments when they

35. C. J. Sisson, *The Judicious Marriage of Mr. Hooker and the Birth of the Laws of Ecclesiastical Polity* (Cambridge, Eng., 1940), pp. 96–108. As to the textual problems of Book VI, see W. Speed Hill, "Hooker's *Polity*: The Problem of the Three Last Books," *Huntington Library Quarterly* 34 (1970–71): 317–36; A. S. McGrade, "Repentance and Spiritual Power: Book VI of Richard Hooker's *Of the Laws of Ecclesiastical Polity*," *Journal of Ecclesiastical History* 29 (1978): 163–76.

36. *Works* I, xxxv–xxxix.

37. *Laws* VI.iii.2–6.

accord with his own merciful and just spirit, although He does not restrict his forgiveness to that obtained through earthly instruments.[38] Such is the spiritual authority attending the minister's absolution of sins, and attending ecclesiastical courts.

According to Hooker, human justice is oriented to divine justice and the body of Christ on earth, the church, must have its spiritual judiciary to complement the temporal. On this Hooker insists, as he defends the ecclesiastical courts that had coexisted with civil courts from the Norman conquest. One need know little of English history to perceive that such an arrangement invited disputes, and these were vividly present during Tudor times. When Henry VIII established the royal supremacy, he took care to establish a royal Court of Delegates to receive appeals from lower ecclesiastical courts. Also, Parliament at this time limited clerical freedom from civil process (the so-called benefit of clergy), undue citations from ecclesiastical courts, and initiation of heresy prosecutions by the clergy. Otherwise, however, the system of spiritual courts remained in good part what it had been, and it was this system slightly modified, if very shaken, that Elizabeth inherited after the revolutions of Edward VI and Mary.[39] I cannot improve upon Bishop Frere's description of the institutions, nor G. R. Elton's statement of their functions.

> The Archbishops held their provincial courts [writes Frere] and the bishops their diocesan courts, and therein was carried on by them or their officials all the legal business which the middle ages classed as ecclesiastical, *i.e.* not only matters of the spiritual sphere and of church discipline in worship, faith, and morals, but such matters as the probate of wills, matrimonial disputes, and payment of tithes. Besides the episcopal courts there were also the inferior courts that had grown up since Norman times: most of the archdeacons held courts, and there was always one archdeacon and sometimes more in each diocese: even rural deans performed some judicial business by virtue of delegation from the bishop who appointed them and from the archdeacon whose deputies they were. Besides these courts, there were the local courts of places exempt from the ordinary jurisdiction and of peculiars: . . . . so that in all it was calculated that the number of ecclesiastical courts amounted to more than two hundred and fifty.[40]

Elton summarizes the functions of these courts Christian as threefold.

> They supervised the affairs of the clergy, punished their misdemeanours, and adjudicated in disputes among them; they protected the clergy in their relations with the laity; and they exercised jurisdiction over the laity in matters of religion, morals, and certain causes

38. *Laws* VI.vi.3 ff., 11; VI.iii.1.

39. Keir, *Constitutional History*, pp. 59–92.

40. W. H. Frere, *The English Church in the Reigns of Elizabeth and James I* (London, 1904), p. 351.

which were reserved from the secular courts. Among the first kind of matters we may mention neglect of duties, worldly behavior, crimes, heresy or lesser offences against conformity in doctrine and ritual. The second covered the enforcement of lay payments to the Church, especially tithes but also oblations, mortuaries and other fees, as well as the punishment of riotous behaviour in church, contempt of the clergy, and attacks on ecclesiastics. The last involved the detection and punishment of heresy and the like among the laity; of adultery, incontinence and other sexual offences; a vast jurisdiction over matrimonial and testamentary affairs; and jurisdiction over such matters as perjury and defamation which in the sixteenth century came to be handled by the Star Chamber. The law administered was the canon law of Rome, until the Reformation ended its study in England. Thereafter (from about 1540) the English Church courts did not quite seem to know what their law was, though after the repeated failure to promulgate canons for the Church of England a body of law based partly on the old canons and partly on statute was used. . . . The courts could inflict only three punishments—forbidding attendance at church, and lesser and greater excommunication—but since all these were redeemable by penance the infliction of various forms of penance is a frequent entry in the records.[41]

These long extracts suggest what we have lost with the loss of Hooker's Book VI: the particulars that show how a Christian order could be made pervasively effective through its own courts, judges, and punishments. No account of the general principles of Hooker's politics, nor of the subtle blending of Christian principle with political power in Book VII on bishops and Book VIII on monarchy, conveys so vividly the religious rule that might thus be massively emplaced. Is not such a scheme essentially medieval, essentially theocratic in tenor? To retain or reinstitute Christian predominance, within a nation receding from the old feudal collection of private spheres under two overlords, royal and papal—that was the English church's, and Hooker's, political problem.

In fact, the church courts were in a rather decayed state to confront their various rivals, old and new. Pungent little allusions by Hooker point out a better direction. It seems, for example, that fees for marriages, for probate of wills, and for other licenses afforded opportunities too rarely passed by, although recent scholars dispute the old reformers' charge of general corruption.[42] Hooker himself observes caustically that the "souls of men are God's treasure" for which his ministers are strictly accountable; "God hath not invested them with power to make a revenue thereof." In general, the legal and rather secular procedures of the courts did not bespeak a very fervent devotion. They seemed especially anomalous to the faithful and godly Puritans, who wished, as Hooker put it, "no lawmakers but the evangelists, no courts but presbyteries, no punishments

41. Elton, *The Tudor Constitution*, pp. 215–16.
42. Ronald A. Marchant, *The Church under the Law* (Cambridge, Eng., 1969), pp. 244–45.

but ecclesiastical censures."[43] To them and many others the church "presented a picture to the world of a vast property-owning organization," as one authority writes,

> with an infinite hierarchy of officers, endlessly absorbing tithes, fees and 'offerings', regulated by a man-made law, existing only with the support of the State. It was a home for hundreds of officials and their underlings, clerical and lay, who made a good living not by extortion but by drawing the legal fees to which they were perfectly entitled.

The example *par excellence* was the infliction of excommunication for trivial offences, such as a mere breach of technical procedure. Evidently this greatest of spiritual punishments was bandied about as an everyday penalty, one dispatched by letter, for instance, to those who did not appear with the required fee to show their penitence.[44]

Our tattered text does not permit a confident detailing of Hooker's response to this situation. Clearly, he thought the church's fundamental task to be spiritual and not temporal, and its temporal instruments to be wielded accordingly. He takes care, for example, to pronounce against abuse of excommunication for worldly ends.[45] Clearly, he also thought that the church in the world had to use worldly instruments, or else abandon them to those indifferent or hostile, and thus in effect abandon its task. In general, then, he insists upon the preeminence of the spiritual and thus condemns what he regarded as the church's fundamental flaw: "the souls of men are not loved," and a temporal desire for place and gain dominates. He insists equally upon a renaissance of the church's temporal prerogatives so threatened by the temporality, quietly bypassing the charges of spiritual interference in matters temporal. For the temporal is directed to the spiritual, and the due claims of church and clerics should predominate, he would think, in matters from other points of view temporal.

Interestingly, both Cranmer and Sandys had chided Hooker for failing to clarify, in the original Book VI, "wherein the distinction lyeth betweene causes spirituall and temporall." In particular Sandys asked him to indicate why "causes of legitimation and bastardie are spirituall" and especially "why matters testamentarie, which is the greatest point of all." These and like matters "are at this day verie strongly impugned," hence the need for "trueth" about them.[46] To explain an invisible passage that Hooker might in any event have varied may appear a trifle presumptuous. Still Hooker would be perfectly in character to refrain from clarifying the unclarifiable, especially if the reasons for the practices in question involved not truth but politics; by some power over things temporal the church sustained the influence of things spiritual.[47]

43. *Laws* VIII.vi; *Hooker's Ecclesiastical Polity, Book VIII*, ed. R. A. Houk (New York, 1931), p. 236.

44. Marchant, *Church under Law*, pp. 27, 245.

45. *Laws* VI.iv.1.

46. *Works* III, 130, 111.

47. Herschel Baker says of Archbishop Laud's later efforts: "The care of the church meant a program of calculated repression. Laud's metropolitan visitations and the various ecclesiastical courts—archdiaconal, diocesan, provincial, and the dread High Commission—might alarm legal-

Several commentators on Elizabeth's reign describe a weakening of church courts (except for the High Commission) and trace it chiefly to a narrowed jurisdiction, increasingly merely spiritual. Evidently there was occurring some laicization of court officials and of law, some loss of disputed jurisdiction and mixed causes to common law courts and especially to the increasingly potent royal Court of Chancery,[48] and some restriction to penalties such as excommunication, ignored or disdained by recalcitrants, reformers, and recusants alike.[49] Elton sums up the tendency: As the ecclesiastical courts ceased to enjoy the assistance of those secular, they

> seem generally to have passed into a state of abstraction—active in a vacuum, vexatious but no longer dangerous or powerful. Probate jurisdiction [with power over every man's inheritance among an aristocracy where power went largely with inheritance] must be excepted from this; that remained real and important enough.[50]

The issue involved was decisive: would the church's priorities be overridden by others? Hill gives some splendid examples. The church's problem was in good part economic. The causes were two: a failure of gentry and nobility to pay decent livings out of the livings and tithes they now owned or leased, and an increasing avoidance of the tithe by the citizenry generally. Now, the various disputes that arose over benefices and advowsons, impropriate tithes, leases of lands and tithes, and the amount and application of tithe, were treated very differently by courts ecclesiastical and civil. Roughly speaking, the former tended to provide for the spirituality, the latter to preserve the lay citizenry's contractual rights and property. As to the church tax, for example,

> the important question before 1640 was how and where tithe cases were to be decided. If they went before the church courts, as the bishop wished, any *modus* (agreement or custom) would be called in question which did not give the incumbent an 'equitable' tenth. If they went before the common-law courts a 'rank *modus*' would be disallowed because too large: no *modus* would be disallowed because too small.

The upward revision of these arrangements between the potent rich and a suppliant clergy was, Hill tells us, the most obvious clerical policy to restore the church's revenue and stature. But the "tremendous effort made by the ecclesiastical courts . . . to revise *modi decimandi* in an upwards direction was frustrated by the issue of prohibitions by the common-law judges."

ists like Coke in assuming judicial power, but in Laud's view they were essential in compelling that religious conformity without which the state would be chaos" (*The Wars of Truth* [Cambridge, Mass., 1952], p. 256).

48. Marchant, *Church under Law*, pp. 112–13; W. J. Jones, *The Elizabethan Court of Chancery* (Oxford, 1967), pp. 393, 399.

49. F. Douglas Price, "The Abuses of Excommunication and the Decline of Ecclesiastical Authority under Queen Elizabeth, *English Historical Review* 57 (January 1942): 106–15; Marchant, *Church under Law*, pp. 236–43.

50. Elton, *Tudor Constitution*, p. 215.

A crucial instance involved London ministers who resorted to church courts to restore their traditional tithe on rents, a tax increasingly avoided through general fraud. The stratagem failed resoundingly: "In 1607 the Court of Common Pleas ruled that ministers might not sue for tithes in the church courts." The potent Archbishop Laud eventually launched a counterattack against prohibitions and common law courts in general; this particular ruling was reversed. The efforts expended, however, and the alliance aroused between reforming enmity and propertied enmity, contributed mightily to the movement that took Laud's head and the head of his master Charles I as well.[51]

Such quarrels and conflicts are not taken up explicitly in Hooker's writings that remain. Book VIII contains, however, a lovely specimen of his tactics. He ignores wretched and controversial particulars, while stiffening the clergy to defend spiritual prerogatives in general—all while defending royal (and political) supremacy against reformers. "There is in England," Hooker intones blandly,

> no cause given unto any to make supplication as Hilary did, that civil governors, to whom commonwealth-matters only belong, might not presume to take upon them the judgment of causes. If the cause be spiritual, secular courts do not meddle with it: we need not excuse ourselves with Ambrose, but boldly and lawfully we may refuse to answer before any civil judge in a matter which is not civil, so that we do not mistake the nature either of the cause or of the court, as we easily may do both, without some better direction than can be had by the rules of this new-found discipline. But of this most certain we are, that our laws do neither suffer a spiritual court to entertain those causes which by law are civil, nor yet if the matter be indeed spiritual, a mere civil court to give judgment of it.

With that crucial if inexact insistence Hooker takes his leave of the relation between spiritual and temporal courts—only to explore, in the next and last section of the *Laws*, the instance that involves all the great conflicts between *ecclesia* and polity that his blandness has hitherto disguised: whether the king "may be exempted from being subject to that judicial power which ecclesiastical consistories have over men."[52]

But we anticipate. Any final discussion of ecclesiastical courts involves discussion of the royal supremacy, as is obvious from the example just noted. First we turn to the bishops, the supreme governors of ecclesiastical discipline beneath the supreme governor.

### Episcopal Authority and Wealth

Defending the bishops involves Hooker in the two essentials of his task: to govern English Christianity in a politic fashion and in governing to assure Christianity's preeminence in England.

51. Christopher Hill, *Economic Problems of the Church* (Oxford, 1956) pp. 280–88, 124, 131.

52. *Laws* VIII.ix.1; VIII.viii.9.

The bishops exercise two kinds of authority, ordination of the clergy and jurisdiction. While Hooker defends episcopal ordination against the reformers' insistence on participation by the congregation, he defends chiefly the bishops' superiority in governing. Despite Keble's suggestion, followed by Shirley,[53] commentators generally recognize that the basis of Hooker's defense is not apostolic succession, that is, the divine status of bishops by virtue of supernatural grace transfused from apostles to first bishops and so on. Hooker supposes that the apostles left something like bishops in authority, and that no form of church government is more in accord with the Word of Christ, but he does not suggest that revelation, or some other supernatural necessity, dictated episcopacy. He defends it as necessary for the sound government of Christianity and as originated by consent of the church.[54] He equates bishops with church governors, especially "the chiefest governors," and such government like all government originates in consent of the whole society.

Book VII has long historical sections which detail the origin of bishops and archbishops and the reasons for both. The essential argument is simple. Bishops are ruling presbyters or priests, and such rule was present in the apostles and shortly instituted in every Christian church. The peculiar cause for this universal phenomenon was "the pestilent evil of schisms," the heresies and sects that almost naturally sprout from Christianity.

> But forasmuch as the Apostles could not themselves be present in all churches, and as the Apostle St. Paul foretold the presbyters of the Ephesians that there would 'rise up from amongst their ownselves, men speaking perverse things to draw disciples after them'; there did grow in short time amongst the governors of each church those emulations, strifes, and contentions, whereof there could be no sufficient remedy provided, except . . . some one were with episcopal authority over the rest, which one being resident might keep them in order, and have the preeminence or principality in those things wherein the equality of many agents was the cause of disorder and trouble.

Such also occasioned archbishops or "metropolitans" and then "in each grand part of the Christian world some one primate, from whose judgment no man living within his territory might appeal, unless it were to a council general of all bishops";[55] thus by the Nicene council originated primates of Rome, Alexandria, and Antioch.

The governors needed by the church from its origin are needed also by the church in England. This is a familiar theme in Hooker's account of English episcopacy. Another theme is rarely discerned: church governance must fit the English regime, civil as well as religious, and the bishops must be restored to important civil power.

53. F. J. Shirley, *Richard Hooker and Contemporary Political Ideas* (London, 1949), pp. 108–11.

54. *Laws* VII.xiv.11.

55. *Laws* VII.viii.10, 5; VII.xiii.3, 5.

One must grasp this political purport of Book VII, however startling it may seem, and however cautiously it is suggested in Hooker's reverent circumlocutions. Hooker's description of England is of what one may call the medieval regime of England, "by the ancient laws whereof, the clergy being held for the chief of those three estates, which together make up the entire body of this commonwealth; under one supreme head and governor." Chief of the estates, the leading clergy should bear "a sway proportionable in the weighty affairs of the land."[56] In plain words, primacy among nobles and in the king's counsels belongs to churchmen, to bishops and archbishops.

Now Hooker's account of the "ancient laws" is not an unfair description of the old English regime prior to Henry VIII's despoliation of church properties. Lords spiritual often had reason for priding themselves as the first estate, superior to lords temporal and the commonality. Grand offices were often held by grand churchmen. The very calling and arrangement of ancient parliaments, according to the *Modus* or order dating from the reign of Edward the Confessor, presumed primacy beneath the king of "the spiritualitie," of the Bishops, Abbots, Priors, and "all other great Clarks."[57]

Yet the reign of Elizabeth during which Hooker wrote exhibited no such civil predominance of prelates. Elizabeth's choice of Privy Councillors is indicative. The way to civil power was through prominence in her Council—"outside of which a man's influence on affairs hardly existed," Elton says. Elizabeth's Council, however, was decisively, and for years exclusively, lay. Between the usurpation of the Council's more important functions by Cardinal Wolsey, under Henry VIII, and Archbishop Laud's decisive influence on Charles I, the status of ecclesiastics among a monarch's highest Councillors never fell so low as under Elizabeth. After Wolsey's fall even Thomas Cromwell had retained the bishops, the remnant of Henry VII's dozen or more spiritual Councillors; "Elizabeth never appointed any ecclesiastic except Whitgift (1586) to her Council,"[58] and that appointment came after twenty-five years.

There were many other signs, during Hooker's time, of diminished episcopal power. Thirteen years into Elizabeth's reign, for example, John Hooker published his "Order and Usage of the Keeping of a Parliament in England," which defined a distinctly subordinate role for clerics. This Hooker was our Hooker's uncle and a patron of his early education. Yet their views differed. John Hooker's publication sharply distinguishes the *Modus* from Edward the Confessor's reign, which he describes as the "old and ancient order," from his own up-to-date version, *The Order and Usage how to Keep a Parliament in England in these Days*. His version never calls the prelates the first estate. Indeed, lords spiritual are inserted into the estate called "barons." The commons

56. *Laws* VII.xv.8, 5–9.

57. "The olde and ancient order of keeping of the Parlement in England used in the time of King Edward the confessor," in John Hooker, *The Order and Usage of the Keeping of a Parlement in England*, ed. Vernon F. Snow (New Haven and London, 1977), p. 136; cf. pp. 129 and 140. See Snow's remarks on pp. 103–4.

58. Elton, *Tudor Constitution*, p. 92. H. R. Trevor-Roper, *Archbishop Laud, 1563–1645* (London, 1963), pp. 226–28.

are implied to be the principal estate; should in extraordinary circumstances the barons be absent, this Hooker says that commons and king can legislate. While he first mentions four "degrees" within Parliament, the clergy being fourth, he then divides in a novel way the estates into three: king, barons, and commons. He silently drops the clergy from the estates of the realm. As the editor of this *Order and Usage* mildly observes, prelates are not presented as an "integral part of the lawmaking process."[59]

Our Hooker, the political theologian, was aware that the policy of his uncle was being forwarded by other and more influential Elizabethans. As his *Laws* affirm the Parliamentary prominence belonging to the ecclesiastical "part," he inserts a bitter acknowledgment: "howsoever now the world would have them annihilated."[60] Hooker may allude to such worldly powers as Sir Thomas Smith and his *De Republica Anglorum*. Smith was a statesman and Privy Councillor. His book had wide circulation and by 1640 had gone through eleven editions. It divides the English regime into various classifications. While mentioning once the phrase "three estates," Smith never includes the bishops or clergy in any list. They are conspicuously absent from the "parts" (gentlemen, citizens or burgesses, yeomen, artificers, and laborers) that he chooses to discuss. Smith thinks Aristotle "prince of all philosophers," praising especially his treatment of "the division and natures of commonwealths." But he never refers to God as the author or giver of authority, nor mentions the Scriptures or natural law.[61] Of such strategies by *politiques* Hooker knows, and he knows also of the singular hazard they pose. "The chiefest cause of disdain and murmur against bishops in the Church of England is that evil-affected eye wherewith the world looked upon them, since the time that irreligious profaneness, beholding the due and just advancements of God's clergy, hath under pretence of enmity unto ambition and pride proceeded so far, that the contumely of old offered unto Aaron in the like quarrel may seem very moderate and quiet dealing, if we compare it with the fury of our own times."[62]

We may suppose, then, that Hooker was also aware that he proposed a revolution while reverently suggesting the clergy as "chief" of the estates, the proper bearer of "a sway proportionable in the weighty affairs of the land." I suspect that he wished more or less what Archbishop Laud later attempted under Charles I. Laud dominated the Privy Council, being "virtual Prime Minister" according to Christopher Hill. And in 1640 the prelates in the House of Lords claimed (unsuccessfully) that by themselves they constituted an estate of the realm. Hill describes Laud's efforts: his

---

59. Vernon Snow, in John Hooker, *The Order and Usage*, pp. 103–4; cf. p. 152 with pp. 181–82; see pp. 66–67, 75, 109–10, and 183, n. 105.

60. *Laws* VIII.vi.12.

61. J. W. Allen, *A History of Political Thought in the Sixteenth Century* (London and New York, 1964), p. 266; Thomas Smith, *De Republica Anglorum* (London, 1583, repr. 1970), pp. 16–30, 7. On the work's influence, see Corinne Comstock Weston, *English Constitutional Theory and the House of Lords, 1556–1832* (London, 1965), p. 16.

62. *Laws* VII.xvii.1.

policy was to get back behind the Reformation in everything but the papal supremacy—recovering impropriations, restoring tithes, if not to a true 10 per cent, at least to what they had been before the rise in prices; restoring the coercive power of church courts, which now meant the complete subordination of the common-law judges to the government, and the ultimate reversal of all the adjustments of the medieval common-law to the needs of capitalist society made in the preceding decades; restoring the privileged social position of priests. . . . Laud was trying to revive the Middle Ages. . . .[63]

That will indicate roughly Hooker's intention, if we emphasize as central restoration of lordly power to the bishops. Hooker knew of the worldly primacy of political primacy; however quietly, this theologian points toward theocracy as a model. Precisely while discussing the bishops he remarks that "in the prime of the world" kings were priests and priests rulers in every sense. There also he praises the "archbishops of Mentz, Colen, and Trevers," being both "archbishops and princes of the empire." The Archbishopric of Mainz, for example, entailed presidency of the electoral college choosing the Holy Roman Emperor, archchancellorship of the Empire, and rule over thousands of square miles. After a war in 1462 between rival archbishops, the city proper was deprived of its old privilege of some free government and became unequivocally subject to the victorious churchman. Simple theocracy, the preferable solution in Hooker's opinion, remained possible.[64]

Yet simple theocracy was not the English solution, and not possible in England. The English bishops were so far from dominant as to be threatened on all sides: by clergy and laity, by commons and nobility, and (more subtly) by monarchy. The picture well known to historians is found also in Hooker's less candid account, making the best of a situation "when the best things are not possible." He defends the bishops' honor and civil power from reformers, and yet also and urgently from laity.

Hooker does not neglect the rot within that weakens the bishops before threats from without. In chapter 1 we noted his bitter indictment of ignorance and mediocrity in the episcopacy, and of their oligarchic tendencies to disdain inferior clergy; to disdain conscientious supervision of the clergy; to exploit for gain duties, courts, and visitations; to acquiesce in the nipping off of revenues by lay patrons; and in general to retreat toward a comfortable innocuousness. This is nicely summarized in Elton's phrase for the ecclesiastical courts: "active in a vacuum, vexatious but no longer dangerous or powerful." Hooker puts pungently the result: "It is a long time since any great one hath felt, or almost any one much feared the edge of that ecclesiastical severity, which sometime held lords and dukes in a more religious awe than now the meanest are able to be kept."[65]

63. Hill, *Economic Problems of the Church*, pp. 340–41.
64. *Laws* VII.xv.5; *Encyclopedia Britannica*, 11th ed. (1911), s.v. "Mainz."
65. *Laws* VII.xxiv.11.

There was rot within, and Hooker responds with a kind of sermon offered firmly and even bluntly to his superiors the bishops. Besides politic instruction in creed and regiment, he gives them moral encouragement and chastisement. Yet Hooker cannot accept as an adequate remedy a merely "voluntary reformation." There remain deeper threats from without that contribute to the rot within. He voices his suspicions as to some mediocrities who discredit prelacy and church alike, "the very cause of whose advancement hath been principally their unworthiness to be advanced."[66] Besides, avarice and truckling in bishops as in ordinaries are encouraged by their relative poverty, and by their dependence on gentry and nobles now unequivocally superior in wealth, power, and dignity. In short, Hooker's defense culminates in an effort at restoration, essentially in the face of the post-Henrician power of nobility and gentry and of the monarchy itself.

Hooker dwells on the bishops' service to English political arrangements; his is a politic address to the self-interest of Christian statesmen. Book VII begins with a warning: the fall of bishops will be followed by that of nobles and lawyers, since reformers aim at all three. It is then impolitic as well as sacrilegious for laity, concealing themselves behind reformers, to reduce the episcopate. Still, Hooker means to restore bishops to a primacy over nobles and gentry. He like Laud must finally rely on the only power capable of such a revolution, the monarchy.

Hooker defends the bishops' primacy in dignity, "next in degree of honour unto the chief sovereign,"[67] and especially the wealth that could maintain such stature. As to titles, distinctions of dress, and retinue, it comes to this: the lords spiritual must be grand to compel the respect and gain the ear of monarch and nobility. For Christian counsel to prevail, even as to Christianity, churchmen must be prominent. "Let unexperienced wits imagine what pleaseth them, . . . with so great personages" these personal differences are necessary.[68] Only thus can exist the ecclesiastical check that amounts to bridle as well as counsel. The reins extend to monarch, as will be shown, but Book VII treats only of the check on aristocracy. An "ornament" when noble, a narrow aristocracy like the English is despotic in the extreme when not. For cherishing of virtues and checking of vices

> what help could there ever have been invented more divine, than the sorting of the clergy into such degrees, that the chiefest of the prelacy being matched in a kind of equal yoke, as it were, with the higher, the next with the lower degree of nobility, the reverend authority of the one might be to the other as a courteous bridle, a means to keep them lovingly in awe that are exorbitant, and to correct such excesses in them, as whereunto their courage, state and dignity maketh them over-prone.[69]

66. *Laws* VII.xxiv.14.
67. *Laws* VII.xvii.5.
68. *Laws* VII.xviii.9.
69. *Laws* VII.xviii.10; Vernon Snow notes the spiritual lords' claims, in John Hooker, *The Order and Usage*, p. 109.

Not only virtue and religion are served. Monarch, laity in general, and the lesser clergy should appreciate this political check on the nobles, and the preeminence in ecclesiastical matters of the bishops. Hooker's remarks to ordinary ministers are particularly revealing. An episcopate often oligarchic in pretension and contemptible in conduct was equally often resented by its clergy, usually miserably poor, and directly squeezed by tithes hard to collect and importunities of bishops no less than gentry. Hence Hooker's sermon to the bishops, and his reminder to the pastorate of the advantages of "such in authority over them as are of the selfsame profession, society and body with them."[70]

The crucial issue, however, was "the honouring of the clergy with wealth"; restoration of the bishops' primacy depended on restoration of church lands, the means of a separate estate. Serious churchmen had intimated this policy from the time of Henry VIII's takings, but it was seriously attempted, with help from the monarchy, only by Laud. Hooker quietly shows the way.

During the sixty years from Henry's dissolution of the monasteries to the end of Elizabeth's reign, more than one-fourth of the land of England changed hands, and a goodly portion comprised pieces lost from church holdings. The stages in this massive takeover by monarchy, gentry, and nobility need not be detailed here. It must be said, however, that Hooker's mistress Elizabeth was no nursing mother of her church. The terrific Henrician reforms had transferred all the monastic property, some one-tenth of the land in England, to the crown, and with that went the rights of presentation to about two-fifths of all benefices. Edwardian laws had in their turn confiscated the properties of chantries (the many small foundations in which a few clergy said prayers for their founders' souls), and nibbled at episcopal lands. There, at the church's vitals, Elizabeth herself made the principal inroads. True, a law of 1559 had stopped alienation of episcopal properties to any subject, but an explicit reservation as to the monarchy allowed what in fact ensued: the "golden stream" henceforth "flowed through the Court."[71] Hill calls Elizabeth "supreme plunderer," although Haugaard thinks this much exaggerated. She and her favorites seem to have despoiled ecclesiastical lands and revenues with a constancy remarked by many and intimated by Hooker as well. She allowed numerous vacancies to persist whereby she could divert the sees' revenues, and during vacancies often exchanged a see's clear lands for impropriate tithes (tithes from old church lands now in lay hands, less valuable and more vexatious to collect). The new bishop's appointment might be conditional upon his acquiescence. With notable regularity a cut of a see's revenues or property was demanded for queen or favorite, and disastrously long leases of church lands were often ordered for favorites. The monarchy was not the only beneficiary, however. Many were the nobles and gentry, merchants and lawyers, who established their fortune and power out of the church's downfall. "The Crown acted only as a channel," Elton suggests, "as recurrent financial crises in the 1540s, 1550s, 1560s, and 1590s compelled it to sell off much of its landed property, and the landed gentry were

---

70. *Laws* VII.xviii.12.
71. Hill, *Economic Problems of the Church*, p. 14; Keir, *Constitutional History*, p. 47.

the ultimate beneficiaries."[72] The net effect was the advancement in power and wealth of monarchy, and especially gentry, at the expense of the church. The bishops in particular "were being transformed from feudal potentates, powerful in their own right as landowners, to hangers-on of the court, making what they could of their office whilst they held it." Christopher Hill's fine remark captures the mixture of economic scrabbling with mean subservience that often characterizes the descriptions by contemporary and historian alike. Hill documents in detail the erosion of episcopal power, dignity, and quality, and the correspondingly disproportionate burden of taxation, both of which followed the loss of ecclesiastical dominance over lands and livings, rights to present, tithes, and other fees and taxes.[73]

This diminishing estate was the product of policy as well as of greed, it seems. "The temporalty seek to make the clergy beggars," Archbishop Whitgift once remarked, so "that we may depend upon them."[74] This no doubt is what Cromwell and Starkey and Smith and Cecil and *politiques* before them and after them had planned. We see again the deep causes for the deep pessimism occasionally displayed by Hooker. Yet he endeavors to restore. His policy to refill the coffers is a little strategic masterpiece of Christian politics, in fact. It is daring in its generalities, in the end to which it points, and in the spirit it means to evoke. Nevertheless Hooker is circumspect and even hedging as to the practical steps so passionately disputed and hence so dangerous in the church's dangerous weakness.

Hooker nerves the episcopacy to fight encroachment and to seek more, urges the pastorate to forbear envy, and beseeches the laity to forbear envy and to give for Christ's sake. The church's wealth is Christ's patrimony, however used or misused by the bishops. He who takes away commits sacrilege, but he who bestows does a holy thing. Twice, at the end of Book V and of Book VII, Hooker plunges feelingly into the justification for honoring God with wealth, by churches, ornaments, and above all, the tenth (or tithe) of whatsoever increase providence should give. There are religious justifications for tithing. It was the practice of Israel. Besides, how better can religion be sustained, and the heart's love of God over gain be shown and developed? Hooker's combination of the pious and the politic shows nicely in a recommendation of payment in kind.

> That which cometh from God to us by the natural course of his providence which we know to be innocent and pure is perhaps best accepted, because least spotted with the stain of unlawful or indirect procurement. Besides whereas prices daily change, nature which commonly is one must needs be the most indifferent and permanent standard between God and man.

While such goods of the earth are commended for ministers, Hooker suggests

72. Elton, *Tudor Constitution*, p. 371.
73. Hill, *Economic Problems of the Church*, p. 28.
74. Whitgift quoted by Hill, *Economic Problems of the Church*, p. 27.

that bishops are due the earth itself. "Of service to God, the best works are they which continue longest," like "the ancient lands and livings of the Church."[75]

To what extent, however, might the church's wealth be carried? A quiet and complicated comparison with ancient Israel softens the blow: the holy tribe of Levites composed only one-twelfth of the people, and nevertheless controlled one-third "of all such goods as the holy land did yield." Hooker draws no very exact conclusions from this except to say that "Christian clergy ought not herein be inferior unto the Jewish," and to conclude that bishops ought to enjoy some one-quarter of "the whole yearly rents and revenues of the church."[76] Is it possible that the church ought to enjoy a patrimony extending to some one-third of the goods of the land, the bishops alone enjoying one-twelfth? Laud and Charles I, one might note, managed to return to the Scottish clergy monastic lands alone equal to one-third of the kingdom. And one scholar estimates that prior to the dissolution of the monasteries the English church itself "owned real estate estimated at one-third the total of the kingdom," and "enjoyed an income two-and-a-half times that of the crown."[77] True, one could go too far: "It hath fared with the wealth of the church as with a tower, which being built at the first with the highest, overthroweth itself after by its own greatness." Some proportion with the other estates must be kept. Yet preeminence meant that in wealth the church could not trail the other estates, and in this as in other things Hooker's advocacy points to Laud's policy. No less a political authority than Cecil had thought that only Henry VIII's distribution of ecclesiastical wealth prevented the church from renewing its rule under Mary.[78]

As a start, however, the church had simply to defend what remained. Every weakening had made it more susceptible to further weakening. Hooker inspired a stern and firm defense against further encroachments. Evidently the bishops needed some such guidance. Stone only echoes a common judgment in saying they "did not show much fight" in the face of lay depredations.[79] While "simonaical corruption" Hooker "may not for honor's sake suspect to be amongst men" of bishops' great place, he inveighs nonetheless bitterly against precisely the sacrifice of episcopal dignity and property for ambition and gain. Elsewhere in Book V Hooker sets forth an old example or two illustrating how

> the best and most renowned Prelates of the Church of Christ have in this consideration rather sustained the wrath than yielded to satisfy the hard desire of their greatest commanders on earth coveting with ill advice and counsel that which they willingly should have suffered God to enjoy.

75. *Laws* VII.xxii.6; V.lxxix.10.
76. *Laws* VII.xxiii.4, 6.
77. Paul Van Dyke, *Renascence Portraits* (London, 1906), pp. 183–84; Hill, *Economic Problems of the Church*, p. 333.
78. Cecil to John Knox, quoted by Conyers Read, *Mr. Secretary Cecil and Queen Elizabeth* (London, 1955), p. 143.
79. Lawrence Stone, *The Crisis of the Aristocracy, 1558–1641* (Oxford, 1965), p. 407.

Martyrdom had been combined occasionally with "virtuous delusion" to invent ways of concealing and saving the church's treasures.[80] Hooker anticipates the saintly Lancelot Andrewes, who refused in turn two clipped bishoprics, offered by the queen on condition he assent to the clipping.

Hooker's treatment of the queen is circumspect. It is even delicious. More than once he ostentatiously presumes, with the elaborate Latin mottoes Elizabeth loved, that to raise a mere suspicion of "any action so dishonorable as this" would place upon her sacred faith and fame an unworthy smirch. Yet he calls attention to "desecrations" by other princes, and he nerves bishops against precisely the "greatest commanders on earth" who make demands like those on Andrewes. When he inveighs against the "colourable shifts and inventions" that have been used to avoid the appearance of open sacrilege, it is hard to suppose him to forget what Stone calls Elizabeth's "less direct, though not necessarily any less effective, methods" of exchanging plump episcopal lands for tithes controlled by lay patrons. "There will be always some skilful persons which can teach a way how to grind treatably the Church with jaws that shall scarce move," Hooker says bitterly, "and yet devour in the end more than they that come ravening with open mouth."[81] Nonetheless, Hooker clearly wishes to avoid offending a monarch on whom the church is already too dependent—and who offers what protection the church has against civil courts, oligarchy, and reformers.

It is understandable, then, that Hooker should offer no conspicuously revolutionary proposals likely to offend those who already dominate the church. Rather unenthusiastically he elaborates reasons for concurring in the dissolution, being most attentive to distinguishing the "human" institution and "superstitious" end of the monastic orders from "that holy and divine interest which belongeth unto bishops." More grudgingly yet he acquiesces in other seizures and transfers that have occurred, until God shall move men to restore "of their own voluntary accord." He calms the landed class, fearful for its new lands; even if its new properties were "taken away from the right owners at the first, . . . such as were after possessed of them held them not without some title, which law did after a sort make good."[82] But against all new encroachments he stands like a rock. The spirit of his appeals is designed to reestablish a climate of giving, to stop the demise of the church's substance, and ultimately to restore it and the church's power.

80. *Laws* V.lxxix.14; VII.xxiv.7, 8.
81. *Laws* V.lxxix.16, 14, 6, 7, 15; VII.xxiv. 22; Stone, *Crisis of the Aristocracy*, p. 407.
82. *Laws* VII.xxiv.25, 23.

# 11

## The Royal Supremacy

### A Christian Commonwealth

To defend a state church from religious purists, while also defending the church from depredations by the state, and somehow reconstructing a purer church by relying upon the state partly responsible for its corruption: that was the gist of Hooker's paradoxical task, and of Book VIII on the royal supremacy. The work that opens with a slashing attack on the most obvious enemies, reforming Christians, ends with a subtle attack on the English monarchy's religious prerogatives, a genuine attack concealed within a genuine defense. Defense was needed. In "ancient" times priesthood may have been "a strengthening of kings"; but "earth hath now brought heaven under foot."[1] For its reputation and power the church was now a suppliant, defenseless before its secular and reforming enemies but for the crown. Attack was also needed. The church's defender had been also its most potent enemy. Now dependent on the monarchy by the monarchy's political and economic strategy, the church needed for its cause a more solicitous and hence more Christian monarchy. Finally, concealment was needed. Hooker had to avoid further alienating Christians from his church, and to avoid further antagonizing monarchy and oligarchy on which the church was all too dependent. Peter Munz has noted Hooker's "opposition to the Tudor State," and has noted too that this "did not take the form of an open criticism but was an attempt to reinterpret it in his own terms."[2] Book VIII moves subtly toward a Supreme Governor who could not be mistaken for Supreme Plunderer.

The text of Book VIII is imperfect. A peculiarly tempting portion at the end, a curious mini-debate on the monarchy's subordination to ecclesiastical

---

1. *Laws* VII.xv.14, n. 2.
2. Peter Munz, *The Place of Hooker in the History of Thought* (London, 1952), p. 96.

courts, shows several gaps and is especially uncertain, while other transitions and the finish of the whole book are not up to Hooker's standard. Still, the unmistakable stamp of his thought is present,[3] and its condition has not prevented extensive commentary by Morris, Shirley, Munz, Allen, and many others. The following chapter attends only to the essentials of Hooker's treatment of the royal supremacy, especially the disputed essentials.

The Act of Supremacy of 1559 was the first great ecclesiastical law of Elizabeth's reign, and became, with the ensuing Act of Uniformity, the rock of her church policy. With minor variations it reestablished the royal headship originated by Henry, extended by Edward, and rejected by the Catholic Mary. It required from all ecclesiastics and state officials an oath "that the queen's highness is the only supreme governor . . . as well in all spiritual or ecclesiastical things or causes as temporal."[4] Particular provisions took back from the pope control of ecclesiastical revenues and appointments, and authorized commissioners to exercise "any spiritual or ecclesiastical power or authority" in the realm. With royal agents thus rested authority for "reformation, order, and correction" of any "errors, heresies, schisms, abuses, offences, contempts and enormities . . . which by any manner spiritual or ecclesiastical power" could redress. Under this comprehensive power the queen appointed the so-called High Commission, the chief instrument (besides the bishops) of her ecclesiastical policy.

Against such a political power over religious doctrines, persons, and properties the Catholics set themselves immediately and forthrightly, the reformers eventually and somewhat less determinedly. Elizabeth's policy was obviously aimed against the Papacy first and foremost, against "all usurped foreign power and authority spiritual and temporal," as the Act of Supremacy said. National church, politically governed, confronted the universal church, headed by the Bishop of Rome claiming succession to the apostles Peter and Paul and thus possession of the keys to heaven bestowed by Christ. The confrontation with "our reformers" was never quite as wholehearted. They depended upon the monarchy for their preeminence over Rome, and through Parliament, counsellors of the queen, and perhaps the queen's inclination, enjoyed considerable influence. Most reformers accepted the royal supremacy, if only from such reasons of expediency. Yet the purists (like Anthony Gilby even under Henry VIII) always bridled at a hierarchical church ruled by king as well as bishop. Elizabeth's enforcement of her middle way made increasingly vivid the contrast between the headship of a monarch and congregations of godly presbyters and laity ruled by the Word of God. Cartwright and Travers had exaggerated and vulgarized Calvin's insistence upon divinely ordained church governance, thus sharpening the issue which Hooker had to confront. The basic issue was common to Catholics and reformers; Book VIII confronts both in turn. "Though

3. J. W. Allen, *A History of Political Thought in the Sixteenth Century* (London and New York, 1964), p. 195.

4. The Act of Supremacy, 1559: I Eliz. I c.i, ix, reprinted in Claire Cross, *The Royal Supremacy in the Elizabethan Church* (London and New York, 1969), pp. 128–29.

they had different conceptions of the 'church,'" as J. W. Allen puts it, "the preservation of true religion was dependent on the church's independence."[5] Be it through pope bearing the keys, or congregations bearing the Word of God, religion within its sphere was to direct polity, church the civil magistrate, and priest the monarch. Elizabeth's supremacy over the English church violated or even reversed that principle. It could seem that the temporal ruled the spiritual; earth ruled heaven. The situation Hooker regrets could seem the one he defends. It is urged in Scripture that things of this world are nothing to those of the next, things temporal nothing to things spiritual, and that the two must not be mis-valued or even confused. "Render therefore to Caesar the things that are Caesar's, and to God the things that are God's."

Hooker's genuine defense of Elizabethan arrangements involves this com-prehensive proposal: to unite the realms of Christ and Caesar not through the Christian prince alone but also and chiefly through a Christian polity that will guide the prince to a Christian governance. Hooker grants and even insists that "things appertaining unto religion are both distinguished from other affairs, and have always had in the Church special persons chosen to be exercised about them." No doubt church differs from commonwealth, and the spiritual ministry of Word and sacraments is not fit for kingly jurisdiction. But this need not imply two realms, "as under heathen kings the Church did deal with her own affairs within herself, without depending at all upon any in civil authority, and the commonwealth in hers, altogether without the privity of the Church." Hooker grants that the received error on this point is common. He attributes the old insistence on separating realm of Christ from realm of Caesar to old circum-stances, however, to the old situation of a persecuted or at least unauthorized faith. Nothing in Scripture precludes a juncture of faith and commonwealth in a better situation, "in such commonwealths as have now publicly embraced the truth of Christian religion." After "the mightiest began to like of the Christian faith," and "whole free states and kingdoms became obedient unto Christ," there could be one realm with two "accidents," religious and civil. "A commonwealth we name it simply in regard of some regiment or policy under which men live; a church for the truth of the religion which they profess." Reason itself calls for such an articulated juncture: a true understanding of politics puts religion as its chief concern, and of religion, Christianity as the true religion. A Christian polity is then a church. "As a politic society it doth maintain religion; as a church, that religion which God hath revealed by Jesus Christ." True, those who identify church with clergy, such as Catholics, will balk. The church comprises the whole body of believers, however, as Marsilius and the reformers affirm. This body contains at once members of politic society and believers in Christ, and thus church and commonwealth can be together one society. Some members may be appointed to one office according to the form of secular law and regi-ment, and some to another after "the spiritual law of Jesus Christ," yet without making "two several impaled societies."[6]

Hooker thus produces a political-theological miracle. He makes essen-

5. Allen, *Political Thought*, p. 230.
6. *Laws* VIII.i.4, 2, 3; VIII.vi.13.

tially Christian the *politeia*, the regime or rulers and ruling way of life that is the chief theme of Aristotle's *Politics*. He makes politic the otherworldly devoutness of the Christian. He manages to inform his flock with both the moderate political wisdom of the philosophers and the theocratic political practice of the Jews. We have discussed Hooker's arts of interpreting the ancient political writers as religious and the ancient religious writers as politic. A passage from Book VIII deserves consideration here:

> For of every politic society that being true which Aristotle hath, namely, "that the scope thereof is not simply to live, nor the duty so much to provide for life, as for means of living well" and that even as the soul is the worthier part of man, so in all commonwealths things spiritual ought above temporal to be provided for. And of things spiritual, the chiefest is religion [Hooker here cites an equivocal passage of the *Politics*]. . . . The heathen themselves had their spiritual laws, causes, and offices, always severed from their temporal; neither did this make two independent states among them. God by revealing true religion doth make them that receive it his Church. Unto the Jews he so revealed the truth of religion, that he gave them in special consideration laws, not only for the administration of things spiritual, but also temporal. The Lord himself appointing both the one and the other in that commonwealth did not thereby distract it into several independent communities, but institute several functions of one and the same community.[7]

### The Distinctiveness of Hooker's Views: Commentators and Predecessors

In the broad outlines of his solution, Hooker had predecessors among earlier English churchmen, including Henry VIII's Archbishop Gardiner and Hooker's own patron Archbishop Whitgift. "I perceive," Whitgift had written, "no such distinction of the commonwealth and the church that they should be counted, as it were, two several bodies, governed with diverse laws and diverse magistrats, except the church be linked with an heathenish and idolatrous commonwealth."[8] This is an advance from the earlier Elizabethan protestations of, say, Bishop Jewel, who had simply defended reformers against Papacy by insisting on the duty and right of Christian princes to govern their churches by the Word of God. Hooker incorporates Whitgift's advance. Yet he goes farther. One must not exaggerate Hooker's immersion in the doctrines of his time.

His difficulty in uniting polity with church was not exactly that set forth by J. W. Allen and Peter Munz: "Then, as now, it would have been impossible to arrive at any definition of 'essentials' which would have been accepted by all who professed themselves Christians."[9] This Hooker knew full well and sought to overcome in principle by arguments we have considered, and in practice by

---

7. *Laws* VIII.i.4.

8. *Defence of the Answer*, in *The Works of John Whitgift, D.D.*, ed. Rev. John Ayre (Cambridge, Eng., 1851) II, 313; I, 388, 391.

9. Allen, *Political Thought*, p. 197; Munz, *Hooker*, pp. 56–57.

Christian governance. He knew that Christianity was understood variously or misunderstood widely among his countrymen. Nonetheless he can treat all Englishmen as subjects of Christian England well understood, through his (admittedly doubtful) doctrine of implicit consent to English laws and Christian customs and thus of consent to his understanding of Christian essentials. Yet the objection can be rephrased, in a manner appropriate to Hooker's awareness and yet also cognizant of the practical difficulties of his doctrinaire understanding. How can he expect English governance to provide in practice for the Christian England he defines in principle? How can he assure that England is a religious regime, not merely a politic regime with religion as secondary part? That is the difficulty for Christians potentially present in the Henrician settlement, ever more visible as Elizabeth's reign wore on.

> It was possible under Henry VIII [Allen remarks] to see in the Royal Supremacy an instrument for the salvation of souls and the construction of a truly Christian commonwealth. It was possible to believe that popular Bible reading would produce general agreement about true religion. It became, under Elizabeth, more and more difficult to hold such views. Increasingly apparent was it that, while royal supremacy involved a power to determine the form of religion for every one and in every sense, that power was being used for quite earthly ends. Visibly the government was seeking lines of least resistance and not, unless with extreme indirection, the salvation of souls.[10]

For this critical reason, Hooker moves far beyond Whitgift in defending the church's wealth and civil power and in combining with his defense of the supremacy a considerable attack. He expands massively Whitgift's presumption that "a wise and godly prince" will defer in religious matters to his wise and godly bishops. He refrains wholly from any statements that "the continual practice" of Christian churches

> hath been to give to Christian princes supreme authority in making ecclesiastical orders and laws, yea, and that which is more, in deciding of matters of religion, even in the chief and principal points.[11]

Whitgift's bald insistence upon princely discretion is replaced by Hooker's own insistence upon a mutual rule of king, Parliament, and Convocation, as regulated in a Christian commonwealth by settled law and Christian custom.

That Book VIII corrects as well as defends is commonly acknowledged, although a few have argued to the contrary. Shirley suggested that Hooker "gives a picture of the working of the English monarchy of his day as the most reasonable rule." While the passage Shirley cited indicates Hooker's intent, it indicates the reverse of Shirley's interpretation. Royal supremacy in church matters must be "strictly tied" by "some certain rule," and such a rule "hath not hitherto been agreed upon" adequately. "The different sentences of men herein I will not now go about to examine, but it shall be enough to propose what rule

---

10. Allen, *Political Thought*, p. 171.
11. *Works of Whitgift* III, 306.

doth seem in this case most reasonable."[12] The legal historian Holdsworth interprets the *Laws* as "an explanation and a vindication of the Tudor polity in state and church; . . . the only book which not only describes that polity but also explains its underlying principles."[13] Holdsworth cannot account for the remark just quoted from Hooker. More generally, Holdsworth thinks that Hooker's work shows the typical Tudor combination of the "medieval idea of the supremacy of law" with "the needs of the modern state," a combination tending toward the modern constitutional state. Hooker becomes another candidate for first Whig. What seems primary to Hooker is Christianity, however, not law or state, to say nothing of freedom of religion, or separation of church from state. His interpreting of law and limiting of state serves his Christianity. The civil power is not understood as sovereign or as representative in the modern sense, the instrument of the individual's rights and interests.

Most recently, Cargill Thompson has called the *Laws* a conservative piece of propaganda on behalf of the "*status quo*," the royal supremacy in particular.[14] Without repeating arguments given in the introduction, I note that Cargill Thompson did not attend to the unpromising mix of Calvinists and *politiques* in the ecclesiastical *status quo* as Hooker presents it. He also overlooked (1) Hooker's implicit agreement with the Puritans as to many of the church's flaws, especially the bishops' flaws; (2) Hooker's various efforts in Book VII to resuscitate clerical wealth and power; and (3) the way Hooker's reinterpretation of English law and custom encroaches, in a manner foreign to Whitgift, upon Elizabeth's prerogative as to her church.

Still, those who agree on Hooker's political originality differ about its content. Houk thought that Hooker defends "not so much the *status quo* as his idealization of Elizabethan England."[15] Yet he characterizes Hooker's ideal as "utopian" or "eternal" (whereas Hooker limits his solution to that defensible in England) or even as imbued with "modern democratic theory." Similarly, Hallam suggests that Hooker wrote "with a temerity that would have startled his superiors" and that Archbishop Whitgift might well have ordered some excising had Book VIII been published immediately; yet he calls Hooker's views "Whig principles."[16]

Peter Munz's reflective study, on the other hand, relates Hooker's work both to the English political situation and to the great Christian political alternatives suggested by Augustine, Thomas, and Marsilius. One could scarcely better his remark on Hooker's procedure:

> He was always intent on interpreting these (existing) conditions in terms in which they would become acceptable to his general philo-

12. *Laws* VIII.ii.16; F. J. Shirley, *Richard Hooker and Contemporary Political Ideas* (London, 1949), p. 117.

13. W. S. Holdsworth, *A History of English Law*, ed. S. Chrimes (London, 1923) IV, 212.

14. W. D. J. Cargill Thompson, "The Philosopher of the Politic Society," in W. Speed Hill, ed., *Studies in Richard Hooker* (Cleveland and London, 1972), pp. 13–16.

15. *Hooker's Ecclesiastical Polity: Book VIII*, ed. Raymond Aaron Houk (New York, 1931), p. 5.

16. Henry Hallam, *The Constitutional History of England* (Paris, 1841) I, 162.

sophical outlook. And he did that by drawing attention to neglected factors and diverting it from those that seemed less pleasing . . . shifting the emphasis from the undesirable to the desirable elements of the status quo.[17]

Indeed, to fully understand the embattled state of Hooker's church, one would have to reinterpret according to that canon not only the *Laws*, but also many of the ostensibly conforming legal-political treatises of the period, going back at least to Sir John Fortescue's *De Laudibus Legum Angliae*, and including Sir Thomas Smith's *De Republica Anglorum*.

Munz interprets Hooker as finally failing in his defense-cum-correction, however, failing even to finish his work "when he discovered that he was no longer a real apologist but had become a critic." Munz suggests that Hooker confronted the Puritans with Thomistic ideas favoring union of church and polity, and Marsilian ideas favoring governance of church by the civil ruler. Arriving at Books VI, VII, and VIII he saw the impossibility of reconciling these, and the incompatibility of a Christian solution with the Tudor Constitution. The *Laws* lay unfinished because "Hooker had not been able to make up his mind as to what to say."[18]

It is true that Book VIII is short, allusive, vague in details as to the power of Convocation, the archbishops, and church courts, reticent as to the competing claims of common law courts and as to controversy over the kind of law that is to rule. Nevertheless, Munz's argument is rather speculative and has decisive difficulties, textual and substantive. While Book VIII may be incomplete, and while we lack most of the original Book VI, the evidence suggests that Book VI and surely Book VII were completed. Hooker completed some of the books that Munz's argument supposes him unable to complete. Be that as it may, it is clear that Hooker understood from his work's beginning the gravity of England's drift to a lay polity, and that neither the first five books nor the last three show him without a solution. Biting attacks upon atheists and a hungry laity appear repeatedly in the early books, as does an effort to reestablish ecclesiastical power and wealth. And what of Book VII's remarkable strategy: to restore bishops to preeminence among the estates in power and wealth, to restore to that extent theocracy? Munz fails to mention the consummate ingenuity and perfect prose of Book VII. Nor does the sketchiness of Book VIII seem due to a defect in Hooker's plan. Some scholars believe the manuscript of Book VIII to have been abused, if not partly suppressed. Or perhaps Hooker died before completing it. Besides, he may have only hinted at controversial particulars, as he does in Book VII, to avoid antagonizing the court or to avoid suppression. In any event, he is not at a loss in what remains of Book VIII. The last section shows him at his most clever, precisely while apparently abstaining from a most diffi-

17. Munz, *Hooker in the History of Thought*, p. 102.

18. Ibid., p. 110. Arguments similar to Munz's have been made by H. F. Kearney, who says Book I's reliance upon reason contradicts Book VIII's deference to will, and by Father Bull, who contrasts Hooker's scholastic beginning with his "Roman Law" ending glorifying the "state." H. F. Kearney, "Richard Hooker: A Reconstruction," *Cambridge Journal* 5 (1952): 300–311; George Bull, "What Did Locke Borrow from Hooker?" *Thought* 7 (1932): 122–35.

cult decision. He blandly presents the arguments *pro* and *con* for the authority (so outrageous to Elizabeth) of church courts over monarch, while ostentatiously declining to decide the matter and as I shall argue, quietly revealing his decision.

Seeking "The Place of Hooker in the History of Thought," Munz interpreted Hooker as governed by historical trends in thought, in this case Thomism and Marsilianism. He missed the distinctiveness of Hooker's thoughts, abstracting especially from Hooker's own understanding of his situation and intention. Munz begins not with Hooker's interpretation of the religious-political situation, but with Munz's interpretation of the "historical" situation. "For it is only the historian who can, in retrospect, understand a thinker in his own historical context more clearly than he could understand himself."[19] With an Hegelian candor now rare, Munz *begins* by assuming his understanding to be superior to Hooker's, his "history" to be the best perspective for judging Hooker's philosophy, his own understanding of history to be superior to Hooker's grasp of his problem.

Still, in his own way Hooker does combine the deep reflections of Marsilius and Thomas and does blend uniquely two versions of Christian Aristotelianism in themselves incompatible. No doubt Hooker's notion of a Christian commonwealth owes much to the spirit of Thomas, as Munz suggested. Thomas moves toward one society, with priests and rulers as complementary parts, and this goes far beyond the first great synthesis of classical philosophy and Christianity, that by the theologian whom Hooker most admired, St. Augustine.

Augustine was evidently the first among Christian theologians to defend political rule and military service as genuine duties for Christians, despite the Scripture's commands to "judge not lest ye be judged," to love your enemies, and to turn the other cheek. Furthermore, Augustine came grudgingly to conceive of the secular power as an aid to the church. It did not provide mere preconditions, but enforced upon heretics the true gospel.[20] Yet all this was compelled by necessity. Rule, force, and coercion of the faithful were but the inevitable consequences of nature's depravity through man's sin. Nature and grace, regime and revelation, polity and church are separate spheres forced to coexist by the sin that alone calls forth rule. It was a coexistence made conspicuous by the victory of Christianity in the Roman Empire. Nevertheless, the world remains decisively divided into a city of God and a city of man. The Christian's worshipping eyes look up to the divine city, even while necessity compels him to drudge with men below. There is absent Thomas's Aristotelianism, which goes farther than does Hooker's in conceiving polity and rule as itself natural. Political rule like church rule cultivates Christian goodness, Thomas said, if not by the sacramentary means peculiar to priests, then by the ruler's enforcement of scriptural law.[21]

19. Munz, *Hooker in the History of Thought*, p. 28.
20. Herbert Deane, *The Political and Social Ideas of St. Augustine* (New York, 1966), pp. 221–28.
21. St. Thomas Aquinas, *On Princely Government*, XV, in *Aquinas: Selected Political Writings*, ed. A. P. d'Entrèves (Oxford, 1954).

Still, Thomas's unity is not Hooker's unity. Thomas's treatment of the relation between priests and rulers, church and polity, is famous for a doubtless intentional obscurity. His thematic treatment occurs in a work enigmatic and unfinished. Yet he clearly moves to restrict church to the clergy and to raise clergy above civil rulers. Does not Thomas yield the spiritual power "a general supervisory function," as Munz puts it, over the temporal power? Furthermore, any inclination to unite church and polity, under either lay or clerical headship, would run smack into the Papacy—head of the Christian empire outside, and yet within, all polities. Thomas defers to the Papacy where present, and this too distinguishes his views from Hooker's.

## Marsilius and Hooker

Precisely the way Hooker defended Elizabeth's Tudor arrangements reminded Munz and others of Marsilius of Padua, the original, spirited, and controversial Latin Averroist.[22] Both thinkers treat the church as the whole body of believers, rule as properly in the whole body (or, for Marsilius, in some part with "greater sway"), and the civil ruler as dominant over the church. Yet a fundamental dissimilarity colors the resemblances and causes decisive rejections by Hooker.

Primarily Marsilius sought to restore sound politics, at least civil peace, by cutting off claims to superiority by Papacy and by clergy in general. No more of the two cities; for practical purposes he subordinates the divine city to the human. Hooker too dwells on the need for one ruler, for order. But the ruler need not, perhaps ought not, be lay. Royal supremacy over the English church is defensible without being best. Hooker defers to Israel as an authoritative precedent, and he praises the theocratic Archbishopric of Mainz. Marsilius, however, insists that Jewish law is no precedent for Christians.[23] He strains every text and gloss to limit clergy to the purely "spiritual" and otherworldly. They are in no way to meddle with "temporals." Civil authority should seize all ecclesiastical property beyond a purely "evangelical poverty" rather strictly construed.

Recall Hooker's opinion that the "chiefest" root of the assault on bishops is an "irreligious profaneness," attacking churchmen's power and wealth "under pretense of enmity unto ambition and pride." "No practice so vile, but pretended

22. See C. W. Previte-Orton, "Marsilius of Padua," *Proceedings of the British Academy* 21 (1935): 137–83, and W. D. J. Cargill Thompson, "The Source of Hooker's Knowledge of Marsilius of Padua," *Journal of Ecclesiastical History* 25 (January 1974): 75–81, and references. Cargill Thompson argues that Hooker borrowed his one express citation of Marsilius and on this ground that scholars have overstated (1) the "historical influence" of Marsilius upon Hooker, and (2) Hooker's firsthand learning. Of this cramped pedantry one may say that as one swallow does not make a spring, neither does one swallow make a spring absent. That Hooker cites Marsilius but once (however that be derived) proves little as to such an accomplished rhetorician. Hooker uses (and misuses) human authority to give authority in the public's eyes to what, apart from Scripture, was authoritative in his eyes, his reasoning. Besides, Hooker might choose not to draw public attention to the Marsilian original, to an insidious attack on Christianity under the guise of an open attack on its temporal power. So my text suggests. In any event, the resemblances noted by previous scholars remain. Those scholars lacked Cargill Thompson's confidence in Hooker's mediocrity of mind, in his commonplace absorption of Marsilian commonplaces.

23. Marsilius of Padua, *Defensor Pacis*, trans. Alan Gewirth, vol. 2 of Gewirth's *Marsilius of Padua, Defender of Peace* (New York, 1956), II.iii.9; II.ix.8, 9.

holiness is made sometime as a cloak to hide it"; then Hooker inveighs against a French king's policy that all "prelates and bishops should be clean excluded from parliaments where the affairs of the kingdom were handled; pretending that a king with good conscience cannot draw pastors, having cure of souls, from so weighty a business, to trouble their heads with consultations of state."[24] The indictment fits best those cast crudely or subtly in the Marsilian mold.

Hooker cites Marsilius by name but once, and then when arguing contrary to the Paduan, that episcopal authority is no new and insignificant invention but existed in the primitive church from apostolic times. Hooker would not have missed what the Catholics had been quick to point out: some connection evidently existed between Luther's doctrines and Marsilius's earlier insistence upon a church of all believers and a purely spiritual Christianity.[25] If this were so, reforming doctrine was more than the unwitting destroyer of a Christianity powerful in the world. Reform was the unwitting bearer of part of a witting destroyer, although it destroyed also the politic subordination of Christianity that was the core of Marsilius's suggestion. As Hooker's immediate enemies among true Christians were "our reformers," so his fundamental enemy among professed Christians seems to have been Marsilius. Under pretense of purifying Christianity, Marsilius took advantage of its otherworldliness and urged the powerful to strip the church of worldly power. Like Hooker's predecessor Thomas Starkey, whose teaching has seemed Marsilian to some scholars, he would not kill the faith (out of concern for its moral and political utility), but would make it utterly dependent.[26]

Hooker struggles against a dependence which puts second things first. He agrees with Marsilius that the "two cities" amount to a political disaster. He accepts part of Marsilius's remedy: rule by the whole body of believers, and thus by one society or community. While Marsilius seeks political rule over the church, however, Hooker, laboring under a royal supremacy, seeks to make powerful the church and thereby to make Christian the polity. He adopts the church of all believers. By his doctrine of consent to government, however, Hooker presupposes a Christian and even Augustinian understanding of man's prepolitical sufficiency, a doctrine not regarded seriously by Marsilius. Hooker also assumes that natural and divine law should limit any ruler, an assumption about which Marsilius is, to say the least, equivocal. Marsilius seems to assume the faithfulness of the legislator; he attempts to reduce to impotence the priests, except as teachers. Hooker attempts the reverse: he would restore the church's potency by hemming in with Christian law the legislator. He intimates need for the help of a true Christian prince; Hooker extols Constantine. Marsilius intimates a low opinion of this the first emperor to exempt priests from civil jurisdiction and to give Christians jurisdiction over lands and property.[27] One must

24. *Laws* VII.xv.7.

25. Alan Gewirth, *Marsilius of Padua and Medieval Political Philosophy*, vol. 1 of *Marsilius of Padua, Defender of Peace* (New York, 1951), p. 303 and references.

26. Leo Strauss, "Marsilius of Padua," in Strauss and Joseph Cropsey, eds., *History of Political Philosophy* (Chicago, 1972), pp. 251–70.

27. Marsilius, *Defender* II.xviii.1; II.xxiii. Cf. *Laws* VIII.v.1.

compare Marsilius's attacks on coercive and economic power with Hooker's strategy to restore church courts and church wealth. Marsilius plans to give fundamental coercive authority over the church itself to the "faithful legislator." The legislator appoints bishops, determines all disputes involving religious persons, and even allows or authorizes excommunication. "A bishop or priest, as such, has no rulership or coercive jurisdiction over any clergyman or layman, even if the latter be a heretic."[28] Hooker's church and polity is fundamentally church, however. In Book VIII as throughout he provides for the laws of *ecclesiastical* polity.

### To Restore a Christian Governance

In "realms like this, where for good and weighty reasons" rule over all has been given to a monarch, Hooker's apology sets forth the sort of reasons that will constitute the duty of a Christian monarch, and the sort of arrangements that will confine him to his duty. These reasons do not include Henry VIII's desires for a new wife and a dynasty through a male heir, or the hunger of king and the rich for the church's wealth, or the jealousy of *politiques* like Cromwell of papal power in particular and ecclesiastical power in general.

Society, like the "whole world," lives by "order," begins Hooker's blander defense, and "this order of things and persons in public societies is the work of polity." By the discretion allowable to any independent multitude England has vested in one civil ruler a power over things ecclesiastical as well as things secular; neither law of God nor necessary argument forbids this. "'No man,' saith our Savior, 'can serve two masters.'" With this curious authority for civil rule, Hooker goes on to illustrate the clashes endemic to conflicting jurisdictions in a manner reminding of Marsilius.[29] He defends the English solution, however, on grounds contrary to Marsilian.

Far from shrinking from coercion, the English church should solicit the sword of royal power; far from devolving sovereignty upon the civil power, the church should guide the monarch by laws of ecclesiastical polity. Hooker's moderation of English kingship amounts, then, to a combination of Aristotle's politic encouragement of rule, of a mixed regime, and of law, with a strict Christian priority of church, of clergy, and of religious law and custom. Against reformers he urges the need for unity and for assistance from the powerful, against old Christian writers he urges the need for some balance or mixing of political powers, and against such an Aristotelian as Sir Thomas Smith he urges the primacy of Christian duty and a Christian clergy.

The civil coercion that often offends modern reformers in principle, Hooker suggests, is nonetheless often sought by them in practice. He points slyly to the "custom which many Christian churches have to fly to the civil magistrate for coercion of those that will not otherwise be reformed," and he draws the lesson. In Christianity as in other religions, ecclesiastical power cannot "do of itself so much as when secular power doth strengthen it; and that," significantly, "not by way of ministry or service, but of predominancy such as

28. Marsilius, *Defender* III.ii.14, 16; II.xxviii.17, 18; II.xxxix, 7.
29. *Laws* VIII.ii.18; VIII.iii.6; VIII.v.2.

the kings of Israel in their time exercised over the Church of God." True, Christ refrained from placing the sword of corporal punishment in the hands of the church of Christ, "as God did place it himself in the hands of the Jewish church." And how does Hooker weigh this concession of a difference between spiritual Christians and more worldly Jews, a difference so dear to Marsilius and the reformers? It seems that Christ denied the temporal sword only because His politic judgment saw it then impolitic! The apostles were to go unarmed into nations "the chiefest governors whereof would be open enemies" for many years.[30] Here and now rulers are friends, however, and temporal coercion is both politic and divine.

Both politic and divine: rule is politic because useful in providing "the order of things and persons in public societies" and thereby in spreading the Word; divine for both of these reasons. "A thing of so great use as government amongst men, and human dominion in government, cannot choose but be originally from (the Son of God)." It follows that kingly dominion as in England is, in its way, divine work. "God doth ratify the works of that sovereign authority, which Kings have received by men." "Unto kings by human right, honor by divine right is due." That the human title to government is human consent is true; that this title is but a kind of ratification of necessary regiment to maintain God's necessary work is also true; both have been discussed. Hooker therefore favors the stricter sorts of government, those more fit to enforce a life dutiful to God's laws (revealed and other), more conducive to "preservation of quietness, unity, order, peace."[31]

This encouragement of an authoritative order is repeatedly paired with another theme in the politic Book VIII, however, one that matches the divine sanction for monarchs with the divine limits and laws supposed to be observed by monarchs. Hooker slights the Old Testament's elevation of tribal patriarchs and kings, and takes special care to criticize some ancient Christian writers who forgot that royalty might become tyrannical or unfriendly. They bestowed in "high and ample" terms "universality of power," being perhaps too conscious of the authority that "God hath towards the world and those things that be in it." Hooker guides his flock away from this analogy of kings to God and toward the moderate teachings of Aristotle, who defines "that most sweet form of kingly government" as "regency willingly sustained and endured, with chiefty of power in the greatest things."[32]

Here Hooker cites a passage from the *Politics* that illumines the sort of limits on English kingship he means to strengthen. Aristotle there considered hereditary kingship according to custom, of the heroic period. Homer is authority for a detail, and this heroic context appears crucial. Such kings were founding kings, outstanding men who drew their tribes or clans or villages into cities and common lands, perhaps by conquest. Their qualities stood out because "in earlier times . . . it was rare to find men who greatly excelled in virtue." Although these heroes brought men out of barbarism into cities and

30. *Laws* VII.iii.4.
31. *Laws* VIII.iii.1; VIII.ii.6.
32. *Laws* VIII.ii.11, 12.

civility, their monarchy to that extent smacked of barbarism, or existed only in the transition from barbarism. Uncanny parallels exist between it and another type that Aristotle mentions: hereditary monarchy according to law among barbarians. Aristotle intimates that only a servility sunk in custom, perhaps Asiatic rather than Greek, could continue to stomach a kingship by custom of merely hereditary right.[33] Such a custom-ridden order differs from the kingship, unmentioned by Hooker, that Aristotle himself intimates as a sort of model at Book III's end: rule by a man of godlike or philosophic political wisdom. We may note that even the term "heroic," used by Aristotle to discriminate ancient Greeks from barbarians, reminds in the Greek original of the customs and myths of Greek religion.

Aristotle notes also that these hereditary kings were distinctly limited in authority, especially as their polities became more civilized. Monarchy becomes more problematic when the monarch is surrounded by equally deserving rivals; it then lasts best by being limited. Yet a monarchy so limited is not much of a monarchy. In an Aristotelian example Hooker expressly follows, Theopompus took away some of the Spartan king's power to enable the kingship to endure. "In a way he did not make it less but greater." Only in permanence, however: a passage unmentioned by Hooker concludes that such a king is really no king; he has lost his chief political offices. The philosopher sums up the remaining duties of general and chief priest as those of "a military commander holding office for life."[34] Further inquiry is dismissed as merely legal (we might say "constitutional"); such a military office can exist under any regime.

Hooker, on the other hand, dwells on moderating monarchy by custom and by law, rather than by other men or classes of men who compete for political rule. From early times men commonly saw "that to live by one man's will became the cause of all men's misery";[35] so seeing, by common consent they instituted laws. While common consent calls for no particular form of rule, it calls for a rule of law.

Hooker takes care to attack such "seedsmen of rebellion" as the authors of the *Vindiciae contra Tyrannos*, who make the voluntary deed of the people the only title to rule. He defends hereditary selection where such is established. Yet his defense of hereditary monarchy only sets the stage for his own limitation of monarchy. "Kings, even inheritors, do hold their right to the power of dominion, with dependency upon the whole entire body politic over which they rule as kings."[36] Established by agreement, kings are subject to the agreement. Even kingdoms founded in conquest may "grow even little by little," Hooker remarks delicately upon a situation like the English, into "the most sweet form" of primacy "in the greatest things, willingly sustained." Small wonder that he cannot choose "but commend highly their wisdom, by whom the foundations of this commonwealth have been laid." Hoary legal maxims are trotted out: "Lex facit regem"—the law makes the king; "Rex nihil potest nisi quo jure potest"—the

---

33. *Pol.*, 1285ª 20–23, 1286ᵇ 7–10.
34. *Pol.* 1285ᵇ 34–1286ª 7, 1285ª 30–34, 1285ᵇ 20–24.
35. *Laws* I.x.5, 14.
36. *Laws* VIII.ii.9.

king can do nothing except what he can do by law. The citations are to Henry de Bracton's thirteenth-century treatise on English law and custom. Are the lawyers the true founders of what is great in England? Houk calls Hooker's Book VIII a product of the law schools of the time, and Sheldon Wolin has suggested the influence of Sir John Fortescue. Yet Hooker nowhere cites or calls attention to Fortescue or to Sir Thomas Smith, then the two best known legal writers on English kingship. Perhaps Hooker rightly suspected their orthodoxy and pointed back to more Christian legal writers. In any event, Book VIII is fundamentally the product of Hooker's own opinions about what is best. "The best established dominion is where the law doth rule the king, the true effect whereof particularly is found as well in ecclesiastical as in civil affairs."[37]

Part of Hooker's strategy, then, melds English royal supremacy with the true duty of a Christian king. "All power is given unto edification, none to the overthrow and destruction of the Church." No doubt English Christians like all Christians should obey the powers above them, but the duty of subjects is matched by that of rulers. "As we by the law of God stand bound meekly to acknowledge them for God's lieutenants, and to confess their power his, so they by the same law are both authorized and required to use that power as far as it may be in any sort available to his honour." Hooker's very terms make his point. The king's power of "supreme dominion" affords "spiritual jurisdiction" as to "externals" alone; he is a principal instrument for "the Church's outward government."[38] All these words are limited by their meaning in Hooker's doctrine of the church.

This subordination of monarchy to the laws of God is accompanied by a certain subordination to the men of God. I state briefly here the argument to follow. Hooker's policy considerably subjects the monarchy to human law, to Parliament as to law in general, to Parliament and Convocation of the Clergy as to ecclesiastical law in particular and to church courts as to judicial matters involving the church. Does Christian kingship in England require a considerable moderating of Elizabeth's English kingship by Christian customs and by the clerical estate? In reading Book VIII one must do what few do, read and recall Book VII. Hooker does not remind us in Book VIII of Book VII's intimation that the clergy is the principal estate, and should be restored to wealth (one-third of the country's lands, perhaps) and power (primacy among the nobles) in proportion to its principality. Unlike Laud, he at least appears to seek alliance with nobles, gentry, parliamentarians, and lawyers. The judicious Hooker insists with the king upon his hereditary and supreme royal dominion, with lawyer's maxims upon the definition of that dominion according to law, and with lawyers, nobles, gentry, and admirers of ancient republicanism upon the rule of law, the moderating influence of the various estates in Parliament, and the king as only part of Parliament. In the course of all this, however, Hooker reinterprets in turn kingship and dominion, law and courts, and Parliament and estates,

---

37. *Laws* VIII.ii.7. As to Smith, see above, p. 144 and below, pp. 170–71. As to Fortescue, see below, pp. 168–69, and Mary Pollingue, "An Interpretation of Fortescue's *de Laudibus Legum Angliae*," *Interpretation* 6 (1976): 11–47.

38. *Laws* VIII.iv.9; VIII.ii.6.

in order that all defer to Christian law, courts, Convocation, and clergy. That is the gist of Hooker's policy for England, and of Book VIII as it remains to us.

## English Law and Politics:
## The Problem of Revising the Supreme Power

Book VIII seems a rather specialized and legal inquiry as to English institutions, as to the divisions of ecclesiastical authority between king, clergy, Parliament, and courts. Yet it also attempts a kind of revolution in the English regime, a reestablishment of the political primacy of the church within its religious sphere, and thereby of religion within the political sphere. The book appears legal because the church does not claim to rule in its own name. The king is admitted to be supreme over the church, and Hooker treats only of the laws and institutions limiting his supremacy. Yet the laws in question are to determine the shape of his rule in the crucial respect. "Whether it be therefore the nature of courts, or the form of pleas, or the kind of governors, or the order of proceedings in whatsoever spiritual businesses; for the received laws and liberties of the Church the king hath supreme authority and power, but against them, none."[39] The king is said to rule, and yet through him the church rules. The king himself is eventually said to only "consent" or "authorize"; as to ecclesiastical matters, he has but a "negative voice." C. S. Lewis had the essentials right years ago: "The Supreme Head of the Church is, in fact, the bottle-neck through which the decision of the local church-nation becomes law."[40]

*Contra* the reformers, Hooker does defend the English king's authority to call ecclesiastical convocations, make ecclesiastical laws, judge ecclesiastical disputes, and appoint bishops. He insists, with the arguments for Christian order in a Christian commonwealth that we have just discussed, that without the king's stamp no counsel (however wise) is law, is more than counsel. Yet his is not understood to be a shaping stamp: the king's is a stamp of approval, not a mold. As to laws, we are reminded that those of nature and God are crucial; they suffice for the everlasting bliss proper to each man. They indicate even what is of greatest necessity for the "outward politic body of the Church"; the visible church prescribes only the remaining deeds and opinions "fit or convenient . . . for public unity's sake." Even those that remain for human making are not chiefly the king's to make. They are the whole society's, and decisively Parliament's and Convocation's. The claim is astonishing, however hedged about subsequently, and it alone (as we will argue) would make this last book repugnant to Elizabeth and her successors. "The parliament of England together with the convocation annexed thereunto, is that whereupon the very essence of all government within this kingdom doth depend." True, Parliament includes the king, and yet now as but part. In practice his is to be a subordinate part, at least in the shaping of law. Laws should be devised by the wise, and thus "unto ecclesiastical persons the care of devising ecclesiastical laws should be committed, even as the care of civil unto them which are in those affairs most skilful." In effect Hooker subordinates king to Parliament and Convocation, and as to

39. *Laws* VIII.ii.17, 6.
40. C. S. Lewis, *English Literature in the Sixteenth Century Excluding Drama* (Oxford, 1959), p. 458.

ecclesiastical matters Parliament to Convocation or at least to powerful church-men like the archbishops and bishops. Parliament's role is characterized as "assent," that "general consent of all" that makes of wisdom law, in the same way in which the king's power of dominion is called that "which establisheth and maketh" laws. Hooker admits only that the king's supremacy in making laws "resteth principally in the strength of a negative voice."[41] So far does he try to raise Parliament, and especially the shaping initiative of Convocation and clergy.

A similar treatment is given the appointment of bishops, discussed in chapter 10, and especially the king's "supereminent authority in commanding, and in judging of causes ecclesiastical." No one supposes, Hooker writes as to judging, that the king might "in person" prescribe services, or dictate "how the word shall be taught, how sacraments administered," or sit in ecclesiastical jurisdiction like a bishop. English monarchy is restrained by the ancient order of law prescribing the Christian order of faith and ceremony. In effect, then, the old faith, the old hierarchy, and the old ecclesiastical jurisdiction is to govern—"what courts there shall be, and what causes shall belong to each court, and what judges shall determine of every cause, and what order in all judgments shall be kept; of these things the laws have sufficiently disposed." Recall the Elizabethan struggles between ecclesiastical and civil jurisdictions, church courts and those of common law and prerogative, and Hooker's bold conclusion: "boldly and lawfully we may refuse to answer before any civil judge in a matter which is not civil."[42]

Still, some kingly supervision of the judgments of ecclesiastical and civil courts is needed, else kings cannot "do as virtuous kings have done." In his circumlocutory way, Hooker slyly defends the sort of primacy in monarchs that will restore the decisive primacy of the church. He recurs to another example from Israel, in particular to an ancient king of Israel who restored priestly wealth. Joas enforced upon his people a church tax and in particular compelled the priestly tribe of Levites to collect taxes owed them. Should a truly Christian king appear in England, it seems, he should govern the common law courts and be the crucial instrument for that restoration of episcopal wealth and power Book VII slyly suggests. Let a future king such as Charles I take note, perhaps as prompted by a knowing bishop such as Laud.

Besides, the ecclesiastical courts also need a supreme governor of judgments. To reformers Hooker gives his customary rebuttal: no law of God or of reason prohibits such authority. More space is given to his favorite theme: the withholding of "the king's person from being a doer of that which his power must notwithstanding give force unto." Royal judgments should defer to received laws, and the task of judgment should be relegated to churchmen. "Such persons must be authorized judges in each kind, as common reason may presume to be most fit; which cannot of kings and princes ordinarily be presumed in causes merely ecclesiastical." In matters civil this is a favorite theme of the republican lawyers, such as Fortescue, Smith, and eventually Blackstone.

41. *Laws* VIII.vi.11, 1, 5, 6, 10, 12.
42. *Laws* VIII.viii.9, 3, 1.

Hooker guards less against political tyranny, however, than against radical variations in the faith when "the highest," possibly "favouring Heresy," incline to judge by themselves. One cannot but think of the swerves made by Henry VIII, Edward VI, and Mary, if not by Elizabeth herself. Our author dwells not on monarchs so near. We are fed instead a tale of old Christian emperors who "from time to time did what themselves thought most reasonable in those affairs; by this means it cometh to pass that they in their practive vary, and are not uniform." Hooker's conclusion is nonetheless very general and very bold. The kind of sentence where some "great person" hears these matters to and fro debated, and decides himself as to the truth, "bindeth no side to stand thereunto; it is a sentence of private persuasion, and not of solemn jurisdiction, albeit a king or an emperor pronounce it."[43]

### Hooker's *Laws* and Elizabeth's Monarchy

Hooker's defense of royal supremacy considerably reduces and reshapes the supremacy actually exercised by Tudor royalty and not least by Elizabeth. Despite his insistence upon a strict ordering by degree from monarch on down, he slights Elizabeth's domination of Parliament, clergy, and Convocation, and especially her rule by royal prerogative over the church. Hooker is distinctive in insisting on the decisive authority in public affairs of settled ecclesiastical law and custom and on the decisive authority in ecclesiastical affairs of ecclesiastical men. We conclude by discussing the controversial relation of his thought to Elizabethan opinions and practice.

The most influential recent scholars reject most emphatically the thesis of Hooker's political distinctiveness. They assert that his theory of the English constitution corresponds with "the traditional medieval and Tudor view," as Cargill Thompson puts it, or, differently phrased, with "the traditional constitutional doctrines of the English common law."[44] Historians of the Tudor monarchy such as G. R. Elton agree; under the Tudors "a doctrine of parliamentary sovereignty—of an ultimate legislative supremacy vested in King-in-Parliament—was half-grasped and wholly practiced" from the 1530s on. Hooker seems hardly novel in circumscribing monarchical prerogative by law, Parliament, and fundamental law. Elton does chide Hooker for somehow missing "the fact that the 'essence of government' in Tudor England was quite independent of the Convocations of the archepiscopal provinces."[45] Is this Hooker's only novelty, however, and but a scholar's mistake, or is it the crucial sign of a deeper originality, perhaps politically fundamental in the Elizabethan context?

Cargill Thompson and Elton share a common peculiarity: to understand the actual Tudor constitution they rely considerably on legal-political writers. Cargill Thompson takes his bearings from Hooker's immersion in "contemporary legal and constitutional ideas." Elton quotes Sir Thomas Smith's characterization of Parliament, "the most high and absolute power in the realm," as evidence of the common understanding of Tudor arrangements, of the "entirely

43. *Laws* VIII.viii.8, 7.
44. Thompson, "The Philosopher of the Politic Society," pp. 46–47.
45. G. R. Elton, *The Tudor Constitution* (Cambridge, Eng., 1968), p. 14, 235n.

new reputation" of Parliament at the beginning of Elizabeth's reign.[46] Writers such as Smith and John Hooker, however, may reflect only one species of opinion, that of lawyers and courts and parliamentarians, as opposed to queen and court and courtiers. They may even reflect their own reflections, their own reformulations of Tudor arrangements to limit the Tudors. If so, Richard Hooker might be similar to these thinkers—and yet quite different from Elizabethan practice, or he might be different from, or similar to, both. I shall argue that he builds upon his similarities to these Tudor thinkers and to Tudor practice and yet differs fundamentally from both.

According to Franklin Le Van Baumer, the very formulation "king-in-parliament" first came to prominence in the writings of a well-known lawyer-publicist under Henry VIII, Christopher St. Germain. Wherever St. Germain "speaks of legislation, he invariably refers to the 'king-in-parliament,' not to the king alone." St. Germaine says roundly more than once that "there is no statute made in this realm but by the assent of the lords spiritual and temporal, and of all the commoners, that is to say, by the knights of the shire, citizens and burgesses, that be chosen by assent of the commons which in the parliament represent that estate of the whole commons." Although these remarks accord somewhat with those of other writers of the reign, they are opposed by remarks of royal servants such as Cromwell and Wolsey. They differed from the king's practice as well. While on the continent "political theory was reflecting practical politics" more faithfully, Baumer says, in England "political theory was slow to reflect the growth of monarchical power." This despite "the sometimes arbitrary rule of ministers like Wolsey and Cromwell, the enhancement of the king's prerogative in consequence of the Reformation, and the increasing power of the royal courts of equity."[47]

Baumer interprets remarks by St. Germain and others as in the tradition of English legal-political thought inaugurated by Sir John Fortescue, especially in his *De Laudibus Legum Angliae* (c. 1465). Fortescue had praised English laws before a young prince, a future king, and had called England a *dominium politicum et regale*, a reign political and royal, but not merely royal. Some scholars thought this to signify Fortescue's quiet recommendation of a republic—not a modern popular and representative government, to be sure, but something after the Aristotelian notion of a mixed regime or mixed monarchy. Most recent scholars reject this view, however. They follow an argument like McIlwain's in his *Constitutionalism: Ancient and Modern*. *Politicum* means not political but constitutional. It signifies a negative check by fundamental law which protects the subject's rights, instead of an "organ of government responsible to the people and independent of the king." McIlwain grants that republicanism ultimately became a part of the English constitution—but only 150 years after Fortescue's works. He supposes that Fortescue in the late fifteenth century could not have so conceived: "for Sir John Fortescue, as for Bracton, there was and

46. Elton, *Tudor Constitution*, p. 230; Thompson, "Philosopher of the Politic Society," p. 46.

47. Franklin Le Van Baumer, *The Early Tudor Theory of Kingship* (New Haven, 1940), pp. 150–52, 165.

there could be no legitimate government in England except the king's government."[48]

McIlwain's whole study supposes a "historical evolution of constitutionalism." The somewhat apolitical notions of governmental powers and private rights, characteristic of liberal constitutionalism, are read back hundreds of years into earlier thinkers. Theirs appears as but an unperfected and undeveloped stage of constitutional thought, and they as but limited cogs in the process of development. This is doubtful in general, as I trust my work demonstrates. Another scholar, Donald Hanson, has suggested that McIlwain's "legalistic prism" blurs essential differences in medieval politics; "the law was neither the immemorial custom of the folk nor was it fundamental. Rather to the extent it was common law it was primarily the king's law." By supposing a developing law one misses "those acts of conflict and cooperation we call politics."[49] McIlwain's thesis seems particularly doubtful in the case of Fortescue. After all, *De Laudibus* is a dialogue of praise, reminding more of what Aristotle called *epeidectic* rhetoric than of a law text. The interlocutor, a chancellor, suggests to the prince whom he is tutoring that the laws of England are to be changed in Parliament. Not the king's household but the Inns of Court, he adds, are the academy of the realm for training and cultivating the nobles and gentry of the realm. These seem important and political balances to kingly power. Also, the English way of appointing sheriffs, and other appointments and arrangements, are said to reflect a judicious balancing or checking of king by the various estates. The liberty and prosperity of yeomen, a lesser landed class somewhat equivalent to Aristotle's essentially democratic middle class, is especially praised for a political and royal regime like England (as distinguished from the simply regal France). The best recent study of *De Laudibus Legum Angliae* suggests that a tension between chancellor and prince, English law and monarchy, balanced arrangements and kingly ambition, pervades the work in form and substance. Fortescue seems himself a kind of lawgiver. He "may be inculcating in the prince and in others a certain understanding of the English regime, rather than describing the regime as it functioned at the time."[50]

Suppose it now has been shown that Fortescue and St. Germain are not merely legal thinkers and not merely reflecting their times. Then the similarity to their thought of Hooker's thought may signify that he too participates in a politic conspiracy, a rather republican conspiracy of the thoughtful against the dangerous ambitions and ideas of unchecked monarchs. The relation of Hooker's thoughts to the practices of Elizabeth we shall take up shortly. First

---

48. Charles Howard McIlwain, *Constitutionalism: Ancient and Modern* (Ithaca, 1961), pp. 87–91.

49. Donald Hanson, *From Kingdom to Commonwealth* (Cambridge, Mass., 1970), pp. 35, 37.

50. Pollingue, "An Interpretation of Fortescue's *De Laudibus Legum Angliae*," p. 30. See Sir John Fortescue, *De Laudibus Legum Angliae*, ed. and trans. S. B. Chrimes (Cambridge, 1949), chs. 24, 29, 33–37, 9, 18; cf. 49 with 45. John Hooker exaggerates the Commons's freedom to choose their speaker, to speak, and to conduct their business (*The Order and Usage of the Keeping of a Parliament in England*, ed. Vernon F. Snow [New Haven and London, 1977], pp. 169 n. 52, 170 n. 68, 179 n. 95, 181 n. 99, 186).

we explore the similarities alleged between Hooker and specifically Elizabethan lawyer-statesmen, in particular Sir Thomas Smith, the most prominent Elizabethan expounder of English politics and law. We have previously noted a contrast: Hooker tries to restore the spiritual estate to lordly political power; Smith implicitly denies that clergy should exercise political sway in the English commonwealth.

Cargill Thompson noted a striking resemblance between some of Smith's language and Hooker's, and it is possible that Hooker in Book VIII intended to build upon Smith's views, which were coming into prominence during the 1590s. Both writers planned the limitation and moderation of the monarchy by law, but they differ as to the kind of limits and the kind of polity. Hooker insists upon the authority of immemorial custom and above all the customs or, as he calls them, "laws" of an ancient English church. While praising philosophy Smith himself is reticent as to Christianity; he was famous as a "Grecian" and statesman, although a priest, and has been called "religiously neutral." He does remark more than once to the effect that "all changeth continually." Also, his famous paean to Parliament's "high and absolute power" includes baldly the power to "establish forms of Religion." Like Fortescue, he celebrates the English common law, solicitous of the subject's liberty, over the continental civil law drawn from imperial Rome. Smith tells us that in England civil law practice exists in the church and its courts, which he implicitly deprecates as also from Rome and hence "externe and forraigne." He dwells on the dreadful writ of Praemunire, originally used against papal privileges, as means of wresting disputed matters from the church courts; he finally attributes the freedom of church courts from such writs merely to the church's authorization by "royall majesty."[51] In short, Smith argues that the authority of the church violates fundamental English laws and customs, and its violations depend wholly on the royal prerogative; Hooker argues that the prerogative is bound and limited by the old laws and customs of England establishing the authority of the church. Perhaps Hooker gives a skillful Christian twist to Smith's *politique* doctrines, by elevating the clergy instead of the lower gentry and yeomanry, courts ecclesiastical instead of civil, and Convocation as well as Parliament.

It may be, to speculate a bit, that Hooker appreciated the growing power of the gentry and middle classes in county and borough. Smith like Fortescue seemed to think these the steadying core of a republic, or at least the power to help moderate an autocratic monarch and a narrow oligarchy. Hooker could not but think them a power in the localities often overshadowing the crown and its ecclesiastical prerogative, a power which the church might ignore or inflame only at the peril that finally engulfed Laud. Besides, a drastic separation from the other estates would increase the church's dependence upon the monarchy— and hence upon the faith, or lack of faith, of the monarch. True, these estates as represented in Parliament tended to be reformers from 1559, and then anti-episcopal from the reformers' failure of 1563 in the lower house of Convocation. Still, after the early years theirs was predominantly a moderate presbyterianism.

51. Sir Thomas Smith, *De Republica Anglorum* (London, 1583, repr. 1970), pp. 116–18, 22, 35.

One might speculate that Hooker sought in political practice what he sought by his book in religious principle—to win over the moderate Presbyterians, especially the pastors, to what he takes care to call a Christian Commonwealth. This would counter the religiously neutral circles of lawyers, gentry, and courtiers, who were gaining in Parliamentary power, no doubt to the pleasure of writer-statesmen such as Sir Thomas Smith. A mild bill requiring weekly church attendance or at least religious observance at home, backed by bishops and reformers alike, could not obtain passage in Elizabeth's last Parliament. Claire Cross has commented on the limited success of Elizabeth's policy of "ruling the church independently through her ecclesiastics alone," without "the co-operation of the laity."[52]

Elizabethan law and politics, like Elizabethan legal and political writings, afford opportunities for scholarly controversy that have not been neglected. Macaulay once remarked that party strife has poisoned every source of information as to early English history, especially sources concerning the "limits of prerogative and liberty."[53] Precisely if one questions the "evolving constitution" school of historical research, which disparages older scholarship as less advanced, unhistorical, or unscientific, one finds oneself in a historical no-man's-land among guns such as Hume's (a monarchy "absolute"), Hinton's (a "decline of parliamentary government"), Elton's ("a doctrine of parliamentary sovereignty—of an ultimate legislative supremacy vested in king-in-parliament—was half-grasped and wholly practiced"), or Neale's (the Commons became "a political force with which the Crown and government had to reckon").[54] Without pretending to an adequate account, one can say nevertheless that Hooker slights somewhat Elizabeth's domination of Parliament, clergy, and Convocation, as I have suggested, and above all her rule by prerogative over the church.

A. F. Pollard remarked that *parliament* in its original meaning involved parleying, and parliament first appears as the parleying between king and the other powers of pre-Tudor England, the great feudal nobles. According to Pollard, the first recorded usage of the term dates from the reign of Henry III and refers to the *parleamentum de Runemed* between John and his Barons. First was the king (if only from William's conquest), then the king's council or *curia regis*, and finally a crown in council in Parliament, as Pollard puts it. This High Court of Parliament met sporadically in accord with the king's need for taxes, and generally met unwillingly. While admitting petitions by commoners, its meeting involved fundamentally advice and counsel from the spiritual and temporal barons. Right up until the sixteenth century and Henry VIII, Parliament consisted of this occasional meeting with barons as the Councillors and powers,

52. Cross, *Royal Supremacy*, p. 85; Sir John Neale, *Elizabeth I and Her Parliaments: 1584–1601* (New York, 1958), pp. 394–406.

53. Thomas Babington Macaulay, *History of England* (New York, n.d.) I, 34, 35.

54. David Hume, *The History of England from the Invasion of Julius Caesar to the Abdication of James the Second* (Boston, 1850) IV, appendix 3, 344–62; R. W. K. Hinton, "The Decline of Parliamentary Government under Elizabeth I and the Early Stuarts," *Cambridge Historical Journal* 103 (1957): 116–32; Elton, *Tudor Constitution*, p. 14; Neale, *Elizabeth I and Her Parliaments: 1559–1581*, p. 16.

and with commons hardly more than suppliants giving consent in a merely formal manner. The power of the magnates was drastically reduced, however, by Henry VII and Henry VIII, who reaped the wealth and power taken from lay rivals and from a church brought to submission. With nobles and bishops reduced, and middling gentry not yet risen, "the absorption of feudal liberties by the crown gave rise to a monstrous growth in the liberties of kings" during the Tudor era.[55]

Pollard's diagnosis was given earlier if in slightly different form by Hume, and confirmed in some parts by Stone's recent and comprehensive *Crisis of the Aristocracy, 1558–1641*. Henry VIII's supremacy over the church not only reduced one rival but yielded wealth to sway the other. The predominance that enabled the sovereign to encroach on the nobles took more direct forms as well, especially as guided by the dissembling Elizabeth. Stone details Elizabeth's manipulation of debts and pensions and of the unrequited burdens of honors, court, and office. He also shows her parsimonious unwillingness to relieve difficulties provoked by the aristocracy's profligacy and her policies. Two-thirds of the total peerage were in serious financial difficulties during the last fifteen years of Elizabeth's reign, and this when the country at large was rapidly increasing in wealth. By 1603 the property of the peers of 1558 had fallen in absolute value by a full quarter. Even after a massive comeback of the aristocracy under the sympathetic, weak, and profligate James I, the House of Commons in 1628 could buy the Lords three times over; the Commons had come to be *the* House and *the* power rivaling the monarchy. Even the number of peers fell during Elizabeth's reign, thanks to her stinginess in replacing lines extinct, lines attainted, and so on. No duke existed after the Catholic Norfolk was attainted in 1572. Furthermore, the peers' old military powers and functions became somewhat subordinate to the crown. Their authority over dependents was eroded by attendance at a court far from their estates, by a shift from service to economic rents, by Tudor laws discouraging maintenance of armed bodyguards and liveried retainers, by new religious doctrines of obedience, and, finally, by replacement of military hardness in many peers with an indulgence in pleasure and luxury or at least with a courtier's dependence and extravagance. "Haughty and independent magnates" had become begging "mendicants."[56] If these words applied to the nobility could be more accurately applied to the bishops, their rough suitability to both indicates the queen's preeminence over the chiefest of the old estates.

Hume attends less to monarchic policy and more to the nobles' "change of manners" as cause of the commoners' new authority, on which he and more recent historians dwell. Luxury dissipated huge estates, and gave subsistence to "mechanics and merchants, who lived in an independent manner on the fruits of their own industry." Yet the new forces did not challenge Elizabeth's authority; far from it.

55. A. F. Pollard, *The Evolution of Parliament* (London, 1926), pp. 12, 261, 262–65, 431.
56. Lawrence Stone, *The Crisis of the Aristocracy, 1558–1641* (Oxford, 1965), pp. 227, 159, 123–26 *passim*.

By all these means the cities increased; the middle rank of men began to be rich and powerful; the prince, who in effect was the same with the law, was implicitly obeyed: and though the farther progress of the same causes begat a new plan of liberty, founded on the privileges of the commons, yet in the interval between the fall of the nobles and the rise of this order, the sovereign took advantage of the present situation, and assumed an authority almost absolute.

For awakening these middle ranks from customary or religious passivity, Hume gives credit to the Puritans, but unlike many historians since Hegel, he does not identify the liberty achieved with that at which the reformers aimed. While acknowledging, then, "the faint dawn of the spirit of liberty among the English" during Elizabeth's reign, Hume draws attention principally to "the jealousy with which that spirit was repressed by the sovereign, the imperious conduct which was maintained in opposition to it, and the ease with which it was subdued by this arbitrary princess."[57]

Neale's *Elizabeth I and her Parliaments* questions somewhat this judgment, because of the courage and independence of some members and the tact as well as the commands of the queen. One should note also the implicit limits on Elizabeth, especially her warlike people confronting a monarch without special mercenaries. Neale grants, however, that the Elizabethan government was fundamentally "personal monarchy." By custom and rumor, punishment and reward, all backed by her power and that of her Council, the queen dominated the two houses until her last years. She summoned them more rarely than any monarch since Henry VIII. Elton estimates that there were ten parliaments, thirteen sessions, less than one hundred forty weeks of parliament, during her whole forty-five years as queen; the mere numerical average of three weeks of parliament per year was the lowest since Henry VIII averaged about two. And despite Sir Thomas Smith's bald assertion that to Parliament belongs "the most high and absolute power in the realm of England," one writer, Sir John Seeley, remarked that "in Queen Elizabeth's reign it would not have been natural . . . in describing the government of England to mention Parliament at all. Not exactly that Parliament was subservient, but, that, in general Parliament was not there." Elizabeth herself used the expression "this parliament" and "parlia-

57. Hume, *History* IV, 133, 141, 374; Macaulay, *History of England* I, 35–39. Hume so judged despite his recognition of the queen's tactical retreat as to monopolies. In appraising his judgments of Elizabeth, one must consider his intention. He sought to wean his own generation, especially Whigs contrasting her reign with the Stuarts, from a politically dangerous admiration for her and for Britain's "ancient constitution." He allows finally that her power "was almost unavoidable" (no doubt because of a still-potent nobility, and religious division and fanaticism). Clearly Hume admires the "singular talents for government" that made Elizabeth perhaps as admirable a monarch as ever ruled. While suggesting that more indulgence of her people, less imperiousness, would have been requisite for a perfect character, he says that her vigor, constancy, penetration, vigilance, address—her energy and prudence, in short—"appear not to have been surpassed by any person that ever filled a throne" (*History* IV, 243).

As to the dangers of precisely a "god-like" English monarch for the popular jealousy and balanced arrangements required by the system of liberty, see Locke, *Two Treatises of Government*, ed. Peter Laslett (Cambridge, Eng., 1964) II, 94, 110, 161, 165, 166 esp., 170.

ments," a usage said by Edward P. Cheyney to have been common. There was not a permanent institution or governing power, Parliament; occasionally a special assembly, a parliament, was summoned by her. "The permanent continuous government was the Queen, her privy councillors, judges, and other officials." The most independent of all speeches made in Elizabeth's parliaments, after all, protested control over the Commons' proceedings, especially its proceedings as to religion, by "rumours and messages" concerning the queen's pleasure. For this affrontery Peter Wentworth was stopped by the House itself—and consigned to the Tower.[58]

The general story of Elizabethan Parliaments, then, is one of submission to the queen and her policies, especially in matters of religion, interrupted by sporadic and fearful endeavors to resist and even to seize the initiative for reform. True, the Commons gradually asserted control over some aspects of procedure and of regulation of members, and with the Armada's defeat the Commons's ambitions were less restrained by their fears. Still, these presaged the future more than they governed the masterful and dissembling queen. The procedural steps were even begun under the tender guidance of Henry VIII and for his own use. "He wove parliament like a garment round his royal carcase for protection" (Pollard says), relying chiefly on the Commons to counter the bitter antagonism of foreign critics and the lords, especially the abbots and bishops. Under Edward VI and the foolish Mary Tudor, the reforming bent of the House, together with its high proportion of independent landed gentry, led away from suppliancy into sturdy opposition. Only at the inception of Elizabeth's reign, however, when she was weakest and most in need of Commons and reformers against Catholic bishops who were also peers, did the Commons compel any marked variation in Elizabeth's *via media*.

It seems that Elizabeth had planned for her first parliament of 1559 a very gradual reformation of the church. She would take back the supremacy and revenues that Mary had given the pope. But she would delay any act of uniformity, thinking perhaps to restore pretty much the old doctrines of Henry VIII's unreformed creed. Her caution did not avail. Neale has exhibited "an organized movement operating through the House of Commons, the object of which was to force upon Elizabeth and her government a complete Protestant programme, at least as radical as that achieved by the close of Edward VI's reign."[59] To obtain the supremacy she wished and the divines she needed, and to ward off various initiatives as to canon law and Christian doctrine, the queen was forced to bow. She managed to get her useful act allowing exchange of crown holdings for episcopal lands. She had to accept, however, an Act of Uniformity that involved a new prayer book. This book went much farther toward the reformed Edwardian prayer books than the queen would have liked, it seems, even if her hand can be seen in its blurring of Protestant with Catholic doctrine. Evidently what some call her *via media* was a compromise between crown and Commons

58. Neale, *Elizabeth I and Her Parliaments: 1559–1581*, pp. 318–32; Elton, *Tudor Constitution*, p. 228; Seeley and Cheyney, as quoted by McIlwain, *Constitutionalism: Ancient and Modern*, p. 107.

59. Neale, *Elizabeth I and Her Parliaments: 1559–1581*, p. 64.

as well as between the faiths. This, however, was the last such political compromise relating to religion that occurred during Elizabeth's reign. She might bestow graciously in response to petition, even when the hand that bestowed seemed occasionally to have been forced, but Parliament in general and the Commons in particular remained decisively subordinate to the queen's own initiatives on religious matters.

Elizabeth had her own modes of legislating, apart from the two houses. In his remarks on the monarch's negative voice, Hooker may allude to the queen's negativing of acts passed by Lords and Commons. This power she used frequently, often merely to remind Commons of its place. Other powers Hooker does not allude to. She could dispense an individual from the effect of a law. And if Sir Thomas Smith defines this as merely an equitable relief from literal interpretation of a law, the Tudors did not. Elizabeth extended it occasionally "in the interests of the Crown" to suspend enforcement of laws.[60] The monarch could also add provisos or amendments that retained legal force despite their failure to receive the assent of Lords and Commons, although this Elizabeth used sparingly, perhaps once.[61] Above all, Elizabeth had her own legislative or quasi-legislative power by virtue of proclamations. These were limited by common law in bearing on person and property, and by existing statute as to other matters. They could, however, create offences with penalties (although not felonies or treasons), and they extended into matters of religion, administration, society, and economics (the famous monopolies). Elton treats these prerogative proclamations as obviously needful for efficiency, while Hume takes pains to condemn them as an absolute "legislative power" dangerous to liberty.[62] Although unenforceable as common law, such proclamations were enforced in the prerogative court of Star Chamber. Through these Proclamations of the Queen in Council, and by her episcopal hierarchy and the High Commission established by proclamation in accord with the Act of Supremacy of 1559, the queen actually exercised her authority over the church. Indeed, she insisted that religion above all must fall solely within her monarchical prerogative.

To understand the famous Elizabethan prerogative, which Hooker barely mentions, one must realize the extensive power that Elizabeth deployed. The queen acted with and by her Privy Council, true. After the Tudors' reduction of nobles and church, however, the crucial members of the Council were counsellors whose wealth and power were often dependent on the queen or perhaps bestowed by the queen. The Tudors had fattened upon their victims' losses, and sale of the spoils could assure a present independence even if it mortgaged the future. While Elizabeth could not quite live off her own, she managed by rigid economy, a cautious foreign policy, and revenue measures of varying subtlety and equity, to come closer than most of the Tudors. Parliament was in session only when summoned, and was summoned only to obtain its assent to taxes. She took advantage of her fiscal prudence to summon only rarely. In the years between parliaments and sessions of any one parliament, she was not exactly at

60. Elton, *Tudor Constitution*, p. 21.
61. Pollard, *Evolution of Parliament*, p. 274; cf. Elton, *Tudor Constitution*, pp. 20–21.
62. Hume, *History* IV, 353–54; Elton, *Tudor Constitution*, pp. 20–24, 170–71.

a loss. She appointed all the chief and highest offices or magistracies, spiritual and temporal. Her Council, sitting as Star Chamber, formed with Chancery one of the two prerogative courts, and was in fact a kind of super-court disciplining especially the old rivals, a still fractious nobility and a church in ferment and decay. She and her Council ruled over matters of war and peace, martial law, feudal privileges like the lucrative mastership of wards, and generally over all domestic affairs from religion to trade and justice. All subjects lived in fear of the queen and her Council. It or its Star Chamber could imprison those who incurred displeasure, be they nobles, ecclesiastics, or members of Parliament. The queen sequestered or imprisoned seven members of the Commons during the one sitting of 1593, all for venturing into the subject of religion that she hugged to herself.[63] One understands how Elizabeth could insist with success that religion especially was to be governed by her prerogative alone, and with more insistence and more success as her reign strengthened its hold.

Elton acknowledges that "'prerogative' was the great Tudor word, stressed in particular by Henry VII and by Elizabeth." Prerogative comprised "those rights enjoyed by the king which acknowledged his superior position and enabled him to discharge the task of governing"; it was the monarch's sphere for ruling by his own will and motion. Elton notes this without explicating it; he comments that in any event lawyers like Staundford and Sir Thomas Smith insist that "these privileges could be defined—were, in fact, defined by the common law of England."[64] Whether the subordination of prerogative to law was itself law or merely the wish of lawyers is a question, however. Whatever be the case with Staundford, Smith is like the great Fortescue in so interpreting the law as to moderate the kingship. He points artfully away from feudal arrangements toward an Aristotelian mixed regime so far as English conditions allow, calling into greater prominence Parliament, common law, courts, and yeomen.[65] Would Elizabeth admit such subordination? She consistently refrained from any endeavor to define her prerogative—that is, to set limits upon it—or even to explain how disputed matters like the succession or church governance fell unequivocally within it. Most historians do not interpret her reticence as mere distaste for bandying words. Certainly the queen's counsellors claimed for her a prerogative unlimited by law, as Hume shows, and in many instances the deeds of the queen and her favorites violated common law and intimidated courts and judges. Hallam insists that Hume drew his evidence from one party only. Unlike Elton he grants nonetheless that the cabinet of Elizabeth insisted on a "high prerogative," which he phrases thus: "Besides the common prerogatives of the English crown, which were admitted to have legal bounds, there was a kind of paramount sovereignty, which they denominated her absolute power."[66]

63. Neale, *Elizabeth I and Her Parliaments: 1584–1601*, p. 278.

64. Elton, *Tudor Constitution*, p. 17.

65. Smith, *De Republica Anglorum*, pp. 23–32, 36–41. On the efforts by earlier writers to subject prerogative to law, see Baumer, *The Early Tudor Theory of Kingship*, pp. 184–85.

66. Henry Hallam, *The Constitutional History of England* (London, 1863) I, 283, 263. Cf. R. G. Usher's opinion: the lawyers' claim that prerogative had to be authorized by law and interpreted by lawyers was met (on grounds more solid historically) by "civilians and ecclesiastics"

As to ecclesiastical matters especially, Elizabeth "would not tolerate the invasion by Parliament of her royal prerogative," as Claire Cross puts the policy on which we have remarked and on which historians agree. Her pretensions did not go without challenge. Aside from the original Act of Uniformity, however, the victories were all the queen's. The sharp and punishing rebukes which she administered to Parliament showed a "deepening alliance between an autocratic monarch and an autocratic ecclesiastic (an alliance, however, in which the monarch never lost the initiative)."[67] Monarch and church joined against a reforming Commons, and common lawyers, a growing class of gentry, and middling people, provoking divisions later exacerbated by James I. It was a policy carried by "thorough" to apparent triumph and real disaster under Charles I and Archbishop Laud. One cannot see parliamentary sovereignty in this prerogative treatment of what, in the eyes of both houses or at least of most of the Commons, was the burning issue of the day.

It is striking that Hooker avoids conspicuous use of the term *prerogative* as he discusses royal supremacy. Hooker's predecessor Whitgift had written in his *Defence*: "The archbishop doth exercise his jurisdiction under the prince and by the prince's authority. For, the prince having the supreme government of the realm in all causes and over all persons, she doth exercise the one by the lord chancellor, so doth the other by the archbishops."[68] Hooker had many reasons to follow his patron and superior in saying what the queen had preached and practiced and no doubt wished to hear. But he did not.

Nor were the ecclesiastical policies of the queen so decisively shaped by clergy in general, and Convocation in particular, as the other half of Hooker's handsome interpretation would have us believe. It is true and important that Elizabeth always held that the royal supremacy meant "royal rule of the church through the clergy." The queen was quick to remove a little sting from her female headship by renouncing Henry's old title of "head," as well as his ecclesiastical pretensions. One of her proclamations denied specifically that she claimed "any superiority to ourselves to define, decide or determine any article or point of the Christian faith and religion, or to change any ancient ceremony." She asserted only a power of jurisdiction to direct all estates to live in "the faith, and the obedience of Christian religion," to enforce the laws of God and man to that end, and

> to provide that the church may be governed and taught by archbishops, bishops and ministers according to the ecclesiastical ancient policy of the realm, whom we do assist with our sovereign power, etc. An office and charge as we think properly due to all Christian monarchs, and princes sovereigns, whereby they only differ from pagan princes that only take care of their subjects' bodies without

---

who "regarded the royal prerogative as the foundation of the State, and the law as an emanation from it. Originally the King had possessed all power whatsoever, and he still retained all possible authority that he and his predecessors had not expressly and finally delegated to administrative or judicial bodies" (*The Rise and Fall of the High Commission* [Oxford, 1913], p. 225).

67. Cross, *Royal Supremacy*, pp. 90, 85–86.
68. *Works of Whitgift*, p. 246, quoted by Cross, *Royal Supremacy*, p. 35.

respect to the salvation of their souls, or of the life hereafter to come.[69]

Hooker could found his doctrine in Elizabeth's words. Yet the words are belied by Elizabeth's deeds. Some commentators suppose that she shaped the church out of policy, while others suppose her motive was religious conviction. No one denies that she shaped the church.

By combining Convocation with Parliament as the essence of English governance, Hooker moderates the ecclesiastical governance of queen and her bishops, as he had moderated the civil monarchy. Convocation is the calling together of the clergy, in its two houses of bishops and representatives of the lesser clergy. Actually there were (and are) two Convocations, of Canterbury and York, originating with the old papal provinces into which the church was divided; of that difficulty we are not told. Nor are we reminded that Henry VIII unmercifully bullied his Convocations into a submission complete and perhaps abject, that Convocation had hardly been consulted under Edward VI ("entirely ineffective," Haugaard calls it),[70] and that Elizabeth's restoration of royal supremacy and reforming doctrines was executed not only without assent of Convocation (Marian in sympathy), but in the teeth of its unanimous opposition. "Cuius regio eius religio" was fundamentally true—and precisely what Hooker wished to halt. Now Elizabeth's own convocations were also supine, or at least decisive neither politically nor religiously. To quote Elton's remark again: "The fact is that the 'essence of government' in Tudor England was quite independent of the convocations in the Archepiscopal provinces."[71] Once the lesser clergy's movement for reform had been beaten in the lower house of Convocation, the struggle was transferred to the House of Commons. For her part the queen ruled through her hierarchy. No one would say that she ruled through Convocation, except as to details that she did not hesitate to vary, or in effect to veto, even when matters of faith and doctrine were involved. In short, the bishops controlled the lower house, and the queen by her appointments controlled the bishops. No doubt Book VII's recommendation to bishops of "moderation" and especially "conference," and Book VIII's elevation of Convocation, were intended in part to raise the lower clergy at the expense of the lordly bishops—a clerical analogy to the raising by Fortescue and Smith of the lower gentry.

Elizabeth ruled her bishops. None of them ever approached the shaping and initiating power which Charles I allowed Laud. Although Whitgift did obtain real authority, it was only in ecclesiastical matters, and even there susceptible to the queen's veto. Until Whitgift's appointment to Canterbury, Elizabeth had often lacked prominent churchmen whole-heartedly devoted to her middle way. At the reign's beginning the old Papists were stiffly opposed on one side, and the new reformers were bent on moving to the other. True, Elizabeth took counsel from the newly returned reformers. She followed them only in part, however, and she disillusioned most. When her second archbishop of Canter-

69. Quoted by Cross, *Royal Supremacy*, p. 25.
70. William P. Haugaard, *Elizabeth and the English Reformation* (Cambridge, Eng., 1968), p. 16.
71. Elton, *Tudor Constitution*, p. 235, n. 1.

bury, Grindal, defied her command to halt the prophesyings (sessions of reformed clergy and laity for godly worship and godly criticism), Elizabeth did
not hesitate. She sent her own letters of instruction to the bishops concerned,
sequestered Grindal (the leading cleric of the land) from his duties for five years,
and would have deposed him altogether if her Council had not managed to
dissuade her. Evidently Grindal's own response hurt him most of all. He touch-
ingly petitioned that the queen refer matters relating to "religion, or the doctrine
and discipline of the church, unto the bishops and divines of your realm" and
that in treating such holy matters she not "pronounce so resolutely and peremp-
torily, *as from authority*, as ye may do in civil and extern matters."[72] Hume
spoke knowingly. Elizabeth was born to command. The magical charms that
Neale has shown her to throw over Parliament have to be weighed against her
famous imperiousness. Consider her note to a bishop who tried to protect his
London garden from the projected house of an encroaching courtier:

> Proud prelate,
>
> You know what you were before I made you what you are: If you do
> not immediately comply with my request by G—— I will unfrock
> you.
>
> Elizabeth[73]

Grindal's suspension in effect ended the possibility that a churchman could
obtain reforms of which Elizabeth "personally did not approve," as Claire Cross
puts it. With the accession of Whitgift, the queen obtained for the first time a
churchman after her own heart, a true defender of her new order. Still she did
not hesitate to intervene years later in a Cambridge dispute that he had settled,
repudiating an agreement concerning articles of doctrine, and forbidding their
promulgation in the university. Here as many times before the queen "made her
incursions into matters of faith to prevent the imposition of precise formularies
and so to avoid controversy within the church," as Cross remarks; "nevertheless
this was an exercise of royal power at which ecclesiastics were the most likely
to cavil."[74] Still, Whitgift's energy and politic judgment materially strengthened
the church's influence on its own behalf. He repeatedly called upon the queen
to check parliamentary incursions upon the clergy—imploring her not to hand
the clergy over to the laity—and by the last session he fomented in the Commons a small but disciplined church party.[75] As lay peers and courtiers gathered
power for themselves and their causes by patronizing a newly potent Commons,
so might the lords of the church. To see the possibilities one must consider
Hooker's attempt to restore the lords spiritual to primacy in riches, power, and
civic office. Against this, however, Elizabeth and her chief councillors always
seemed to set themselves. Only in 1604 did the devout James I pass an act
forbidding archbishops and bishops to alienate their lands to the crown, and

72. Quoted by Cross, *Royal Supremacy*, p. 63.
73. Hallam, *Constitutional History* I, 224, cf. 225.
74. Cross, *Royal Supremacy*, pp. 75, 63, 76.
75. Neale, *Elizabeth I and Her Parliaments: 1584–1601*, pp. 406, 409, 83, 273–74,
409–10.

only Laud tried seriously to recover church lands and revenues previously alienated.

Nor did Elizabeth's control over hierarchy and Convocation in some other way reflect the guiding spirit of ecclesiastics. The influence of churchmen in the Privy Council never fell so low among the Tudors or Stuarts as under Elizabeth. After a quarter century Elizabeth finally appointed Whitgift to her Council. Whatever his influence finally came to be, and no one suggests that it approached that of Cecil or Hatton or surpassed such patrons of reform as Walsingham, Knollys, or Leicester, the governing tone of queen and Council as to matters ecclesiastical did not depend upon the clergy. During the first and decisive years after Elizabeth's succession, Usher suggests, "the Privy Council had virtually administered the Church, by means of laymen and the paramount civil authority." Laud under Charles I eventually arranged that the clerical voice possess a commanding influence in the administrative lawcourts in general and Star Chamber in particular, three bishops constantly attending; Elizabeth never permitted more than one bishop at a time to sit. It was, after all, the queen's own Lord Chancellor's Court, subject to the pervasive influence of Elizabeth and her Council, that "perhaps more than any other single court, was slowly robbing the spiritual courts of their instance jurisdiction," and that "had shared, perhaps helped to initiate, the 'creeping invasion' of the common law."[76]

By the end of Elizabeth's reign, however, one great exception existed to the subordination of church to a royal prerogative shaped by laymen: the High Commission. Originally the Commissioners of Ecclesiastical Causes, to this prerogative court Elizabeth delegated enforcement of her settlement. It was an investigatory and judiciary body and succeeded similar commissions established by Henry VIII, Edward VI, and Mary. The High Commission too seemed little more than a creature of queen and Council during the first half of the queen's reign. With three or four bishops, eight lawyers, and eight laymen, the interest and diligence of the ecclesiastics did not give it great independence, although their enthusiasm for reform occasionally took them farther than the queen wished. The Commission was allowed little if any discretion up to 1580 or so, according to Roland Usher, and was very closely and immediately controlled by the Council. Usher suggests that it defended the *ecclesia* only as political unity and loyalty required, which may be an overstatement. Nevertheless, the rise of Whitgift to Canterbury and Bancroft to London brought a change. These two moved to restore to ecclesiastics the decisive governance of the church, building on developments that yielded the Commission control over ecclesiastical matters and shuffled off lesser duties. From about this time the lay members of the Commission absented themselves, "three or four bishops and half a dozen civil lawyers" being the influential commissioners.[77] Powers of great territorial reach,

76. W. J. Jones, *The Elizabethan Court of Chancery* (Oxford, 1967), pp. 393, 389, 328–38; H. R. Trevor-Roper, *Archbishop Laud, 1563–1645* (London, 1963), p. 271; Usher, *High Commission*, p. 100.

77. Usher, *High Commission*, pp. 83–87, 104, 47–50, cf. 61; Elton, *Tudor Constitution*, p. 107.

enforceable by temporal punishments, were sustained by the Queen but controlled by ecclesiastics. Its initiatives were of a kind to be opposed occasionally by the Council, or by councillors as powerful as Cecil. Elton characterizes the Commission thus:

> It carried the authority of the Crown and could depend upon the support of Star Chamber and Privy Council at a time when the ordinary ecclesiastical courts were losing whatever hold they had once had over the lay power. In fact, it did for the Crown's ecclesiastical jurisdiction very much what Star Chamber did on the secular side.

For the first time under Elizabeth bishops felt they could speak, act, and punish with authority. Said Whitgift: "The whole ecclesiastical law is a carcasse without a soul, if it be not in the wantes supplied by the commission."[78] In the practices of the High Commission, although not in the lay bent of Parliament or the impotence of Convocation, Hooker had reason to suppose that churchmen might govern while monarch assented. Here were teeth for ecclesiastical laws, here governance, that would enforce church articles and laws and judgments. Through the High Commission, under the aegis of Elizabeth I, James I, and Charles I, Archbishops Whitgift, Bancroft, and finally Laud sought to restore the predominance of faith and church.

What if this decisive royal patronage were not forthcoming, however? The Commission was soon surrounded with enemies, among reformers, recusants, lawyers, and gentry, in Council, Parliament, and the law courts above all. A flood of prohibitions deluged it no less than the ordinary ecclesiastical courts. Without royal support the Commission could be neutralized or killed, as Sir Thomas Smith had envisioned, its teeth having been blunted or extracted. Its lay component could be reinvigorated, its subordination to Council reestablished, the bishops brought to heel or made innocuous through appointment of mediocrities, or (as with George I and Hoadley, Bishop of Bangor) themselves made reducers of the church through appointment of enemies. To take the worst case, suppose the supreme governor were supreme plunderer or supreme enemy. By custom, law, Parliament, Convocation, and ecclesiastical courts, Hooker sought to hem in royal supremacy so it would serve only for "edification of the church." Power remained nonetheless with monarch and council. What if the supreme power put down the church rather than elevated it?

In the last chapter of Book VIII, the present conclusion of the whole *Ecclesiastical Polity*, Hooker considers a question dangerous even to raise. "The last thing of all which concerns the king's supremacy is, whether thereby he may be exempted from being subject to that judicial power which ecclesiastical consistories have over men." The text is more abused than any other portion of Book VIII, or than any portion of any book except almost all of VI, which also examined the jurisdiction of ecclesiastical courts. Modern commentators have either missed this section, perhaps because they looked for a modern right to

---

78. Quoted by Usher, *High Commission*, p. 110, see pp. 107–99; Elton, *Tudor Constitution*, p. 219.

rebellion, or supposed that Hooker did not decide the question, or supposed that Hooker decided simply against the subjection of kings to ecclesiastical authority.

The blandness of Hooker's opening seems to me revealing. He will confine himself to setting down, first, the reasons why some maintain that kings ought to live in no subjection, and, second, the arguments of those who judge it necessary, "even for kings themselves, to be punishable, and that by men." And the merits of these opposing views? "The question itself we will not determine. The reasons of each opinion being opened, it shall be best for the wise to judge." Here is new modesty in one who pronounced the essence of English governance to lie in Parliament, and king and Parliament alike to be bound by ecclesiastical law and the judgments of wise ecclesiastics. There is irony here and, more serious, strategy. There is only the appearance of modesty. For here too the wise are to judge. Hooker throws open to wise ecclesiastics, who will grasp his meaning, a question that Elizabeth had to regard as closed by herself. To claim for the church a coercive authority over the prince implies denial of the prince's supremacy over the church—"in the days of Henry VIII . . . a capital offence," Hooker observes of the reformers' version, and nothing less in the days of Elizabeth. Sober resolution, that could appear to queen or Council other than treasonable affrontery only if obscured by a modesty that seems not to resolve.

Hooker has been tasked with mediocrity or complacency or even pusillanimity for failing to consider resistance, or the right of resistance, to a state church grown more politic than religious. Here he considers the problem, albeit in a manner so politic and religious that few commentators notice. Those who so easily recommend to others resistance to queen and Council might ponder the truth in the substantially untrue thought of the liberal Hallam—"Hooker, as may be supposed, does not enter upon the perilous question of resistance."[79] Perilous indeed, before an imperious queen and Council who threw members of the Commons into the Tower for even questioning the queen's religious policy. Yet the peril, as Hooker might think, is less to him than to his faith and church; the church now depended for its faith and power upon the monarchy. Also, a teaching more obviously resolute would not only infuriate queen and Council, but would also encourage in various ways the various attacks against the church, by reformers and recusants already in a kind of rebellion and by the sly *politiques* engaged in subversion. Hooker expressly attacks the reformers' and recusants' rebellion, while indicating only to the wise the prince of problems in royal supremacy.

To those politic reasons for caution must be added the civil passivity encouraged by his Christianity. "Let every soul be subject all unto such powers as are set over us," he quotes St. Paul, because "all powers are of God." Still, there is a limit to caution and obedience. Render not unto Caesar what belongs to Christ. "Howbeit, not all kind of subjection unto every such kind of power." Hooker concludes in general (in a sermon not part of the *Ecclesiastical Polity*) that rulers who exceed their authority need not in conscience be obeyed.

79. Hallam, *Constitutional History of England* I, 162.

Usurpers of power, whereby we do not mean them that by violence have aspired unto places of highest authority, but them that use more authority than they did ever receive in form and manner beforementioned . . . as in the exercise of their power to do more than they have been authorized to do; cannot in conscience bind any man unto obedience.[80]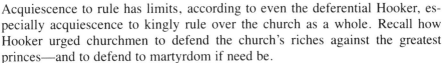

Acquiescence to rule has limits, according to even the deferential Hooker, especially acquiescence to kingly rule over the church as a whole. Recall how Hooker urged churchmen to defend the church's riches against the greatest princes—and to defend to martyrdom if need be.

In sketching reasons for and against a monarch's subordination to ecclesiastical courts, Hooker indicates his own views, and it is hard to see by whose wisdom he would prefer to be guided. One must nonetheless speak hesitantly and tentatively; who knows what is missing from this section? What remains amounts to a bald statement of one argument *contra* the king's subjection, and a lengthy discussion of the Puritan Cartwright's argument *pro*. Kings are not subject to human judges, for in politic societies some final authority must exist; otherwise no superiors, no order, no justice. In kingdoms, then, no subjection of kings. An argument reminiscent of Hooker, and of the English royal supremacy, this insistence upon order nevertheless does not provide against an irreligious order.

The rough outline of such provision is subtly intimated precisely as Hooker seems to counsel deference. He rebuts Cartwright's contention that princes are subject to the excommunication pronounced by ecclesiastical courts. A settled judicial authority, whereby ecclesiastical judges should "call their own sovereign to appear before them into their consistories, there to examine, to judge, and by excommunication to punish them," is impossible in the English regime. "Kings of England are within their own dominions the most high and can have no peer; how is it possible that any, whether civil or ecclesiastical person under them should have over them coercive power, when such power would make that person so far forth his superior's superior, ruler, and judge?" With this concludes Hooker's work as we have it: "For which cause, till better reason be brought, to prove that kings cannot lawfully be exempted from subjection unto ecclesiastical courts, we must and do affirm their said exception lawful."

This last and obvious word is not the only or final word, however. In his concluding paragraphs Hooker distinguished from usual and settled judicial authority an unusual and extraordinary authority, a visitation of excommunication upon kings for unusual and extraordinary sins. Long extracts from ancient writers recount the excommunication of two emperors by churchmen of the empire. Hooker stresses the exceptional nature of the incidents: the crimes were rare and unwonted, the proceedings sudden (occasioned by personal confrontations as the emperors sought to worship), the bishops not within the ordinary jurisdiction of the emperors chastened. Here, Hooker insists, is no case of ordinary judicial

80. *Works* III, 457–59.

authority, no model for regular ecclesiastical jurisdiction. Yet it is a model for extraordinary ecclesiastical jurisdiction. This "excommunication, which princes ought patiently to suffer at the bishop's hands, is no other than that which we also grant may be exercised on such occasions and in such manner as those two alleged examples out of antiquity do enforce." Although the last paragraph ends by defending the rule of English law and monarch, it begins by insisting on the subordination to Christ's ministry, in crucial cases, of any earthly ruler. Concerning such an excommunication: "This we grant every king bound to abide at the hands of any minister of God wheresoever through the world." To provide for severing from Christ the unchristian monarch of a Christian commonwealth—it is Hooker's final bridling not only of mortal man but also of English governance.

# Index

Designer:   Jane Bernard Rockwell
Compositor:   Graphic Composition, Inc.
Printer:   Thomson-Shore, Inc.
Binder:   John H. Dekker & Sons, Inc.
Text:   VIP Times Roman
Display:   Palatino Bold (Linotron 202)